BETSY CADWALADYR
A BALACLAVA NURSE

AN AUTOBIOGRAPHY OF ELIZABETH DAVIS

Betsy Cadwaladyr

BETSY CADWALADYR

A BALACLAVA NURSE

AN AUTOBIOGRAPHY OF ELIZABETH DAVIS

Edited by Jane Williams (Ysgafell)
With an introduction by Deirdre Beddoe
Revised edition with preface added
edited by Gwyneth Roberts

WELSH WOMEN'S CLASSICS

Published by Honno
'Ailsa Craig', Heol y Cawl, Dinas Powys,
South Glamorgan, Wales, CF64 4AH

1 2 3 4 5 6 7 8 9 10

First published in Great Britain by Hurst & Blackett, 1857
First published by Honno in 1987, reprinted 2007
This edition © 2015

© Introduction Deirdre Beddoe 1987

British Library Cataloguing in Publication Data
A catalogue record for this book is available from the British Library.

Print ISBN: 978-1-909983-27-4
Ebook ISBN: 978-1-909983-28-1

Published with the financial support of the Welsh Books Council.

Cover image: Miss Nightingale and the nurses in the East (engraving),
Armytage, Charles (fl.1857-74) / Private Collection / Ken Welsh /
Bridgeman Images. Reproduced courtesy of
The Florence Nightingale Museum Trust, London.
Betsy Cadwaladyr image, p.2: Engraving from a photograph,
1857, in National Library of Wales.

Text design: Elaine Sharples
Printed by

Contents

Introduction

by Deirdre Beddoe

This book is the work of two nineteenth-century Welsh women – Elizabeth Davis (Betsy Cadwaladyr), a domestic servant from rural Meirionnydd who travelled the world and who gained fame as a nurse at Balaclava during the Crimean War; and Jane Williams, writer and scholar, who interviewed Elizabeth Davis and preserved for posterity this account of her fascinating life. Both women broke out of the confines imposed upon them by sex and class – the one through travel and adventure and the other through education and a serious literary career. Through Jane Williams's appreciation of the significance of Elizabeth Davis's tale, and through her pioneering pursuit of oral history, we have in this book a unique record – the authentic voice of an early nineteenth-century Welsh working woman recalling the events and experiences of an action-packed life. It is a life which echoes the everyday experience of many Welsh women, in that Elizabeth Davis was in domestic service, and it is a life which was exceptional in that she was a world traveller who came into contact with international events in the horrors of the field hospital at Balaclava, where she served under Florence Nightingale.

In 1856 the paths of these two very different women crossed. They had met before, some five years previously, but the second meeting took place 'under circumstances which led the writer to appreciate more fully the extraordinary character and history of Elizabeth Davis'. Presumably this meeting took place in London, where both women were living in 1856, and presumably, what led to Jane Williams's greater appreciation of Elizabeth Davis's character and life, was the fact that Elizabeth Davis was newly returned from the Crimean War, where she had worked as a nurse under the aegis of the heroine of the day, Florence Nightingale. It is important for the reader of today to appreciate the fury and rage in Britain when the facts of the 'mismanagement' of the Crimean War, and particularly the appalling neglect of the sick and wounded in the pest-houses which passed for hospitals, became known. The practical response at home to the full horror of the situation in the Crimea was the setting up of a fund for providing comforts for the sick and wounded and the despatch of a party of nurses, under Florence Nightingale, to the Crimean front. The peace, an unsatisfactory and generally unpopular one, was made only in March of 1856. When Jane Williams met Elizabeth Davis, who had served as a nurse in Miss Stanley's party and who had worked in the field hospital at Balaclava, she realized the topicality and significance of Elizabeth Davis's story. The result was a series of lengthy interviews which Jane Williams recorded and edited and which were published in two volumes by Messrs Hurst & Blackett in London in 1857.

In this introduction to *An Autobiography of Elizabeth Davis,* I should like first to comment briefly on the life and literary career of Jane Williams and to pay particular attention to the way in which she set about the task of recording Elizabeth Davis's life-story. Secondly, I should like to draw the reader's attention to the exciting and in many respects amazing life of the heroine of this work, Elizabeth Davis. Thirdly, this is an important book, which I am delighted to see being reprinted and I should like to point out why and how I think this book contributes to our knowledge of Welsh women's history.

Jane Williams (Ysgafell) was born in London in 1806, the daughter of Eleanor and David Williams; her father was a clerk in the Navy Office. She was brought up in comfortable circumstances, but the loss of most of her family's money, apparently when she was in her teens, changed her life and prospects for ever. She lived in the parish of Glasbury (then partly in Radnorshire and partly in Breconshire) for some years before moving to the house Neuadd Felen, in Talgarth, Breconshire, to join her mother and sisters who had moved there several years before. Here she learned Welsh and engaged in scholarly pursuits. Here too she became acquainted with Lady Llanover and became a member of that lady's literary circle, with its concern for Welsh learning and its romantic pursuit of Welsh tradition. Jane was to become a scholar, a linguist, a poet, a historian and a writer. She had her first volume of poetry published when she was eighteen, in 1824. Her religious devotion and her scholarship led to the publication of a serious devotional work, *Twenty Essays on the Practical Improvement of God's Providential Dispensations as Means to the Moral Discipline to the Christian* (1838). In 1848 she was stung to reply to that slur on the morality of the Welsh people *The Report on the State of Education in Wales* (1847).

This report, better known as 'The Betrayal of the Blue Books' depicted the Welsh as irreligious, drunken, immoral and lacking in even the most basic education. The report was particularly scurrilous, by Victorian standards, in its remarks upon the moral laxity of Welsh women, whose indulgence (along, of course, with Welsh men) in the practice of 'bundling' (or 'courting in bed') was alleged to be responsible for unacceptable levels of illegitimacy in Wales. Jane Williams joined the chorus of condemnation of this report and leapt quickly into print. In the curiously titled, *Artegall:* or *Remarks on the Reports of the Commissioners of Inquiry into the State of Education in Wales,* published by Longman & Co. in London in 1848, she denounced the report as partial, and accused the commissioners of perverting the evidence. The report, she alleged, was not an impartial investigation but a case for the prosecution. Jane Williams made a spirited defence of the Welsh people and of the Welsh language. She produced a clear and reasoned document in which she systematically dismantled the evidence of the commissioners. In her scholarly way she even added an appendix devoted to the shaky grammar and inelegances of style of the commissioners and asserted, 'A set of exercises upon grammatical errors might indeed be compiled from the writings of the Commissioners, for the cautionary use of Welshmen studying the English language.' It is more relevant to note here that the biographer of Elizabeth Davis championed Welsh womanhood. Welsh illegitimacy figures, she noted, compared very favourably with those of England – a comparative exercise not included in the report. Welsh women, she maintained, were clean and 'tidy'. Contrary to the impression given by the Commissioners, they did not regularly keep farm animals indoors: she only knew one household where a chicken resided indoors with its elderly mistress. Jane Williams demonstrated the ignorance of the Commissioners concerning the habits and lifestyle of the rural population. She picked up these two points regarding women. One of the Commissioners wrote, 'it would appear that household duties of a material nature (whereof several are naturally picked up in the common routine of agricultural employment) were not altogether neglected.' Jane Williams sharply responded, 'Any Welsh matron would readily inform him, that practical skill in domestic occupations was never yet "picked up" in the fields.'

Secondly she showed that the Commissioners assumed that boys left school earlier than girls in rural areas – because they did so in mining areas – yet 'any cottager could have told him that the girls' home services became first available, that they have not "more leisure", and cannot "be better spared".' In short, Jane Williams's response to the 1847 Report shows not only a clear and scholarly mind but a familiarity with and an understanding of the life and the people of Wales: she drew on this to defend them from the sneers of the Commissioners.

Jane Williams, though never very strong, continued to pursue a literary career. In *The Literary Remains of the Reverend Thomas Price, Carnhuananawc* (1854-55) she gained her first experience of biographical writing. This consisted of one volume of the collected writings of this Celtic scholar, eisteddfod enthusiast and member of the Society of Cymreigyddion – and one volume of his biography written by Jane Williams. She, who had always shown a Victorian disregard for the snappy title, also produced the cryptically named *The Origin, Rise and Progress of the Paper People* (1856): this described a game which she and her siblings had devised and played throughout their childhood and it was illustrated by Lady Llanover.

In 1856 Jane Williams met Elizabeth Davis for the second

time. We know little of the circumstances of either meeting
but we learn from Jane Williams's Preface that in this second
meeting she came to appreciate fully 'the extraordinary
character and history of Elizabeth Davis'. I have referred
above to the newsworthy story which Elizabeth Davis had to
tell of events in the Crimea but I think Jane Williams's interest
in Elizabeth Davis goes deeper. She was not only interested in
Elizabeth Davis because of the Crimean episode in her life:
she did, after all. write her life history in two volumes, only
one of which is devoted to her Crimean War Service. The first
volume is devoted to the story of her father's life, the
Calvinistic Methodist preacher David Cadwaladyr, to
Elizabeth's early life on a hill farm outside Bala, to her early
work experience in domestic service and to her extensive
travels as a servant all over the world. The whole life of
Elizabeth Davis is full of adventure and is highlighted by her
courageous and enterprising character. Jane Williams, the
delicate scholar and Welsh culture enthusiast, was clearly
captivated by this working woman whose life was brimming
with action. But having said that, I think one must realize that
Elizabeth Davis had very controversial things to say about the
popular heroine of the day, Florence Nightingale, and that her
testimony to events in the Crimea would have been of great
interest to the Victorian reading public, who were still
discussing the war. It was the section on the Crimea which
made this book eminently publishable and Jane Williams
realized it. Jane Williams herself explains in the preface her
working method in interviewing and recording the life of
Elizabeth Davis.

She faced difficulties – Elizabeth Davis was old and ill;
'she possessed no written records of her life, no memoranda,

no letters, no tangible and visible helps to memory'; there were gaps in her memory of past events. She told her story in a 'desultory and digressive manner'. Jane Williams points out to the reader that she did not simply sit and listen and record, but had a considerable job on her hands. In her own words, and using a craftsman's metaphor, she tells us that she had:

> To seize the first floating end of each subject that chanced to present itself, to draw it out, to disentangle it, to piece it, to set the warp straight and firmly in the loom, and to cast the woof aright so as to produce the true and original pattern of such tapestry, has required sedulous application. The winding of silk worms' cocoons without a reel, is scarcely a task of more difficult manipulation.

Jane Williams undertook what was clearly a lengthy series of interviews with Elizabeth Davis. She had to guide and discipline her respondent's answers, and to piece together what was not always a coherent narrative. We can measure her great success in this by reading the 'autobiography'. Then she was faced with the decision whether to transcribe literally Elizabeth Davis's words. Nowadays the oral historian, with recording equipment, would opt for a word for word transcription. In the middle of the nineteenth century when readers' expectations were for a more polished prose, Jane Williams chose a free rendition. Yet the language of this book is clear and simple – very different from the biography of Carnhaunawc. Jane Williams opted to convey the 'genuine sense' rather than the exact words, though the heroine's very words were retained when they were 'apt and striking'. One other problem faced Jane Williams as an interviewer: namely

how to verify certain incidents. This became particularly
necessary when Elizabeth Davis was describing events at
Scutari and Balaclava in the Crimean war and it is to the great
credit of Jane Williams that she went to considerable lengths
to check out Elizabeth Davis's version. Hence the accounts of
Elizabeth Davis's experiences in the Crimea are interspersed
with other evidence from the period and by quite lengthy
notes. Jane Williams therefore found herself not only as an
interviewer but as an assessor of the accuracy of the accounts
of near contemporary events.

In assessing the career of Jane Williams I would
undoubtedly recognize her *Autobiography of Elizabeth Davis*
as her most significant contribution to Welsh history. She
performed an important rescue operation in recording the life
of Elizabeth Davis, a woman whose class would normally
have prevented her from leaving such a record of her life. Yet
Jane Williams would have very likely valued her later literary
works more highly. Apart from translations and from verse,
she produced two more large works. The first of these was
The Literary Women of England (1861) – a survey of British
women writers from the ancient Britons down to 1850, which
she was inspired to write because of the scant attention
hitherto paid to literary women. The second of the major
works from her later years was really the culmination of her
life's scholarship, *A History of Wales derived from Authentic
Sources* (1869). *The Welsh Dictionary of National Biography*
notes that this history was not superseded until the publication
of Sir John E, Lloyd's research on the subject in 1911.

In this edition of *An Autobiography of Elizabeth Davis,*
Jane Williams's original Preface and Introduction have been
included. Her Introduction is a paean to Welsh Protestantism

and its defence of the religious feeling of the Welsh people (backed up by the numbers of Sunday schools and chapels in Wales as recorded in the 1851 Census) has more relevance to her response to the 1847 Report on the state of education than to the life of Elizabeth Davis.

It is not necessary for me to write at length about the life of Elizabeth Davis or Betsy Cadwaladyr (1789-1860) here: she tells her own story, with Jane Williams's help. But it is necessary to stress that she was altogether an amazing woman: she was physically striking, with her tall dark looks and she was possessed of a remarkably strong personality, characterized by enterprise, courage, honesty, a great sense of adventure and an enormous capacity for hard work.

She was the daughter of the Calvinistic Methodist preacher, Dafydd Cadwaladyr, and his wife Judith. She spent her early years on the hill farm of Pen-Rhiw near Bala. There, life was meagre and hard and the puritanical Dafydd Cadwaladyr forced a stern regime on his daughter. Although she speaks of him with admiration, resentment comes across during the years when she tells of him hauling her out of a dance when she was a young girl. The death of her mother, who had borne sixteen children, when Elizabeth was only about five years of age, distressed her greatly and since she did not get on with her older sister, who kept house for her father, she left home at the earliest possible opportunity. From the age of nine to fourteen she lived in the house of her father's landlord at Plâs-yn-Drêf. Here she learned domestic skills, reading, writing and how to speak English. At the age of fourteen she left the protection of Plâs-yn-Drêf. Typically she left because 'a sudden thought occurred to me not to stay there any longer, and that I must see more of the world'. And so she did. Taking the only work open to a young girl of her station, she began to see the world through entering service. In taking such a job she was in fact part of a large migrant workforce of Welsh women, though her self-confidence and the freer social relations between the classes in her home area, made her disdainful of the more rigid class relations she encountered elsewhere. No mistress ever succeeded in lording it over Betsy Cadwaladyr – a name she changed to Elizabeth Davis for the greater ease of dealing with the English.

Employment in domestic service took her to Liverpool, Chester and London but her desire to see new places, coupled with the vagaries of her employers, was to take her much further afield. She visited the continent in 1815, the year of the Battle of Waterloo; she sailed as a nanny to the West Indies and visited plantations worked by slaves; she travelled to New South Wales and Van Diemen's Land in Australia, when the convict system was at its height – her travels took her to India, China, to South America and to Africa. Her visits to all these places were attended by lurid adventures, which she managed, sometimes barely, to survive. I shall not pre-empt the reader's pleasure by telling of these but her encounter with a villainous convict in Australia – which resulted in her laying him flat – and her experience in a Chinese opium den, in the presence of the Emperor of China, from which she had to exit backwards, are recounted in a lively style and make memorable reading. Amorous adventures also figure largely in her story: failed suitors were littered from Liverpool to Lima but the most persistent was one Barbosa, who seems to pop up all over the globe and who was even driven to kidnapping her – but Elizabeth Davis remained single.

In 1854 Elizabeth Davis embarked upon a new phase in

her career. In that year Britain and France (and later Sardinia) became involved in a war, in support of Turkey, against Russia. It was a war hallmarked by disasters. Even while it was in progress, four Parliamentary Commissions of Inquiry investigated the appalling events and conduct of the war. The British public were kept in ignorance of the horrific conditions pertaining there until William Howard Russell, the first war correspondent, published the story of conditions at the barracks hospital at Scutari, on the Black Sea, in the weeks following the Battle of the Alma (1854). The wounded and sick were without food, medicine or beds. They lay in filth and were further subjected to cholera and fever. Russell's reports burst on a horrified nation and one response was the despatch by the Secretary of War of a party of forty nurses under the supervision of Florence Nightingale. Elizabeth Davis followed the newspaper accounts of the Battle of the Alma and read of Miss Nightingale's departure. She made a quick decision. 'I was determined that I would try to go to the Crimea.' She joined a party of nurses under Miss Stanley – who were not in fact under the command of Florence Nightingale. This was perhaps just as well since from first hearing her name Elizabeth Davis took a dislike to her. 'I did not like the name of Nightingale. When I first hear a name, I am very apt to know by my feeling whether I shall like the person who bears it.'

Elizabeth Davis travelled with Miss Stanley's party by land and sea first to Therapia and then to Scutari on the Black Sea. Scutari was the main British war hospital, where the nurses were under Florence Nightingale's control. This was the hospital where Florence Nightingale wonderfully reformed conditions and gained the affectionate epithet, 'The Lady with the Lamp'. But Elizabeth Davis chafed at being kept away from the main scene of action – the Crimean peninsular, which lay across the Black Sea and, without Miss Nightingale's blessing, she left for the hospital at Balaclava in the Crimea. She may well have been anxious to escape from Florence Nightingale's control. At Balaclava she set to work immediately to bathe the maggot-infested wounds of the wretched soldiers. She was appalled to find that no man had a bed so she demanded, and got, bedding from the army purveyor. She nursed the men for six weeks on the wards and then she was placed in charge of the special diet kitchen. She made sure that food in ample quantities was made available. She made lavish demands upon the stores – on one occasion, ordering 'six dozen of port wine, six dozen of sherry, six dozen of brandy, a cask of rice, one of arrowroot and one of sago and a box of sugar'. She was an excellent cook and her hard work and liberality was a blessing to many. But overwork and ill health forced her eventually to return home. She left with a recommendation from Miss Nightingale for a government pension.

One of the main points of interest in this autobiography is that Elizabeth Davis heartily disliked Florence Nightingale and levelled some severe accusations against her. She had little good to say about 'The Lady with the Lamp'. She alleged that at Scutari, 'Miss Nightingale had a French cook and three courses of the very best of every kind of food were served up everyday at her table…'; whilst Elizabeth Davis and the other nurses lived off filaments of meat boiled down to make the patients' broth. She was appalled at Florence Nightingale's strict adherence to the system of requisitions of food and clothing, and she protested when Florence Nightingale tried to extend this regime to her (Elizabeth Davis's) kitchen at Balaclava. She tells of how Florence Nightingale let the stores of clothing, food and other gifts donated from Britain rot in the stores at Scutari, and says that very little of these actually reached Balaclava. (When she returned to England she found clothing which had been donated for the Crimea for sale in dockside shops and auction houses – though she does not blame Miss Nightingale for that.)

In order to appreciate better what Elizabeth Davis was complaining about it is necessary to explain that the British army was hamstrung by incredibly elaborate procedures in distributing goods to its hospitals. The Commissariat provided food rations for soldiers in hospital if they were well enough to eat normal rations but if they were too ill to eat normal foods their diet was provided by the Purveyor, who provided 'medical comforts' such as rice, port-wine, arrowroot. Not only was this complicated enough but there were also the Free Gifts. The Free Gifts were donations from people all over Britain who sent shirts, pots of jam, Christmas puddings, herrings, handkerchiefs, gloves etc. to the soldiers in the Crimea. Queen Victoria herself had sent water beds and she and her daughters had knitted mittens for the troops. Florence Nightingale was appointed as Almoner of the Free Gifts – as well as Superintendent of the Nursing Establishment! Miss Nightingale regarded what she termed 'these frightful contributions' as not worth the freight. She was expected to acknowledge and account for them all.

Elizabeth Davis's opinion of Miss Nightingale's administration of the stores and free gifts greatly interested Jane Williams, who went to considerable lengths to

corroborate Elizabeth Davis's account and to supplement it
with an analysis of contemporary government reports and
other sources. Jane Williams, as her work on the 1847 Report
on the state of education in Wales shows, was familiar with the
language and procedures of government reports or 'blue
books' as they were popularly known. She concluded that
Florence Nightingale was wrong in adhering so rigidly to
army procedures (see Appendix B): Florence Nightingale's
practice was only to issue stores upon obtaining a requisition
signed by two medical men. Jane Williams attributed this strict
adherence to bureaucratic procedures to a 'self protective
principle of rigid observance'. In short, Miss Nightingale
could never be accused of breaking regulations. Jane Williams
argued that in the emergency conditions of the Crimean war
a more liberal interpretation of the rules would have helped
the men. Jane Williams believed that she was performing a
public service in publishing this material and was anxious to
avoid any repetition of the situation. She states:

> We are conscious of no bias, no partiality, no prejudice.
> Our investigations have fairly led to the conviction that
> the method of administration did not produce the largest
> amount of benefit which ought to have been
> communicated by the means at its command; and that the
> Barrack Hospital at Scutari continued to present the
> greatest amount of least alleviated misery of any war-
> hospital belonging to the British Army of the East.

In short Elizabeth Davis with her common sense, her practical
skills and her spontaneous generosity towards the wounded
appears in great contrast to the bureaucratic Florence

Nightingale. It is not my brief to defend Miss Nightingale nor to sift through the many great tomes of contemporary evidence on the conduct of the Crimean war. In fairness to Florence Nightingale, I would point out that she had the absurd double responsibility of being in charge of all the nurses and administering the gifts. She was the standard bearer of British women nurses and in the face of undisguised hostility from the male doctors she probably felt obliged to keep the regulations. It was all a long time ago and Elizabeth Davis's story is one contribution to what was then an urgent debate. There can, however, be no doubt that both women performed sterling service in the Crimean war.

Finally I should like to draw readers' attention to the poignant notice at the end of this book. The elderly Elizabeth Davis was appealing for work or public charity. I do not know the outcome of the appeal. Elizabeth Davis died in 1860.

Deirdre Beddoe
Penarth, 1986

Preface

by Jane Williams

The writer first became acquainted with the heroine and narrator of these adventures in the year 1851. In the year 1856 they met again, under circumstances which led the writer to appreciate more fully the extraordinary character and history of Elizabeth Davis. Though worn by time, and oppressed by illness, her indomitable energy still shone in her eyes, and bore her fine form erect; still manifested itself in industrious activity, and in buoyant cheerfulness of spirit.

She possessed no written records of her life, no memoranda, no letters, no tangible and visible helps to memory. In a desultory and digressive manner, she gave, to the best of her recollection, an account of the principal facts of her own remarkable history. She knew that lapse of time and intermediate events had cast their shadows over some scenes; she was aware that here and there a link in the chain was bent or broken; but she trusted in her vivid impressions of the past, and in her own sincerity of purpose.

Discrepancies and mistakes may be detected in the details, errors in chronology, errors in geography, and errors in the orthography of names and in the designation of persons; but the writer believes that for all thorough students of human nature, the narrative, as a whole, bears internal evidence of the light of its truth. With the guidance of its heroine, and the light of analogy, the incidents have been arranged in consecutive order.

It has been the writer's object justly to apprehend the meaning of the narrator, and faithfully to express it.

It is well known that a free translation often renders the sense of an original with more truth than a literal one.

It was impossible in all parts to give the exact language spoken. The writer has therefore aimed at conveying a true reflex of her exact meaning, preferring the genuine sense to literal precision.

Wherever the very words of the heroine were apt and striking, they were retained.

Footnotes have been added in order to identify persons, to verify facts, to correct exaggerations, and to show the probability of some extraordinary statements.

The important matter contained in the Appendix tends both to place the public services of Mrs Davis in a just light, and to prove the worth and weight of her opinion upon a great public question.

The narrative of a pure-minded woman, of thorough integrity and of dauntless resolution, and one to whom the Bible formed the chart of life, cannot be altogether useless to society; although like every other record of real experience, it affords matter for warning as well as for example.

A cursory reader may suppose that the writer had merely to listen and to record, but the task of preparing the narrative has really involved much care and labour. To seize the first floating end of each subject that chanced to present itself, to draw it out, to disentangle it, to piece it, to set the warp straight and firmly in the loom, and to cast the woof aright, so as to produce the true and original pattern of such tapestry, has required sedulous application. The winding of silkworms' cocoons without a reel, is scarcely a task of more difficult manipulation.

The reader who supposes the text of the narrative to have cost the writer little trouble, may probably expect that all its most remarkable passages should be illustrated or explained by notes. Extensive inquiries have been instituted for this purpose, and some valuable results have been obtained, but the circulation of a whole edition can alone be expected to bring in the contributions of diffused and personal information necessary for the full execution of this desirable object.

It may be necessary here to call attention to the peculiar character of the heroine – a character as different from the ordinary type as are the events of her history.

The extraordinary combination in her of the spirit of enterprize, self-dependence, and mental alacrity, with great bodily strength and activity, a commanding figure, noble aspect and perfect self-possession of manner, never failed to exercise a powerful influence upon her associates; and its uniform effect upon her employers, in levelling the usual barriers which divide the classes, is shown throughout this work. To those who are unacquainted with her, the fact may seem incredible. To those who have experienced the power of her blended dignity and deference, no further evidence is necessary.

In her autobiography, the absence of sentiment and air of unsympathizing indifference, must not be taken for the want of kindness and humanity.

Her nature was undoubtedly peculiar, imaginative, impulsive and adventurous; but the mountain region which produced her, and the state of society which surrounded her in early life, moulded and impressed upon the native metal the form and stamp which it has never lost.

Introduction

by Jane Williams

A story, fruitful of events, attend!

Pope's *Odyssey* XV. 423.

The Welsh have been in all ages a religious people.

They were so in Druidic days, and, with the joy of sincere and earnest hearts, they welcomed Christianity as soon as it reached their shores. Its ministers succeeded promptly to the charge of districts which Druids had held before.

Church history records that Wales was one of the last countries in Europe which yielded to Romanism, and among the first to cast it off.

From the Reformation until the beginning of the eighteenth century, a series of devout and diligent native bishops succeeded in dispelling supersitition, in arousing its recent victims from moral torpor, in giving the people good Welsh translations of the Bible and the Book of Common Prayer, in enforcing the use of the native language; also in preaching, and in the administration of all religious ordinances. By these wise and simple means they gained all hearts, and won the whole population to become good and zealous members of the Established Church. The exceptions were few and insignificant; Welsh dissenters bearing much the same proportion, perhaps, in those days to Welsh churchmen, as the churchmen now do to the dissenters.

After more than one hundred and fifty years of Protestant life and prosperity, a deadly change was wrought in the Welsh Church.

Bishops foreign to the Principality, ignorant of the language, the cast of thought, the habits and the feelings of the people, were appointed to the Welsh sees; not casually or occasionally, but systematically and in succession. This is no place for detailing the process by which they wrought the ruin of the Welsh Church. They reproved the active zeal of apostolic men, and rewarded their faithful labours with deprivation and expulsion. They bestowed the best Welsh livings upon strangers to the country, who often held them in plurality; hiring Welsh curates at miserable stipends to visit parishes far distant from each other, to christen, and marry, and bury, and to perform divine service here and there, now and then.

It is touching to observe, in the midst of this withering change, how constantly the people resorted to every means of grace which the Established Church still afforded.

In 1768, the Hon. Daines Barrington estimated, from statistical returns, which he obtained from the local clergy, that the proportion of communicants in the Principality, was as two-fifths to the congregations.

The piety of one or two generations sufficed to keep alive that national attachment to the establishment, which, in the course of time, flickered like a lamp unsupplied with its proper oil.

The earnest, imaginative, and social qualities of the Welsh people, required mental interests and active occupation. The scanty ministrations of the clergy, and their dry ethical dissertations, dropped upon the hearts of the hearers like the chill waters of petrifying springs. Deprived of the advantages of religious occupation and instruction, the people fell back upon the wayward exercise of their national talents, and upon the traditionary lore of their land, accumulated through revolving centuries.

Sundays, being holidays from manual labour, were more especially appropriated to amusement. Then were held the Chwarae gamp, sports for the trial of strength and activity among the young men, to which spectators thronged from distant parishes.

The old town-hall of Bala often – and especially on the seventh day – was used for reverberating tennis-balls.

Dramatic performances, called 'Coeg Chwarae' or 'Interludes', composed for special occasions by local Welsh poets, were acted on Sundays, in summer time, by the country squires, yeomen and peasants together. Singing to the harp, was a favourite amusement; and dancing parties were frequent; the harp, on such occasions, being usually accompanied by the violin, which is the modern representative of the ancient Welsh 'crwth'. Not only on Sundays, but after working hours on week-days, the nimble Cymry used to delight themselves by going through country-dances, some of which had no less than four-and-twenty variations.

There were quiet households too, where the sounds of the harp and voice were enjoyed without dissipation, and the old national tunes, the old traditionary tales of wonder, and the poems of the ancient Welsh bards, proved alternate sources of intellectual pleasure to the little circle formed around the hearth.

The revival of religion in Wales was wrought by native preachers, previous to the occurrence of a similar event in England, under the influence of Whitfield and Wesley.

Gruffydd Jones, rector of LIanddowror, William Williams, curate of Pantycelyn, &c.; Daniel Rowlands, curate of LIangeitho, &c.; and Peter Williams, curate of Swansea, &c.; with other men of kindred spirit, would have retained the whole nation in the unity of the church, had they not been prevented by the infatuated dignitaries.

Even Howel Harris, the originator of Welsh Methodism, shrunk from the appellation of 'Dissenter', and regularly led his whole 'family of love' from Trefecca, to attend public worship, and to receive the sacraments in the parish church of Talgarth.

Discipline was in those days the episcopal idol, and to it were ruthlessly sacrificed all the most zealous members of the Welsh Church, and with them expired its glory.

The eagerness with which the Welsh people of all ranks and ages seized the opportunities of instruction, as soon as they were offered in their native language, is attested by their teachers. The old and the blind came, the vigorous wrestler, and the skilful musician; servants paid other servants for doing their work, in order to gain time to attend the Welsh Circulating Schools, which were originated by the Rev. Gruffydd Jones, rector of LIanddowror, and afterwards revived in North Wales, by the Rev. Thomas Charles, of Bala.

"The Circulating Day-Schools," said Mr Charles, "have been the principal means of erecting Sunday-schools; for, without the former, the state of the country was such that we could not obtain teachers to carry on the latter; besides, Sunday-schools were set up in every place where the Day-schools had been."

The distribution of religious books in the native language, personal exhortation, district visiting, and public ordinances, administered with zealous piety, soon changed the social state of Bala, and of the whole Principality.

The 'avidity' for learning, which John Wesley afterwards remarked as a characteristic of the Welsh people, was strong, from infancy until death, in Dafydd Cadwaladyr.

His parents kept a farm in the parish of Llangwm, Denbighshire, and he was born there in the year 1752.

When he was a little child of four or five years old, he was awakened from sleep one night, in the midst of a violent thunder-storm, by his mother, who came into the room in an agony of terror, and, falling upon her knees at his bedside, began to pray aloud to God for mercy. In answer to his questions, she told him that she believed the Day of Judgment was come, and God would punish sinners.

This was the first time he had ever witnessed prayer, or heard of religion. With the ready sympathy in strong feeling which is natural to children, he listened to her repetition of the Creed, the Lord's Prayer, and petitions from the Litany, and joined with her in saying them over and over again, while the long and dreadful storm lasted.

The mother's devotion ceased with her terror, but the mind of the child was indelibly impressed with the fear of God. Day after day, and night after night, he continually uttered in Welsh,

"Oh, God the Father of Heaven, have mercy upon us miserable sinners!

Oh, God the Son, Redeemer of the world, have mercy upon us miserable sinners!

Oh, God the Holy Ghost, proceeding from the Father and

the Son, have mercy upon us miserable sinners!" repeating
also the Lord's Prayer, and the Creed.

His father, weary and irritated, silenced the poor boy at last
with a whipping.

His parents attended morning service at the parish church
once a month, or as often as service was performed.

Their children had no other stated means of instruction,
either religious or secular.

Eagerness for knowledge overcoming all obstacles,
Dafydd, at six years old, while watching with an elder brother
their father's sheep upon the mountain, learned a great part of
the alphabet from the initial letters marked with tar upon the
sheep's sides to distinguish the flocks of the several owners.

He afterwards was accidentally led, while idly turning over
the leaves of the Llyfr Gweddi Gyffredin (Book of Common
Prayer), to recognize there the same letters, and finding out
their sounds in combination, he taught himself to read in the
course of two months by this extraordinary method.

It is a custom among Welsh farmers to give their eldest
child the first ewe lamb that is weaned after his birth, and all
the produce of that one lamb when it grows into a sheep; so
that in a few years the child becomes the owner of a little
flock. Dafydd Cadwaladyr's eldest brother was named Robert,
and this was marked at full length upon his sheep. It was
consequently the first word which Dafydd learned to spell.

At eleven years of age he became a farm-servant boy to
Mr Wynn, of Garthmeilio. There he soon met with the
celebrated Welsh poem, *Bardd Cwsg*, and subsequently with
John Bunyan's *Taith y Pererin*, and other valuable books. He
hoarded every shilling he could save to purchase more, and

found himself in two years the happy possessor of a Welsh Bible, and of several religious works.

A pseudo-prophetic rumour reached him soon afterwards, that the papal power would some day be re-established, and that Bibles would be burnt. Alarmed at the thought, he determined to make sure of the contents, and set to work with indefatigable diligence at the task of committing them to memory. He learned the whole of the New Testament, and a great part of the Old Testament. Meanwhile, he never relaxed in his daily labour; and his mistress, pleased with his industry, allowed him, in the winter evenings, as a reward, to attend the social meetings in neighbouring houses, where men and women alike, plying their knitting-pins in the twilight, used to sing Welsh songs and tell legendary tales.

Dafydd distinguished himself at these parties, by repeating select passages from the *Bardd Cwsg*, and the *Pilgrim's Progess*, working up the feelings of his hearers to terror, softening them to sadness, or soothing them to peace.

Garthmeilio was a favourite resort of the ball-players on Sunday evenings. One evening they accidentally broke a window, and Dafydd, on his way to Bala the next morning to fetch the glazier, fell in with a person who told him that there were preachers about to hold a religious meeting in the neighbourhood. His curiosity was strongly excited, and he went to hear them. He was afraid that his master would be angry with him, for the value of instruction was at that time little known, and the feeling of the people was strongly against dissent. He felt tempted to tell a falsehood to account for his prolonged absence. Conscience, however, gained the victory, and he spoke the plain truth. The struggle strenghtened his principles, and confirmed him in the habit of sincerity, which was his characteristic through life. His master did not punish him, but respected his straightforwardness; and thenceforth attendance at such meetings constituted the greatest enjoyment of his life.

He pondered much on serious subjects, and, like all thoughtful and earnest men, his faith was sometimes overcast. He chanced just then to read the *Life of Mahomet*. It awoke in his mind sceptical doubts. Perplexed and distressed, he listened, prayed, and read, in agonizing anxiety, to find out whether the New Testament or the Koran was the true revelation, whether Jesus Christ or Mahomet was the true prophet. At last, the patient study of the Bible brought before him Hebrews vii 26, which dispelled his doubts for ever.

He lived six years at Garthmeilio, and being then afflicted with the small-pox, went home to his parents to be nursed. While recovering from the disorder, he made so much use of his eyes in reading,that he was in danger of blindness. When he got well, the Wynns wished him to return to them, but his heart was set upon gaining more frequent opportunities of religious instruction.

His next place was at Nant y Cyrtiau, where he lived two years. His six days' labour, heartily done, was rewarded by liberty to go where he chose on the seventh, on the condition that he did not come home to take his usual meals. He gladly accepted the privilege, at the cost of the privation.

At nineteen years of age, he became farm-servant to William Evans, of Bedwarian, the first preacher – except the drowsy clergyman of Llangwm – whom Dafydd Cadwaladyr had ever heard. It appears probable that at this period Dafydd acquired the art of penmanship, in which he was entirely self-taught.

Like many of his countrymen, he had a fine poetic mind, and a turn for epigrammatic satire. Fearing to become uncharitable by the exercise of this power, he afterwards confined himself solely to elegiac compositions.

While living at Bedwarian, he appears to have made great progress in the life-long work of self-improvement. He read a great deal; and, having deliberately chosen his lot, became a member of the Welsh Calvinistic Methodist Connection.

In words much resembling the shorter of the two forms given in that invaluable book – Dr Doddridge's *Rise and Progress* – he also wrote and signed a private deed of self-dedication to God's service.

Being attacked by severe illness, he obstinately refused all medicine, and drank great quantities of water to allay his parching thirst. He soon got well, and ever afterwards entertained so high an opinion of the healthful and curative properties of water, that he used it as a daily beverage, and recommended it to others as the most efficacious of all remedies.

When Dafydd was twenty-five years of age, he married an excellent young woman, and took the little farm of Pen Rhiw, near Bala.

His great talents, his consistent piety, his genial temper, and strong, enthusiastic character, had now won for him a high position among his former teachers and masters. At their solicitation he entered upon the ministry, and for fifty-two years he laboriously, zealously, and successfully fulfilled its functions. He continued, meanwhile, carefully to cultivate his farm; giving the most sedulous attention to the guidance of his own house; maintaining his large family in frugal sufficiency of all things; and showing, both at home and abroad, the edifying example of a blameless life, and of unremitting industry. His body was as strong as his mind, and he needed and took no other rest but a short allowance of sleep, and frequent change of occupation. He was the last to leave his scythe on a Saturday night, during the hay-harvest, and, after walking thirty miles on Sunday, and preaching three times, he was the first at his out-door work on Monday morning.

He always walked his journeys, and, in the course of years, he traversed the Principality through and through, and visited the Welsh marches, and many parts of England; preaching three times a day, and going several miles on foot between the services. His walking staff was a cane, given to him by Selina, Countess of Huntingdon. It had a watch in a silver case under the knob at the top of it.

His sermons were eloquent, earnest, and useful. His prayers were the simple outpouring of deep personal devotion and hearty good-will; and they are said to have won more converts than even his preaching.

Instead of reading the chapters of Scripture, as usual, in the meeting-house worship, he used to say them from memory. By the exercise of indomitable energy, he found time for everything. He never broke or infringed upon a promise, and was always strictly punctual. To avoid breaking an engagement, he would, in an emergency, walk all night long, and cross the high and dangerous mountain passes of Merionethshire, through all weathers, snow and storm.

He appears to have assisted Mr Charles in collating various editions of the Welsh Bible.

From one particular copy, Dafydd Cadwaladyr read for many years to his family, and marked his progress, from the beginning to the end of it, twenty-five times.

We have not space for a tenth part of the anecdotes which are on record of his quaintness, his courage, his home virtues, and his ministerial usefulness. He was ready to become all things to all men, as far as his conscience would permit, and would leave higher offices for school-teaching, or to visit the most ignorant and unkind, in order to do real good.

He was consequently beloved by all his neighbours; and by many who disliked religion and all its dissenting professors, he was tolerated and esteemed.

His power of encountering fatigue was marvellous. One day, after having walked from Penrhiw, through Dolgellau, a steep and tedious way, to Abermaw (Barmouth), he climbed the mountainside, where cottages peep down the chimneys of other cottages, and, entering the kitchen of an old acquaintance, sat down to talk with her.

She asked him how he did. He replied that he knew not what was the matter, but he felt a sensation of weariness and sinking which was altogether new to him.

With true Welsh acuteness, she inquired, "Why, Dafydd, how old are you?"

"Well, I am turned seventy."

"And how far have you walked today?"

"Only twenty-eight miles. I used to think nothing of such a distance as that; but, I suppose, it is no wonder that I am tired with it now!"

He lived in health and vigour far beyond the usual three score years and ten; continuing to walk long distances, and to preach energetically until the last; so that his Welsh biographer declares his loss was felt as heavily at the age of eighty-two, as if he had passed away in the fulness of manly strength.

Not long before the close of his earthly life and labours, he took a walk one day to Bedwarian, and went round once more the fields which, in days gone by, he had mown and tilled, and sown and reaped, to look at his 'hen allorau' (old altars) places, where, in his youthful fervour of spirit, he had frequently offered up the sacrifice of prayer – places where he had planned and forecast the life of duty which he had subsequently led. The old man felt hurt at finding overthrown several of these little stone piles, which he had raised in imitation of patriarchal monuments of gratitude. The regret was human, but needless, for many hearts bore the impress of his piety, and his own soul, in its probationary course, had received those divine inscriptions which will glorify God for ever (Heb. x: 15, 17).

Perhaps the soft sorrow, which the Welsh generally experience at the death of friends, may take that mitigated form, not only from the steadfast hope of immortality, but also, in some degree, from the tranquil beauty of their churchyards, where growing flowers are planted and cherished by survivors, as perpetual remembrances of resurrection.

Dafydd Cadwaladyr's daughter Elizabeth arose upon the yet unsmoothed surges of two periods, before the efflux of the one had subsided into the flowing course of the other, and neutralized its strong contrast of colour.

Such eras ever tend to produce determined characters, as the necessity for resistance to opposing power follows the choice of party, and stimulates the exercise of strength.

Impelled by the conviction of conscience to regard the world as the property of God, Dafydd Cadwaladyr, her father, made it the chief object of his life to win men back to their rightful allegiance, by preaching and teaching the great truths of salvation through Jesus Christ, and the renewal of the human will to holiness by the Divine Spirit. He joined himself with other reformers of his day, living like himself for immortality; and dreading for their converts the social sins from which they had themselves escaped, they surrounded their ground with fences, so high and closely set, as to exclude also many harmless and healthful social practices.

Within these strait boundaries, his daughter Elizabeth was trained; but with her, as with Rasselas in the happy valley, the monotonous safety of captivity provoked an irrepressible longing for dangerous adventure. Still anxious to find something new, she broke her boundaries; and, at last, leaving home and friends, moved from place to place, until she had repeatedly compassed the globe, and seen almost every land, and sailed on almost every sea of the south, the east, and the west. Yet, wherever she went, she never forgot that she was Dafydd Cadwaladyr's daughter.

Good-will, sterling integrity, and perfect rectitude, were evinced in her whole course of conduct. In principle, in moral excellence, and in religious orthodoxy, she was always steadfast. The influence of her home-training was manifested amidst a thousand inconsistencies, and many apparent contrarieties. She always sought her countrymen and her fellow sectarians, with true and faithful affection, wherever she went; and she found in India, in Africa, and in Australasia, that the name of her father was a passport to recognition, hospitality, and kindness.

The people of Bala have, from generation to generation, been famous for their industry. In a single year they have been known to sell no less than 32,000 dozen pairs of stockings, 10,000 dozen pairs of socks, and 5,500 dozen pairs of gloves, besides unnumbered Welsh wigs, muffetees, and other articles of hosiery, all knit by their own pins, from yarn spun on their own wheels, from the wool of their mountain sheep.

Few persons who have chanced to travel through any part of the Principality can forget the pleasant sight of Welshwomen knitting with unremitting industry while walking along the roads carrying burdens upon their heads. On summer evenings, before the husband returned from his work, while the children, released from school, played together out of doors, the Bala housewife would often take her baby and her knitting to enjoy an hour or two of social converse at a neighbour's cottage; or a group of matrons and maidens would assemble together in some pleasant nook where sunshine and shade softly mingled,

'And whilst the nimble Cambrian rills
Danced hy-day-gies amongst the hills' [1]

around them, ply their work with busy fingers, and sing together the sweet national airs of their country, pausing at times to relate to each other some wild legendary tale, connected by tradition either with the place, or with the tune.

On such occasions Cadwaladyr's daughter was often a listener, though forbidden to attend their regular parties. Her habit of incessant useful occupation may be traced to such early examples. She excels, like a true Bala woman, in the use of her knitting-pins. It is still customary in many parts of the Principality – and in her younger days it was general – that all the materials of clothing for the family, and all the woven fabrics used in the house should be prepared at home.

[1] *Drayton's Polyolbion*. Argument to the fifth Song.

The sound of spinning-wheels was heard in every cottage – yea, in every dwelling – and busy housewives and their daughters spun the wool of the native sheep into yarn. Reserving what they required for knitting, they dyed some of it bright red for children's socks, blue or grey for their husband's stockings, and black for their own.

The chief part of the yarn they took to the village weavers, who, like the Welsh housewives, were skilful in the preparation of vegetable dyes from native plants. At their looms it was woven into cloth, for coats, and cloaks, and riding-skirts; into flannels of various sorts and patterns, for under-clothing and gowns; into blankets, and bed-rugs, and counterpanes.

Flax and hemp, being purchased at the nearest town, were also spun at home, and taken to the village weaver to be made into different sorts of strong linen cloth for all family uses.

Then, also, as now, the village tailor took his seat on the kitchen table of every household in its turn, to shape the home-made materials into clothes for the master and his boys, or to patch their old suits. In Elizabeth Cadwaladyr's days, he also cut out the petticoats and bobtails, and bedgowns, for the mother and her girls.

Dwellers in mountain lands often notice heavy masses of cloud pausing and settling over the summits, and shaping themselves to imitative forms. They are not equally observant in tracing the effects of those mountains upon their own minds.

Besides the effect wrought by geographical position upon the inhabitants of certain districts, there are peculiar influences of situation and scenery which affect only individuals – as the lightning from the skies finds not an answering flash from every soil.

One of the highest mountains in Wales, Aran Benllyn, so called from its situation at the head of Bala Lake, overshadows the source of 'ancient, hallowed Dee', to which river many marvellous tales are attached, well remembered by the peasantry. The lake itself, and many places around, have also their romantic legends of heroic deeds and preter-natural beings. Ghosts, goblins, fairies, and witches were not extinct in the days of Elizabeth Cadwaladyr's childhood.

The fire-eyed 'dogs of the sky' (Cwn Wybir), the 'corpse candle' (Canwyll Corff), the doleful 'death-warning voice' (Cyhyraeth), the 'knockers', and other gloomy and terrific things were still dreaded and spoken of, though not often perceived.

Her strong imagination, once touched by such wonders, became for ever endowed with a sort of Archimago faculty of transforming creatures of unusual shape into monsters. Interludes, which were often performed in the open air to celebrate a rustic wedding, awakened her dramatic faculty.

The Welsh know few sorrows apart from sickness, and with them the terms are almost interchangeable. It is through no vast effort of self-denial, but a natural and general duty, that the good Welshwoman, whose home is still healthy and happy, should go forth after her daily work and spend the weary night in watching and waiting upon her sick neighbour, expecting no other recompense than similar help when her time of need arrives.

Elizabeth Cadwaladyr, therefore, without a notion of meritorious self-sacrifice, was early prepared for the performance of deeds which the world calls beneficient. Both use and temperament led her to think so lightly of fatigue, hardship, and danger, that only when they became extreme, did she deem them worth mentioning. Her surprise was great when she found that an up-hill walk of about forty yards, from the hospital at Balaclava to the huts, was complained of by anyone, and that the descent could be deemed dangerous when covered with snow.

Accustomed from infancy to traverse the mountain wastes alone, and to cross the deep-channelled brooks, without handrail or help, upon a tapering fir-pole, which rocked to the tread, her well-balanced frame and exact step, rendered all ascents, and descents, and horizontal movements easy. She would – if ever woman could – have trod securely the bridges of St Patrick's purgatory.

Her character may appear to resemble rather the strength, the sternness, and the varied aspects of the mountains, than the soft sunshine of the Lake of Bala. Yet she was eminently social, and had the most engaging qualities as a companion.

The kindliness of her nature was manifested in daily acts of spontaneous service. She was the ever ready friend of the forlorn, the helpless, and the afflicted.

Persons whom she has nursed in sickness, speak with warm gratitude of her never-failing assiduity, her noiseless movement, her gentle touch, her hope-inspiring words, her encouraging smile, her true compassion, her great humanity, and her elevating piety. She thought so little of laborious exercise, of spending successive nights in watching, of striving cheerfully against personal illness – in order to alleviate the sufferings of others by her attentions – of undergoing privations, and of sacrificing her own comfort in every way for their sake, that some benefits thus rendered, not only without complaint, but with cheerful looks and indefatigable hands, cost her no effort, and resulted merely from the exuberance of bodily strength and mental alacrity. The writer of these pages has experienced her care and kindness, and can, therefore, appreciate her self-denying character.

There is an ancient Welsh triad, which declares that the blessing of God follows upon three things – these have already descended upon the head of Elizabeth Cadwaladyr – "The blessing of father and mother, the blessing of the sick and infirm, and the blessing of the necessitous stranger".

It may be well to offer here a few particulars of the present state of the Welsh Calvinistic Methodists, frequent reference being made to their 'Association' in the following autobiography.

The ministers of the Welsh Calvinistic Methodists are itinerant. They are chosen by local societies, approved at monthly meetings; and, after a probation of five years, some among them are authorized at the Quarterly Associations to administer the sacraments. They are severally appointed to particular counties; but each minister makes annually a missionary tour to distant parts of the Principality – thus giving their respective congregations the much-valued excitement of variety; no minister, on such occasions, preaching more than two sermons, both delivered in the same day, in any one chapel.

They are remunerated for their services by small sums, paid to them after each sermon out of a fund formed by the collection of monthly pence from the congregations. The Quarterly Association is considered to embody the whole connexion, either personally, or by means of representatives.

At the last census, the number of chapels was 828, containing upwards of 211,951 seats. The attendance on the

Census Sunday, 1851, was, in the morning, 79,728; in the afternoon, 59,140; and in the evening, 125,244.

The Calvinistic Methodists of Wales support various Home and Foreign Missions. Among the latter may be mentioned their stations in Brittany, and at Cassay and Sylhet in Bengal. In the year 1837, a college for the education of ministers was established at Bala, and in the year 1842, another at Trefecca; the latter under the presidency of the Rev. David Charles, a grandson of the great North Wales Reformer.

The number of Sunday-schools belonging to the Calvinistic Methodists, is, according to Mr Horace Mann's 'Table Q', 962; and the number of scholars on the books, 112,740.

PART 1

Chapter 1

He who loves the young must
love also their sports

Translation of a Welsh Proverb

Bala

Birth – Ancestral Localities – Dafydd Cadwaladyr – The Revd Thomas Charles – Riots at Bala – Domestic Habits – Death of Judith Cadwaladyr – Schoolfellows – Early Indications of Peculiar Character – Dancing – Obsolete Superstitions – Plâs yn Drêf.

I do not exactly know the year in which I was born. Some children of the family tore the spare leaves out of the old Bible in which my father had entered his marriage with my mother, the birthdays of the children, and the dates when several of them died. There was one of their daughters before me who was christened Elizabeth, and she died long before I was born. I believe that I am now about sixty-one years of age – reckoning by the times spent in various places, my known age at the occurrence of certain events, and putting my life together in this way; and I know that the twenty-fourth of May is my birthday.

The history of a Welshman, and of a Welshwoman too, must always begin with the pedigree, so I may as well state at once, that I am descended by the father's side from the royal race of Tewdyr, from which our most gracious Queen also traces her lineage.

My paternal grandfather bore the name of Cadwaladyr Dafydd. He rented a farm called Erwd Dymel at Cerrigydrudion, in the county of Denbigh.

My grandfather's farm had been held by his family from generation to generation, for several hundred years; part of the time as owners, and the rest as tenants.

In this long course of time, his family and the other inhabitants of Cerrigydrudion had intermarried so frequently with the parishioners of Llangwm and Llanfihangel in the same district, that every individual in the three parishes was a cousin in blood to the rest. The eldest son of my grandfather succeeded him as tenant of the hereditary farm.

Surnames were at that time so unsettled in Wales, that each of his five sons bore a different one.

My father, Dafydd Cadwaladyr, was the second of them. He removed into Merioneth, and took a farm called Pen Rhiw, in the parish of Llanycil, near the lake of Bala.

He was a godly man, and a great preacher among the Welsh Calvinistic Methodists. In his person he was thought to be very like the Tewdyr race. He was tall and handsome, of a fair complexion, and had rather light-coloured sandy hair.

He lived to be eighty-two years of age, was active in mind and body to the last, and continued to preach until three days before his death. He never lost a tooth, but kept the whole set of thirty-two in his head as white as ivory. He did not see the use of dentists and tooth powder, and never used anything but salt and water. He had no faith in a coach, or a crazy boat; and, therefore, made the most of his long journeys on foot. In the course of his life he walked twice from Bala to London and back again; and he used to reckon towards the close of his life that he had walked altogether as far as twice round the world.

My father, in his youth, married Judith Erasmus. Her father was Humphrey Erasmus, whose house stood on the point of ground where four counties meet, and four gates opened near it, into four fields of his farm; one in the county of Denbigh; one in the county of Montgomery; one in the county of Radnor; and one in Shropshire. My grandfather, Humphrey Erasmus, was a very godly man, and his daughter Judith – my mother – was a very godly woman.

I was born at Pen Rhiw, within sight of Aran Benllyn, and Llyn Tegid; and in the midst of the fine scenery which tourists admire so much, among the highest mountains, and near the largest lake in the Principality.

The Rev. Thomas Charles[1] was then living at Bala, and doing all the good he could by establishing schools, and preaching in that neighbourhood; he was at the head of the Welsh Calvinistic Methodists, and a most particular friend of my parents.

---

[1] The Rev. Thomas Charles, well known to the world as one of the originators of the Bible Society, was born in the year 1755, in the parish of Llanfihangel, Caermarthenshire. He was educated at the Welsh schools of Llanddowror and Caermarthen, and at Jesus College, Oxford, where he took the degree of B.A. He was ordained to a curacy in Somersetshire, and afterwards became curate of Llanymowddwy, in Merionethshire. An injudicious rector caused him to quit the Church, and he subsequently devoted himself as a Dissenting Minister to the energetic promotion of works of piety and charity. He preached extensively himself, and assisted in organizing the Welsh Calvinistic Ministry. He established Circulating and Sunday Schools throughout the Principality; he edited two editions of the Welsh Bible; he wrote and compiled several excellent religious tracts and books, and set on foot the first periodical magazine ever published in Wales. Previous to his death, in 1814, no less than 320,000 copies of his works were in circulation.

When I was two or three years old, my father accidentally left his licence at home while he went into Caernarvonshire to preach. He was, in consequence, taken before Justice Humphreys, and committed by him, as a rogue and a vagabond, to some prison neal Capel Curig. Mr Humphreys sent to Pen Rhiw for my father's Bible, and my mother, thinking that my father wanted it, and not knowing of his arrest, sent it immediately. Mr Humphreys ordered my father to be again brought before him, showed the book and said that he intended to burn it. Welsh Bibles were scarce in those days, and perhaps he thought that by destroying this one he should put a stop to my father's preaching. However, David Cadwaladyr told him, he might indeed burn the paper and print, but that he could not burn his Bible, as it was not only written in his heart, but in his head; for he had learned it off book from beginning to end. The Justice then altered his manner, and said, "Well, you are a brave old fellow! Take your book and this five-pound note in it."

While my father was thus imprisoned, riots took place for some cause or other – I am sure I don't know what[2] – at Bala; and I have been told that the mob burnt the Bull inn, the old palace of the Welsh princes, I think, also Mr Price's house at Rhiwlas, and the books, registers, and papers belonging to the magistrates' office.

The night it happened, my mother, fearing for her children's safety, took us out into the woods, and hid us in a sort of summer-house, where there were stumps of trees

[2]   These riots were led by some young men who had vainly appealed to the magistrates against the ballot for the Militia. A very old man now living at Bala was one of the ringleaders, and has certified the fact.

placed for seats. The place belonged to a neighbour. We were afterwards told the history, and used often to go and play there. We called it 'The Temple'.

My parents had sixteen children. I knew only by hearsay about my eldest brothers, for they went away from home before I could remember anything. One of them, who had enlisted as a soldier, rose to be a captain in the army; and when he was taken prisoner with the rest at Flushing, he broke his heart with indignation. He said, "I could have borne to die in battle, but not in this way," and he was dead in a moment.

My eldest sister left home so early that I, as a child, could scarcely remember her. She married a man named Nelson, and went out to India.

I was my mother's favourite, and I remember her advice and her exhortations to this day.

I loved her with all my soul; her words have always lived in my heart, and helped to direct my conduct through life. I was very fond of a brother eleven months younger than myself, and had a liking for my younger sisters, who looked up to me for protection.

My elder sister always disliked me; and I returned the feeling very cordially. I had no particular concern about the other members of the family. When any of them affronted me, I used to steal away to a neglected corner of the yard, and sit down to think resentful thoughts, careless of food and of everything, until I crept back in time for bed. My mother found out my sulking corner, and whipped me for my frowardness. After that, I discovered a more secret hiding-place, within a cavernous hole of a neighbouring rock, in a field on my father's farm. Here I regularly resorted for several years, to brood over my occasional causes of displeasure, and to think of all sorts of things. Often and often, while sitting there in utter solitude, strange visionary scenes and beings flitted before me. I had never known of any other country than my own, or of any other people, excepting those I sometimes heard my father read of in the Bible. Yet in my cleft of the rock I used to imagine beings which I believed to have no other existence than my own thoughts gave them. I saw black people, and brown people, and yellow people, with strange-looking and various dwelling-places; and trees and flowers, such as I had never seen or heard of. Especially I remember to have been very much struck with the look of one tall tree, with all the leaves at the top, and bearing numbers of big nuts.

My mother became very ill, and one of her parting charges to my father was, not to bend Elizabeth's spirit. No one could comfort me when she died; and it was my eager desire to die too. I always thought I should have done so, had not Mr Charles, of Bala, by the exercise of some mysterious power prevented me.

I was then a little more than five years of age. When I found that she was dead, I could not bear to stay in the house with her corpse; I stole away to my hiding-place to weep and cry over her loss, and to indulge my angry feelings against Mr Charles, of Bala. I did not think of killing myself, but I believed that I could have died by willing it, if he had not overpowered me. After a long search, my uncle found me and carried me home, famishing and faint, but still resisting his intention, from dread of being in the same house as my dead mother. I was not naturally a gloomy child, although I had these odd fits of anger and melancholy. I was indeed a very merry one, and I have loved a bit of fun all my life, as many odd freaks and adventures will show.

As soon as we came out of chapel on a Sunday morning, my father used to lead all his family to church. He did not approve of separation, and used to take the sacrament at church, or from a clergyman.

My mother was buried in the churchyard of Llanycil, and many years afterwards, he was laid in the same grave.

My father was an excellent, and very fast knitter, and he always composed his sermons as he sat in the chimney-corner over his knitting-pins. We knew what was going on by his not talking to us, and by his saying at intervals in Welsh, "One, one, one," until he reached the clock of the stocking; and "Two, two, two," until he finished the foot. He never wrote them down.

I was sent to school at Bala with the neighbours' children. The two sons of Mr Charles were among my school-fellows, although they were older than myself. Tegid, the poet, (afterwards the Rev. John Jones,[3] of Nevern) and his two pretty sisters were also with us. I was always quarrelling with him and fighting, but I would not hear anyone else speak uncivilly to him, nor suffer anyone to strike him without bestowing a blow in return. He was even then much respected among the children, for his character and abilities. He used to make beautiful verses, and I was always very fond of poetry. I never read any that I liked better than his verses called 'My Native Land'. Our constant squabbles caused a shrewd old

---

[3] This eminent scholar and admirable poet was best known among his countrymen by the bardic name of "Tegid". He derived it from the lake of Bala, which is called Llyn Tegid, in traditional memory of Prince Tegid, a Welsh sovereign who was drowned therein many centuries ago.

lady to say that we two should be sure to come together in after life; but she was mistaken.

I was quick and sharp, and liked to learn to read and write, but the writing master himself spoiled my progress. It seemed that he was not pleased that I got on so fast. He was always finding fault with me; and one day he provoked me so much, by striking me on the face, that I blotted my copy-book on purpose. He got very angry, and threw his cane at me. I threw it back again at him. He took it then, and stuck it in my pinafore, placed a fool's-cap on my head. and stood me up upon a form, where I amused myself by doing the soldier's exercise. He was really cruel to me; and one day he shut me up in the black-hole – a coal-cellar below the schoolroom. I was not penitent or submissive; and so I was left there. That evening, a large religious meeting was held in the school-room, and when the people began to sing I heard them; and, being very fond of music, I tried to sing also as loud as I could. These odd sounds coming up disturbed the meeting. When the writing master divulged the cause of the interruption, one of the elders then came to fetch me out of my prison, but I refused to accompany him, and said that Watkins had put me there, and that Watkins must come and release me, or else I would stay where I was. So at last he was obliged to come. Mrs Jones, the girls' schoolmistress, taught us wholly in Welsh, and all the English I knew in those days was the name for a horse, a cow, or some such words which we learned, now and then, from old Jones, who called this short, general lesson, 'a pennyworth of English', and made each of us pay a penny for it.

I used to invent games to divert myself and my schoolfellows in play hours. My favourite amusement was playing at funerals. On such occasions I always officiated as the parson, and the others were bearers, mourners, spectators, and sextons. To get something to bury often exercised my ingenuity. The butcher had, one day, killed a bacon-pig for my father. I was bent upon having the snout; so I went with a knife alone and secretly to the place where the huge pig was hanging to cool before cutting up. I was very little, and the scaffolding which I had reared to reach it, gave way under me while I was haggling to get the head off; so that the pig and all were very near falling and crushing me. However, I got the snout, and ran off with it. An aunt of mine, my father's sister, was staying at our house. She had company to tea one evening, and on looking for her caddy, in which she kept a pound of the best tea, which had been sent to her from Chester by her sister, she failed to find this caddy. It was searched for in vain. At last I was asked if I knew what had become of it.

"Oh, yes," said I, "I buried it a fortnight ago, under the sycamore tree, and there it is."

The caddy was of china, in a mahogany case; the ground was very dry, so it took no harm there, and they found it safe enough.

I was always a good walker; and I learned to ride when I was very young, on the ponies that used to be about my father's house and farm. I was very active, and used to climb the trees with the boys, and to run races on foot with the swiftest. I learned among them many tricks of skill and strength, such as passing through a stick held behind the left foot, threading a needle while sitting on a rolling bottle, balancing a ruler on the chin, putting my heel to the nape of my neck, and the like. A gentleman once gave me a five-pound-note for my activity, and my father bought a cow with the money.

In those days there lived at Bala an old man who used to be called Shôn Fideldee. He was in the habit of going about the roads and everywhere, playing Welsh tunes. He often went round the farm-houses, to see whether anybody wished to bespeak a jig; he never called at my father's, but he used to pass along the footpath below the garden, in going elsewhere. Whenever he came in sight of our house, my sister would send me upstairs out of the way, for fear I should run after him. Coming from school, through the town of Bala, I often peeped into his cottage, and joyful I was if I found him at home; if not, I used to ask the old woman which way he was gone, and then ran to meet him, as I was ever on the watch to get a tune from his fiddle. Wherever I chanced to find him, whether on the roads or in the fields, or anywhere, he would play for me. Seeing how nimbly I frisked about to his music, he taught me the positions and steps, and would dance with me and play his fiddle going along the lanes or highroads. He taught me to dance the jig, the minuet, the hornpipe, and all sorts of things, at different opportunities, wherever I chanced to meet him.

Mr Simpson, the supervisor at Bala, was a very handsome man. His wife was an Englishwoman; it was reported that she had been born and brought up a gentlewoman, and had ran away with him against her friends' consent. A ball, for the benefit of the County Infirmary, was given in the commercial room at the Lion inn, and people attended it from all parts of the country. A gentleman who was passing through the town, making a tour of pleasure and sketching through North Wales, stayed a day or two at the Lion, and he opened the ball with Mrs Simpson. The four windows of the room were very low and faced the street, and a crowd of people and children assembled outside to look on. The ball began at five o'clock in the afternoon. The people kept early hours in those days. Coming out of school, I stood with the rest of my schoolfellows, and my interest in the scene was so lively that I pressed forward close to one of the windows, through which I saw Mrs Simpson – the fine English lady – at faults in the steps and figure. Instantly I cried, "Stop, stop! Mrs Simpson, that's wrong. I'll show you the way." As quick as thought I sprang in at the window, and did the right steps on the floor.

The dancers were very much amused, and the strange gentleman spoke with Mrs Ellis, the landlady, and then led me by the hand to a shop kept by Kitty Jones, loan Tegid's mother. She kept eight workwomen, and speedily dressed me up, by his direction, in a white book-muslin frock, a white satin sash, white stockings, red morocco shoes, and a white necklace. She lent me a white petticoat belonging to her daughter Helen, to make my frock look well, as my own was of dark Welsh woollen. The gentleman left me for a while in Kitty's hands, and then fetched me back again to the ballroom, where I danced with him and with many other persons, until Mr Charles came to fetch me. He led me out, and said, "My dear child, I did not think you were so naughty." He then desired me to go straight home as I was. I did so, and felt very proud of my fine clothes. I had nothing on my head but my long, thick, and curly black hair. People used often to give me sixpence for letting it fall down for them to look at. I was rosy,[4] and in high spirits, when I arrived at Pen Rhiw, for I fancied that even Gwenllian would be glad to see me so smart. I soon discovered, however, that I was sadly mistaken; for she

---

[4] This fact was probably ascertained either in a pool by the way, or in a pewter plate on arriving.

looked fiercely at me, stripped me of all my finery, even my white stockings, and sent everything back to Kitty Jones. I never saw or heard of my ball-dress again, but I grieved for a long time over the loss of my pretty necklace. My sister was not content with inflicting this mortification – she took a stick and beat me with it severely, so that I was sore as well as sad. When my father came home, he expressed much displeasure at her having beaten me, scolded her, and told her she would ruin me. He talked to me very seriously, said that I ought not to have gone into the ballroom, and asked, "What made you go?"

I replied, "I could not help going, for the telynau (harps) were there." He wanted me to say that I would never do so again, but I only answered, thoughtfully, "I do not know", feeling that very likely I should, under a similar temptation, do the same thing.

The strange gentleman made inquiries about my family, and offered to bring me up and provide for me, but my father would not consent to part from me.

Not very long afterwards, I got into trouble again by my dancing.

A neighbouring farmer's daughter called at our house one evening and asked my sister's leave, as my courage was well known, that I should walk as far as the town with her, because she was afraid of a ghost which haunted that part of the way. My sister consented, understanding that Margaret was merely going to buy some thread and other trivial things, and would return with me directly. Margaret had a bundle, which she carefully left outside when she came to our house. She took it up again when we set out, and carried it to the cottage of an old woman at Bala; the bundle contained fine clothes, in which Margaret dressed herself. She at first intended that I should do her small errands and return home, while she went to a dance, which was to take place that evening to celebrate a wedding; but she forgot everything when we met some young men, who were of her acquaintance, in the street, and took me with her to the public house, where, seeing people dancing and hearing the harps, I could not help dancing myself. Gwenllian became very uneasy when nine o'clock came and I had not reached home. About half-past nine my father returned from preaching in the chapel at Bala, little thinking what I was about at the time, close at hand there. He ate his supper, prayed, and was retiring to bed, when Gwenllian told him that I had gone out with Margaret, and she knew not what had become of me. He immediately set out for Bala, and seeing the old woman, who was watching at her cottage-door for Margaret's return, learned from her where it was likely I should be found.

It was past ten o'clock, and I was going merrily down a country dance, when, suddenly, I beheld the awful apparition of my father, Dafydd Cadwalydyr, standing in the doorway. I made a rush to get out, but there was no space to pass, so I dived, and escaped through his legs, and ran as fast as my feet could carry me to Pen Rhiw.

My sister kept me up until he came in. As he entered, he exclaimed, "Dear me, how the devil does help this girl along, and enable her to use her feet!"

He talked to me very gravely, and asked me how he could go into the pulpit and speak of the wickedness of the world, while his own child did such things. He remarked that his other children did not want to go to dances, and he could not think why I did.

I said, "I can't help it – when I hear music, something tickles my feet, and I can't keep them quiet."

When I was about eight years old, I was taken on a visit into Denbighshire to the house of my father's eldest brother. They used to play interludes there. The people were ungodly, and used to do also some very strange things.

One night the dairy-maid put me to bed, but told me not to go to sleep, as she should want me to go out with her after my uncle and aunt had gone to bed. She came between eleven and twelve o'clock, and took me up and dressed me. At the outside of the house-door, she had put ready for me a pail of water, a beetle,[5] and a pair of stockings without feet; and she had another set of such things for herself. We carried them off, and she sent me into a field with directions to dip the old stockings into the pail, and to beat them on a stone with the beetle, saying certain charming words in Welsh. They began, 'Come and live with me, come and work with me,' &c. The dairy-maid went into the next field. I called out now and then to ask her if I had beaten enough; but I heard no answer. I beat so hard that I broke the beetle. There was a little rivulet at a good distance from me in the field, and at last I saw a tall man coming from thence towards me. He wore a buff waistcoat, and had bright buttons on his coat. I was very much startled, and ran away back to the house, leaving all the things behind me in my fright.

At other times the servants would go in a party of five to the church, taking me with them, and put me to sit in the porch

5   Golchbren – washing-stick. A wooden instrument used in the process of *beetling* – that is, washing and beating house linen and clothes in running water, after they have been *bucked* – steeped and soaked in lye, made of fern ashes.

by myself, while they passed backwards – saying the Lord's Prayer backwards – round and round the church; always turning so as never to cross the porch.

They placed me there, they said, to keep Satan away. One night I contrived to pull a sheet off my bed. and to take it with me under my pinafore to the porch. While they were going backwards round the church, I put it on, and went to meet them jumping along like a frog, having the sheet over my head and trailing around me. They all took fright, ran away, and never stopped until they came to the village. There they stood and called loudly for me. I took off the sheet, rolled it up again, and followed them. They questioned me whether I had seen something terrible in white, but I said "No," and did not tell what I had done. That night it struck me that such tricks were very wicked, and I steadfastly determined never to go out at night with the servants again.

Soon afterwards, my father came to see me, and I told him all these things. He was much troubled, and very angry. He rebuked my uncle and aunt for suffering their servants to practise such wickedness, and took me home with him, giving me good advice not to be a partaker in other people's sins. I had high spirits, but meant no evil.

One day, at Pen Rhiw, my father was out in his ground planting trees, and I was with him. There was a very steep heap of stones hard by, and I amused myself with climbing to the top of it and jumping down. My father called to me and said, "Betsy, don't do that, you will hurt yourself." I said, "I will only do it once more." I did so, fell, and broke my left arm. An old woman set it for me; it was soon well, and as straight and as strong as if it had never been hurt.

My second sister had the care of my father's house after my mother's death. She did not understand my disposition, which might have been led to anything by kindness. She worried me into obstinacy, and then beat me, and often she used me very harshly. My favourite brother died, I became very unhappy, and desired very much some change of circumstances. I would not humble myself to her, and she would not treat me with kindness.

Finding my sister's tyranny intolerable, and longing to be a woman and to provide for myself, I ran away from my father's house, when I was about nine years of age, and sought refuge at Plâs yn Drêf, the residence of the Rev. Mr Lloyd,[6] a gentleman of large fortune at Bala, and my father's landlord. Mrs Lloyd questioned me closely and kindly as to my purpose, and said that I might remain in her household, and learn to be useful.

She had me instructed in all sorts of housework and needlework, in cooking and baking, in brewing, washing and ironing. It was here that I first learned to speak English. She was an invalid, and kept me much about her person, not suffering me to live among the servants. I was taught, besides, to read and write; and, as I delighted in music – always having felt that the sound lifted me off my feet – Mrs Lloyd allowed me to take lessons upon the Welsh triple-stringed harp; and I have often sat to play her to sleep when she was ailing and wakeful.

One day, Bishop Luxmore said to Mr Lloyd, "If you suffer your wife and family to attend the Methodist meetings, sir, I shall strip off your gown."

"Very well, my lord," he replied, "then from this time I shall go with them there."

---

[6] This gentleman was intimate with the Rev. Thomas Charles, and the means of bringing him first into the neighbourhood of Bala.

Chapter 2

Things will have their first or second agitation. If
they be not tossed upon the arguments of counsel,
they will be tossed upon the waves of fortune.

Lord Bacon's *Sentences.*

Liverpool
**Flight from Plâs yn Drêf – Liverpool – Burglars –
Hardships – New Friends – Burglars again – Lancaster
Assizes – Mr Canning's Election – Welsh Preachers.**

I had been at Plâs yn Drêf for about five years, when I agreed
with Mrs Lloyd one Saturday, to live there another twelve
months. In the course of the following Sunday night, a sudden
thought occurred to me that I was not to stay there any longer,
and that I must see something more of the world. I instantly
got up and tied a few clothes in a bundle.

Before Monday morning dawned, I had thrown my bundle
out of my bedroom window, and jumped out after it. I
immediately set off for Chester. I ran the first part of my
journey, fearing to be pursued and taken back; then by walking
and getting a lift now and then in a passing cart or waggon, I
arrived at Chester at last, and went to the house of my aunt.

She received me with astonishment; the very same
afternoon she gave me two pounds ten shillings, and sent me
off to go by the coach from Chester to my father's house.
Instead of obeying her directions, I went straight to the quay,
and took my passage for Liverpool.

When the packet boat arrived at Liverpool, the passengers stood upon deck, and the captain in the midst of them. I held myself aloof throughout the voyage, from everyone on board; and now I felt more upon my guard than ever, lest I should be led into some sort of trap. A gentleman asked me many questions, and seemed to pity me because I was so young and all alone there. I answered him very shortly, and not very civilly. When we had been landed upon the pier, he renewed his inquiries, offering me to take me with him and to give me lodging for the night. I answered that I had relations in Brisbane Street. He said that was three miles off. I replied "Never mind – what's that to you?" and rushed away.

It was about four or five o'clock in the morning when I thus found myself alone in the streets of Liverpool. I wandered for a long time, and, chancing to look back, I saw the same gentleman following. This sadly frightened me, and I turned suddenly into a dirty court, which was ankle deep in mud.

All was still in the town, every house was shut up, and not a creature visible in the streets. Passing along the alley, I saw a door open: a woman came out and threw some water on the ground out of a basin; I recognized her directly.

My father was in Lady Huntingdon's connection. He often made long journeys to preach at different places, and took a leading part in the large religious assemblies held in those days at Bala. He was consequently well known to all the Welsh people in Great Britain. I thus became acquainted with numbers who came from far and near to hear him preach; among them not a few were kinsfolk of our own, for we own cousins to the ninth degree in Wales. The woman I had seen was not my cousin, but her husband and herself were well known to my father, and I instantly called her by her name, as my countrywoman and acquaintance. She had risen before day to get breakfast for her son, who was to sail that morning from Liverpool on a distant voyage. She hospitably took me in, fed me, and gave me a bed, and the next day accompanied me to the house of my cousin in Brisbane Street. He was at the time in the West Indies, and his wife was much surprised at seeing me. She, however, received me very kindly, and while I remained at their house I found that the person who had shown so much concern for me on my landing, was a respectable sea-captain, and their lodger.

My cousin's wife took so great a liking to me, that she wished me to live with her as a companion, feeling often lonely when her husband was away. I did not like her fidgetty habits, and resolved on going to service. This made her angry, and hurt her pride. While I stayed with her, a Mrs Edwards, a friend of hers, asked her as a favour to allow me to go and take care of a house in Church Street while she and her brothers went to a party. Mrs Edwards had given her own servant a holiday; so, when she and her brothers went out, I was left alone in their house. The front part of it was a woollen-draper's shop, which they kept. As I sat quietly in the kitchen, learning by heart the Book of the Prophet Isaiah, out of my Welsh Bible, I suddenly heard a noise of breaking glass. I took the candle in my hand, and walked into the parlour. There I saw a hand and arm stretched through the broken window, trying to catch hold of the key, which stood in the lock of the door close by. I never thought of thieves, and called out, "Stop, stop, I'll help you!" The hand and arm were quickly drawn back out of sight, and everything was still. I went back to the kitchen, not thinking anything was amiss; and after ten minutes had elapsed, went to see whether the man was coming to be let in. I then found that he had removed a whole panel shutter, glass and all, out of the shop window, and I saw him taking a piece of waistcoat-cloth through the window. He put his hand through again, and seized a piece of corduroy. Then I knew he was a thief. I took a great stick, which Captain Edwards had brought from the West Indies, opened the front door, and rushed out. He ran away, and I ran after him down the street calling, "Stop thief, stop thief!" as loud as I could bawl. He turned down St Peter's Alley. I flew after him, caught hold of his heel, threw him down on his face, and jumped upon his back. Two watchmen came up, and I told them what was the matter, where the robbery occurred, and where I lived. They took the thief to the French prison – there being no other at that time. I returned to the house in Church Street, where I had left the door wide open, and stayed there without fear until after three in the morning, when Mrs Edwards and her brothers came home. I told them all the history, and Mr Hugh Jones sat up afterwards until sunrise to watch the premises.

The next day, a watchman came to take me before the magistrates; and Mr Hugh Jones, Mrs Edwards's brother, went with me. Soon after I had got into the court, a magistrate said, "Swear her." I said "Oh no! I won't swear; that would be wicked." He then explained the nature of an oath. I said "I will tell the truth without kissing the book."

I took the oath, and was examined. The prisoner was present, and I was asked several questions concerning him. I told the gentleman exactly what had happened, and what I had said and done. The thief was committed to take his trial at the next Lancaster assizes, and I was bound over to appear as a witness against him. "Ah!" said I to the thief, "you are a wicked man; you have broken the commandment, 'Thou shalt not steal'."

At this the magistrates and lawyers laughed.

I was always known in Meironeth as Betsy Pen Rhiw. On coming first to Liverpool, I called myself by my proper name, Elizabeth Cadwaladyr; but on finding that the English people could not pronounce that surname, I afterwards adopted my father's Christian name instead, and signed myself Elizabeth Davis; my elder brothers and sisters having done the like, in changing Cadwaladyr for Davis.

My cousin's wife refused to assist in getting a place for me; but an acquaintance, whom I had met at her house, made inquiries, and recommended me, as a servant of all-work, to an elderly gentlewoman. I went there accordingly, and found it a very hard place; for my mistress had a daughter, and her daughter had two young children. My mistress had also a son, and two gentlemen as lodgers, all living in the house. She was of a very bad temper, and often scolded and beat me. One day, she provoked me so greatly that I gave her a good beating in return. However, she found me so hard-working and useful that, even after this, she begged of me not to away. I replied that I would go. She reproached me, and said that she knew I had no place to go to, as my cousin would not receive me.

I had not been there many weeks, when, on the Wednesday preceding the Friday on which it was settled that I should leave my place, I knelt down in a very disconsolate state to wash the outer doorsteps. I felt how forlorn and desolate I was, and I cried very bitterly. I thought of my mother, and afresh upbraided Mr Charles, of Bala, in my thoughts, as the cause of all my wretchedness, because he had prevented me from dying with her. In the midst of my distress, two ladies, coming along the pavement, stopped to ask me the cause of my weeping. I told them all my troubles and all my history. One of them remarked to the other, "Poor thing! she is quite a child of Nature." The elder lady spoke most to me, but the younger looked at me very kindly. They asked me the work I had to do, and the hours at which I went to bed, and got up. I said I did all the work of the house, and went on the errands of five grown persons, and two children; and that I lay down at one o'clock every morning, and rose at five. They concluded the interview by telling me, that after I had fetched the muffins and crumpets, as usual, at eight o'clock that evening for my mistress, I was to call at the house by itself, and ask to see Mrs Jackson.

I did as they had bidden me. It was a large mansion. I was shown into the housekeeper's room, and received by a person who asked me many questions as to my capabilities for service. I was disappointed, and asked to see the pretty lady; but Mrs Jackson said she was commissioned to engage with me, and she promised to send a man to fetch me and my box on Friday evening. This was done, and I found myself a member of a very large household, in the service of Sir George and Lady_____. She was the young and pretty lady who had first noticed me in the street; and the elder lady was a friend on a visit to her. Mrs Jackson was the housekeeper.

Lady _____'s favour soon promoted me to the place of head housemaid; I formed a close friendship with her own maid, Sarah Owen, and had a very happy life there.

I have heard that Sir George was born at the Hall, near Preston, in Lancashire; and I believe he had property about there. His lady was a native of the East Indies – I believe that she was born a princess. Her brother, the prince, was staying at Sir George's house when I first went there, and for some months afterwards. He took such a fancy to me, that he proposed to Lady _____ to make me his wife according to the English law; but I was afraid of the very look of him, and would not hear of it.

His lands were, I believe, in the presidency of Madras. I cannot remember his names. He had about four dozen of them. His servants were not Mahometans. They told me that the people of their tribe lived to a great age, and were not subject to epidemic diseases.

The prince was very rich, and Lady _____ was his next heir.

During the first month of November that I spent in Sir George's service, I went very early one morning, with the housekeeper's permission, to assist the servants of Mr Roddy in preparing their master's house in Williamson Square, for the return of the family. The cook had gone out to buy some rolls for our breakfast, and the housemaid and I were on our way upstairs, when, resting on the landing-place of the second flight, I looked out at the leads, and remarked to the housemaid how easily thieves might come in by that way.

The housemaid was timid, and begged of me not to talk of thieves. While were speaking, we heard from below a sort of cracking sound, which caused us to wonder whether the cook could have returned so very soon from her errand. I said, "Suppose it should be thieves!"

The housemaid replied, "Oh! I hope cook hasn't—" *left the door open*, she would have said; but, dropping all her cans, and pots, and pans, in her fright, she fell, speechless.

I set down my load, and ran downstairs. I found the front door wide open, and I ran into the square hallooing, "Stop thief!" It was so foggy that I could scarcely see my hand; and whether there were thieves in the house or not, I did not really know, but I believed them to be there, and ran towards Pitt Street, calling out "Stop thief!" as I went along.

In that street I met two watchmen, guarding a man, who had been running, unseen, before me in the fog. They heard my cries, and stopped him; and, on approaching me, they inquired whether that was the one I meant. I said I did not know, and told the circumstances. They came back with me to Mr Roddy's house, bringing the prisoner with them. They discovered that the countinghouse had been broken open, and found three crowbars and a bunch of skeleton keys behind the door. The large desk had been forced, one of its hinges was wrenched off, and a draft for a large sum of money was hanging partly out of it. I picked up a knife on the floor. It had a metal plate on the handle, marked with the initials 'J.F.H.'. The prisoner tried to snatch it from me saying, "That's mine".

"You commit yourself, my man," said the watchman.

They took him away, and the next day I was obliged to appear before the magistrates again. Twenty houses had been broken into on the previous night. I was questioned concerning the prisoner. I said I did not see him in the house.

"Did not see him?" said another magistrate, scornfully.

"Let her go on," exclaimed the first. I related the facts of the case and he observed, "I knew I could get the truth from that girl."

They bound me over to appear at Lancaster. I said, "Oh! I am going there already at that time."

In the beginning of March, accordingly, I was taken by Mr Roddy to the assizes at Lancaster. Many other people from Liverpool went at the same time. The Church Street trial was brought on the first day. I was not asked many questions. The thief was sentenced to fifteen years' transportation. He had been for many years a Liverpool watchman, and was said to have been the chief of a gang of housebreakers. He was an old offender, and had been several times convicted.

On the second day, the Williamson Square trial came on.

Many questions were put to me. The counsel for the prosecution having said, "Brother Watson, have you any questions to ask this witness?"

Mr Watson said to me, "You opened the door for him?"

I exclaimed, "Oh! what a lie. If you say such things you will go to hell; my mother told me that everybody that told lies would go there."

He continued, "You showed him where the desk was, and you helped him to open it, didn't you?"

I burst out crying violently, and the judge told me I might go down, adding kindly, "Keep to the truth, my girl, through life;" and remarking to the court, "I would rather believe that child's evidence than that of many grown people. I should like to know who her parents are." It was Judge Barrow.

The thief was sentenced to be hanged. He had robbed Dr Solomon's house in the course of the night, before he broke into Mr Roddy's.

Sir George took Mr Canning's part in the contested election for Liverpool. Sir George's brother, Captain John James was then at the house; and Mr Canning with his family, and his mother came and stayed there at the time of the election. Mr Canning was very fond of his mother, and would not be separated from her at any time if he could help it. She was a nice woman, and I liked her better than any of them. Mr Canning and General Gasgoigne were returned together for Liverpool, (1812). There was a great dinner afterwards, and the merchants and principal people sent their servants to wait on the company; all Sir George's footmen went – he kept four – and the men out of livery were sent also.

All through my childhood and early youth, I cherished a very high opinion of my own goodness, and I was more especially proud of my honesty and truth. While I lived at Bala, no one could persuade me to receive the Lord's Supper; but during my first year's residence at Sir George's, I heard the famous John Elias preach a sermon in the Welsh chapel at Liverpool, which wrought a great change in my principles. The text was from Lam. iii, v: 27. In English, the words are, "It is good for a man that he bear the yoke in his youth." That sermon convinced me of my sin, and showed me my Saviour.

I still distinctly remember many of the remarks which John Elias made in it. The one that struck me most, as more especially applicable to my case, was his comparison of unholy people enjoying the pleasures of this world, to oxen that were fattening and rejoicing in their pasture, not knowing that they were preparing for the slaughter. After that I became a communicant, and learned to attend sermons so intently, that I could repeat long passages.

Sir George's family were good, religious people, and belonged to the Church of England.

The house-steward used to read prayers for the servants, every morning and evening.

A Sunday or two after having heard John Elias, I was very much impressed by a sermon on the subject of the 'Sword of the Lord', preached at our Welsh chapel by David Rhys, of Llanfynydd; especially that part of it which described people young and old doing the ways of the world, and practising all sorts of iniquity; never thinking that all the while the 'Sword of the Lord' was hanging over them. This often recurred to my mind, and checked me in my freaks and frolics.

Chapter 3

I rather would intreat thy company
To see the wonders of the world abroad,
Than living dully sluggardized at home,
Wear out thy youth with shapeless idleness
      Shakespeare, *Two Gentlemen of Verona, Act i. s.1.*

Foreign Travels
**Scotland – Mrs Siddons – Ireland – Captain Harris –
Calais – Spain – The O'Rourkes – Paris – St Cloud –
Continental Travels – Brussels Waterloo – Mysterious
Fellow-traveller – Italy – English Homeward Tour.**

I went to Sir George's house in June, and stopped there until
the following March: I then went with the family to Scotland,
and stayed there until the November of that year. Sir George
had a cottage on the Clyde, about three miles from Glasgow
and from thence visited Argyle Castle,[1] where we spent a
fortnight; we then went to G_____ Castle.

The duke was a very old man; he used to wear a little short
wig every day; on state occasions he wore a long wig, like the
Lord Chancellor's – all curls and powder. He had large
buckles in his shoes.

One day, while we were at the castle, there was a great
hunting party. I stood to look at the gentlemen when they were
mounting. After they were gone, I said to one of the grooms,
"I wish I had a horse to go too."

[1] Query – Inverary.

He answered, "There is a horse, if you would really like to go."

I told him that I would go and put my things on by the time he had the horse ready. I ran upstairs to my mistress's room, and found there a riding-habit of Indian nankin which the maid helped me on with. I got a Scotch hat somewhere or other, put it on, and hastened down to the courtyard, where a beautiful little horse was waiting for me. The groom helped me to mount, and showed me the way by which the hounds and hunters had gone off.

I rode a long way without seeing or hearing anything of them. At last, my horse made a dead stand, cocked up his ears, became very much agitated, and, before I was aware, jumped a little rivulet which ran down through some craggy rocks just by: however, I still found myself safe on his back. He became unmanageable, or, at least, I could not guide him; for he rushed among the woods and through the bushes, and I was obliged to lay the reins on his neck, and try, with both hands, to save the habit from being torn to pieces. He went flying along, up the mountains and down again, and over all sorts of steep and dangerous places. My hat was knocked off; my long, black hair streamed behind me, and my habit hung in a hundred shreds about me. In this wild way, I rode across the country from eleven o'clock in the morning until four in the afternoon – chasing the hunters, I suppose, for we only caught sight of their backs just as they were returning to the castle. I tried to hold back the horse, but I could not stop him, and he rushed with me into the courtyard where all the gentlemen were alighting. Much merriment was caused by my odd figure, and some of the gentlemen laughed until they could hardly stand. I went to my mistress afterwards, and told her about the habit; she did not blame me, but laughed, and said, "Oh, never mind the habit. I only wish that I had seen you come back."

The horse was a regular hunter, and not a bit the worse for the run.

One evening at the castle, while playing at hide-and-seek in the gallery, with Martha, the handsome housemaid, we ran out at the part which opened upon the rocks, and I saw there what I thought must be a white cat. I caught at it, seized it, and carried it into the house to look at. It was a short white wig. I stuck it on a stick and carried it out into the gallery. The housemaid said, "Oh! it belongs to the duke – he has been watching us."

The duke's valet saw us with the wig, and came and asked me for it. I refused to give it up. He tried to take it from me, and I ran away, and he ran after me. In taking a turn of the gallery he very nearly overtook me but I rushed against a door, and ran in, carrying the wig on the stick. It was a drawing-room, in which the company were assembled. They received me with shouts of laughter; I was surprised and frightened, but afterwards, finding they took my rude entry so well, I walked round the room showing the wig. The duke was not there as he had gone to his dressing-room. A young gentleman of the party asked me where I got the wig. I said, "On the bush. I will go and see if I can find some more."

The young gentleman at last took the wig; I think he was the duke's son, I then made an apology to the company for intruding, and Sir George, who was among them, laughed, and said, "My servant is a real child of nature!"

Between our visits we went back to the cottage on the Clyde.

We stayed a week at Stirling Castle, and then went to a castle by the sea-side – waiting there a fortnight for fine weather to cross over to Ireland. The lady of the castle was one of the biggest women I ever saw; fine-looking, but tremendously stout – a regular Scotch giantess.

At Edinburgh, I was taken for the first time in my life to a theatre. I saw there, Mrs Siddons, as the 'Tragic Muse', and wished very much that I could look as handsome and noble as she did. At Glasgow I saw her again on the stage, in the character of Queen Catherine.

At chapel at Glasgow, I met with Charles Mackenzie. He was a partner with his father and brother in a wholesale Scotch warehouse and factory. They were respectable people, and our housekeeper at the cottage tried hard to persuade me to marry him. He afterwards followed me to Liverpool on the same errand; but I could not like him.

When we reached Ireland, Sir George and his family travelled about visiting at noblemen and gentlemen's houses.

In Wicklow we went to see a famous well, near the mountain where the gold is. All the people in that neighbourhood, masters and servants alike, went to that well. They took fern with them, and each person threw one sprig into the charming well, and then howled. They could not explain why they did so, but they expected some good to happen as a consequence. We crossed from Kingston to Holyhead, and went to Plas Newydd to visit Lord and Lady Uxbridge. From thence we went to Sir William Bulkeley's house at Baron Hill. We crossed the Menai Strait into Caernarfonshire, and travelled straight home to Sir George's house, in Liverpool. We remained there quietly until March, 1814.

The second summer after I returned from Ireland, I went one Sunday as usual to the Welsh Chapel in Pall Mall, at Liverpool, and there met my friends, Mr and Mrs Jones, of Gee Street. He was a retired tradesman. They had no children. They invited me to go home with them to tea: I agreed, and went on with Mrs Jones.

I was sitting by their fire-side, reading a discourse on the subject of the first chapter of the gospel according to St John, when Mr Jones – who had stopped behind – came in and told his wife, that he had brought their friend, Captain Harris, to tea.

Captain Harris followed him into the parlour. I did not look up when he came in, but continued reading and bending my head down over the book. I felt very odd, and trembled all over. Mr Jones said to Captain Harris, "I have got here a daughter of a friend of yours."

The captain inquired who I was. Mr Jones said, "Look at her and see whether you know her."

The captain replied, "Then she must raise her head for me to see."

Captain Harris wore a buff waistcoat and a blue coat, with bright buttons. He was a fine-looking man. He sat and gazed very intently upon me and, afterwards, took a chair beside me at tea. That night we went to chapel together. I liked him, and would not allow another person to sit next to him there. After service was over, he asked whether I intended to stop for the society's meeting. I said, "Yes." He told me that he could not stay, as he must go to the docks, and he wished me goodnight.

I had three miles to go from the chapel to Sir George's house, and was running quite by myself down Pall Mall, when, there he stood waiting for me. I took no notice of him, but hastened on to pass through the Exchange before it was closed.

He overtook me and talked as we went along, about the sermon, and other matters, but did not say a word about love.

He saw me to my home, and asked leave to come and see me again; so I invited him to come the next day to tea.

Accordingly, he came about five o'clock. He was a friend of my father's and I introduced him into the housekeeper's room as my father's friend, Captain Harris.

Mrs Jackson had wished me to marry James Smith, a rich upholsterer's son; she told Harris about that affair, complained to him of my obstinacy, and bade him try to persuade me to accept of Smith. I went to chapel that evening with Harris, who brought me back, and we settled to walk together the next day to the Old Swan. On Tuesday he came, and I went out to talk with him. He had never spoken a word about love before; but then he told me that seven years before, when he was in Russia, he had dreamed of me, and that he had been looking for me ever since. He mentioned the exact time, and I knew that it was the very night on which I had seen his figure in the field, when I was a child, in Denbighshire. He asked me to promise to marry him – I made no answer, not knowing what to say. He came constantly to visit me, and whenever I displeased the housekeeper, she used to threaten she would tell my father's friend; and she often did so.

In January, he sailed for the West Indies, on board his own ship. When we parted, he said to me, "Have nothing to do with Smith." Harris was a very godly man, and my father had a great friendship for him and his family. While I had so much of his company, I did not care a great deal for him; when he was gone, I liked him better. He used often to write to me.

In March, 1814, I went abroad with Sir George and his
wife. We crossed from Dover to Calais. A number of French
porters, with leather caps on their heads, and plates on their
arms, came down to take the luggage. Among them was a man
without these badges. He was pointed out to me, and I saw
him in the act of walking off with a trunk which contained my
mistress's jewel casket, and with a hat-box of Sir George's. I
pursued him swiftly up the hill, came up with him, caught hold
of his leg, and pulled him to the ground, fought and struggled
with him, and took the trunk and box from him. Setting them
aside, and forgetting them for a moment in my rage, I beat
him, and pushed him rolling down the hill, crying with anger
while I did it, and all the people laughing.

The next morning we went to Paris, and, finding the king
was not yet come, we proceeded by way of Bayonne into
Spain. We travelled chiefly by night, on account of the great
heat, and therefore I did not see all the places; but the sea was
in sight during a part of our journey. I remember Vigo,
Saragossa, Salamanca, Cuidad Rodrigo, Seville, and Granada.

We visited the queen's palace – the biggest they have in
that country. There is no upstairs to it, and it stands upon
several acres of land. We stopped longest at Madrid, where
we put up at a hotel adjoining the King of Spain's palace.

One day, Sir George and Lady_____ attended a court
drawing-room. He wore a uniform, and she was most
beautifully and richly dressed in green velvet and gold, with
a train.

General O'Rourke and his wife had lodgings in the same
hotel, and the room occupied by Lady _____'s maid and
myself adjoined their apartments. Lady O'Rourke used often
to call us in to come and sit with her. She asked Owen to dress

her for the court drawing-room, and I went to assist. She wore a white-muslin dress and pink flowers; upon her head a very high muslin cap, with fifteen red bows in it; and had on a Brussels' lace tippet, a red scarf, and red slippers. She had no train – only a little bit of muslin hanging down behind – and her dress was shortened by her figure in front. She was about thirty years of age, had red hair, and a very red face. General O'Rourke was about thirty years older than his wife – a handsome man, and a perfect gentleman.

He came into the dressing-room, and, looking at her, said, "Have you not a better dress than this to put on?"

She answered, disdainfully, "If you don't like it—"

I did not hear the rest of her speech. They went along a gallery to the palace, and we heard her calling out to the guards and people, with her loud, iron voice, "Make way for Lady O'Rourke!" She looked like a sack of wool tied in the middle. After the drawing-room was over, she went out to drive in the same dress.

When Owen and I went to her room, we generally found her sitting alone, with a bottle and glass beside her; and she was very liberal in offering us what she had, but we did not take it. She was fond of talking of herself and her money; we learned from her that General O'Rourke was an Irishman, and had been from his youth an officer in the Spanish service, where he had won great estimation.

She told us that she was half tipsy at an inn in London one day, when General O'Rourke, who was returning to Spain, had not money to pay for his reckoning, and offered a fine ring to the landlord. She said to the general, "If you will marry me, I will pay the money, and you shall never want money any more, and you may keep your pretty ring, for it is a pity to part with it." He took her at her word. They were married immediately, and she embarked with him on board the next packet for Spain.

From Madrid, Sir George took us back to Paris. The day afterwards, 3 May, 1814, I was on the bridge of St Denis, and saw Louis XVIII come into the city. One night the king gave a grand entertainment at St Cloud, to celebrate his restoration. Sir George and his wife were invited and went to it.

After their carriage was gone, the lady's-maid expressed to me her eager desire to go too, adding that nothing should prevent it, if she had but a proper man to accompany her.

"If that is all," said I, "you shall soon have one, for I will myself be your beau, and we will both go."

We held ourselves much too high on all occasions to associate with the men-servants. The valet had gone out. I knew where our master's things were kept, went to his dressing-room, took out his Spanish uniform, put it on, and also his moustache and whiskers, took his hat, and sword, and cane, and set off with Owen to St Cloud. We gained admission without difficulty, and I made my way through the crowd with an air of authority. We walked about among the company, enjoying ourselves extremely. I amused myself by flirting with some young ladies, who were evidently gratified by my attentions. We went to the saloon for refreshments, and passed so close to Sir George and Lady_____, that we were very much frightened, but fortunately escaped their notice. They got home before us, however, for our cab did not go so fast as their carriage. The lady's-maid was missed, and did not dare to meet her master and mistress. I took courage, and went to show myself just as I was, so that they laughed so much, that they could not be angry with either of us.

We were four days in Paris on this second visit; and we went to see the Tuileries and other fine places.

We then went to Brussels, and from thence we travelled about to various places, which, at this distance of time, I do not exactly recall to mind in due order. We passed two months at the house of Sir George's friend, Mr Elliott, at Toplitz: it was the only place where we did not reside at an inn, through the whole course of our continental travels.

We spent a long time at Trieste, we visited Messina and when we were at Naples we saw Vesuvius. I am sure of the facts, but not of the times of their occurrence. We came a second time, after several months had elapsed, back to Brussels, and arrived there about twoo'clock in the morning. We were delayed for a draw-bridge to be let down before we could get to the Queen's Hotel. On the night of that day there was a ball, and Sir George and Lady_____ had tickets, and attended. Their servants, also, had tickets for the gallery, to view the scene. The room was the largest I ever saw in my life. About midnight, orders came for the 10th Hussar officers to march. At that moment, the dancers were forming all hands round. There was much confusion, and the party broke up.

We returned to the Queen's Hotel, and were very dull and anxious until we heard of the battle of Waterloo. Five days after it had been fought, we left Brussels on an excursion to visit the field. It was thickly strewn with dead bodies. Soldiers were carrying them into corners, and laying them together. Many persons were there searching among the killed for their friends. Broken bayonets, and other things, were scattered about.

From Brussels we went up the Rhine, to Berlin, and then to Vienna, where we saw young Napoleon. He was a fine, delicate looking boy. We obtained permission to see him from his preceptor, Mr Hill, an Englishman.

A French gentleman, whom I fancied to be Monsieur Talleyrand, had joined Sir George's family at Brussels after the battle of Waterloo, and he travelled with us, in disguise, for many months afterwards. Folks used to say that he had pigs' eyes, and could discern what people wanted of him before they spoke. An evil spirit seemed to be in him, he was so very clever; but he was full of jokes, and very pleasant.

We went to Milan, and there Sarah Owen and I made two young students at the University provide us with fine clothes and a carriage for the opera. They were much disappointed when they found that we were setting out the next day for Venice. We had a cottage, for five weeks, at a little distance from that city.

A large nunnery stood near; the grounds belonging to it were very beautiful, but they were surrounded with high walls. At night we used to watch a light, which moved from a high tower down to a lower building, and passed along a row of little narrow windows; for, after seeing it, we always heard the music of a lute or guitar, and songs sung by a very sweet voice in the convent grounds. It began about nine o'clock at night, and lasted for two hours at a time; and then Sarah Owen and I used to watch the light passing back again along the little windows, to the tower where the poor young lady's prison was.

There were sentries at the doors of the convent, and one day, in passing towards Venice, we noticed that they were doubled, and saw a gentleman lurking near the wall, as if he wished to conceal himself. He had attendants, but we did not see them. That night he set fire to the convent (it was a terrific sight from our cottage), and, in the confusion which ensued, he got in and rescued the lady who sang those mournful and beautiful songs. She was an Austrian, only sixteen years of age, and her father had imprisoned her there to keep her out of the way of her French lover, and because she had refused to marry one whose suit he favoured.

St. Mark's in Venice, is the prettiest place I ever saw. We went there every day. From Venice we returned to Milan; thence we went to Berne, and visited a hermit on the top of a mountain. We reached Rome in carnival time. There I first saw ladies riding astride on horseback: they were English women – the Marchioness of Salisbury and her daughter. We met them on the bridge that crosses the Tiber. I was disappointed in Rome. I dare say the Campagna must have been a fine place, and looked well in its glory; but, excepting St Peter's, the new city is nothing worth mentioning. The most curious thing I saw there was the ceremony of the Pope himself making a nun, who belonged to some great family. I pitied that poor young lady. She was only sixteen years of age. It was said she was unwilling to renounce the world, but her father forced her. We visited Bologna, and other places, Aix la Chapelle, the Hague, and Ostend, where we left the pretended Talleyrand.

We cross the channel to Plymouth, and visited Cheltenham, Warwick, Worcester, and Birmingham, spending a fortnight on the way to Liverpool, and seeing everything that was worth seeing as we travelled along. This was the month of November, 1815.

Chapter 4

Come, Disappointment, come!
Though from Hope's summit hurled,
Still, rigid nurse, thou art forgiven,
For thou severe wert sent from Heaven
To wean me from the world,
To turn my eye
From vanity,
And point to scenes of bliss that never, never die.

Kirke White

Liverpool Again

A new Lover – Prospect of going to India – Intended Marriage – Wreck of the Perseverance – David Cadwaladyr's visit to Liverpool.

On returning to Liverpool, I heard Lloyd of Beaumaris preach at the Welsh Chapel, from the text, 'Go and sin no more'. I spoke to him when it was over, telling him I did not see how what he said could be done. He replied that, indeed, it could not, if we strove only with every separate act; for sin was like the blood in our body, and we could not pull the bad away; but that the whole body of sin might be controlled and subdued, if we constantly prayed to God for the help of his Holy Spirit, through the merits of our Saviour.

I found Captain Harris just returned from the last of two voyages, which he had made to the West Indies during my absence. He wanted me to promise to marry him in March. I would not do that; but I did promise to marry him in May. He took a house in New James Street, and furnished it, and had his portrait and mine taken in oils, and hung them up there.

After having made these preparations, he tried to persuade me to go into Pembrokeshire to see his parents; but I excused myself, and he took his ship off to Bristol, and to Solva Porth Glas, to visit his friends.

On Easter Sunday I took it into my head to go to the Quaker's Chapel in Hunter's Street. I was soon weary of the silent meeting, and went out. I set off running, and the street was so very steep that I could not stop myself. A young man stood across my way with outspread arms, and caught me as I came, calling out, "I have caught my wife!" I burst away from him, answering, indignantly, "No, you have not." His name was James B_____. He was a house-painter, in good business at Chester. He was then working at Dr Solomons', Gilead House, at Liverpool. From that day, he used to come every Saturday night, when work was over, to Sir George's house, where he stood about the door to look after me; and on Sundays he used to watch me as I went to the Welsh Chapel, and walk by my side; but I would not notice him, and several times I made a round on purpose to avoid him.

While Captain Harris was away, Sir George received information of the death of his Lady's brother in India, and immediately took measures preparatory to going out with all his family to spend the remainder of his life upon his new possessions. He sold his English estates, and engaged several of his servants to accompany him, Sarah Owen, myself, five nurses, one for each of his five children; the house-maid, Jane, four footmen, the secretary, the house steward and some others. He gave us three weeks' holidays, which began the first week in May, that we might see our friends, and get ready for the voyage. He owned many ships, and had one of them fitted up for the conveyance of his family.

I had not told anyone at Sir George's of my engagement with Harris, and I cannot account for the fact, that under these circumstances, I hired myself to go to India, excepting by a sort of presentiment, which told me that something would come between him and me. Mrs Jackson and my fellow servants supposed that I was going to my aunt at Chester, and from thence, to Bala, when I quitted Sir George's house that Friday night, but I went to my cousin's house in Brisbane Street, and told her that I was going out to India with Lady____, and the family. My cousin's wife knew nothing of my engagement with Harris, and was not even aware of my attachment to him. She invited me to spend a few days with her before I went to Chester, and to return to her house after my visit to Bala. On Friday night, the 12th, I wished very much to tell her that I was going to be married on Tuesday 16th; but I could not speak the words.

I had received a letter from Harris telling me to expect him to arrive either on Saturday night or Sunday morning. I wished on Sunday morning to tell my cousin, but I could not; and I determined to defer so doing until night, when I thought I could do it more easily in the dusk. I went to chapel, but he was not there, and I did not hear one word the preacher said. I felt more agitated and miserable that I can tell. In the evening I could not speak of Harris to my cousin, and I felt very anxious and unhappy.

On Monday morning I put my things on to go out, and as I was leaving the house, my cousin asked me if I chanced to pass by Jones's shop, to buy a pound of tea for her there. I went straight to the Old Docks, and inquired after the ship *Perseverance*. The dock master said he had not heard of her coming in, but directed me to go to the pier-head and look out. I went instead to the churchyard, which commanded an extensive view. I turned away heavy hearted, walked to James Street and went into Jones the grocer's shop. He was a friend of my family, and used to call me Morddrwg, because I was so full of fun. However, I was sad enough that morning. I asked for the pound of tea for my cousin, and while Mr Jones put it up, I looked at the Liverpool newspaper, which had been just brought in, and was lying on the counter.

The first thing I set my eyes on was an account of the wreck of the *Perseverance* on the Black Rock in the fog, on Sunday morning, the 14th, between two and three o'clock; all hands lost, excepting one boy, who was washed upon the rock, and clung to it. I knew nothing more for a long time. When I became conscious, I saw three doctors standing over me. I could not utter a word. I was carried in a sedan chair to my cousin's house. Nobody could think what was the matter with me. All that day I lay speechless. About seven o'clock in the evening, a shopman came from Mr Jones's, and said that a person had arrived there who wanted to see me. My cousin answered, "She cannot possibly go. She is very ill."

I heard what they said, and I cried out, "I will go." She was so glad to hear me speak again, that she ordered a sedan chair and walked by the side of me to Jones the grocer's. I fancied that Harris had been saved, and running to the stranger, I threw my arms round his neck, exclaiming, "Oh, Tom, you are come!" Then, in an instant, I saw that it was not him.

Old Dr Morse, who had attended me in the morning, not knowing that I was removed to my cousin's house, called in at this time to see me. He said, "Let her cry, it will save her mind."

The stranger was James Harris, brother to my lover, and he had come at his invitation to be best man at the wedding.

James Harris had not heard of Thomas Harris's death until that moment, when I told it in my passionate grief; and my Liverpool friends never heard of my intended marriage until he informed them of it. He stayed a week in Liverpool trying to comfort me, and arranging his dead brother's affairs. He wanted me to go back with him to his parents' home, and to be their daughter and live with them. He took his brother's portrait and mine away with him. I had afterwards many kind letters from the old people, pressing me to come to them, but I was fully determined then to go to India.

Mrs Jackson, the old housekeeper, had been dreaming that I was in trouble, and she came to see what was become of me on Saturday; she was very much surprised to learn what had happened, but very sorry for me.

On Monday evening, Lady_____ herself came in her carriage, and fetched me back to her house. She blamed me for not having informed her of my engagement with Harris, but showed me very great compassion and kindness. I knew it was foolish to grieve for him, as it could not bring him back. I could not bear the thought of remaining in Liverpool. and was very glad to have the prospect of going with such good friends to India.

Jones, the grocer, did not approve of my going, and he wrote to my father, and told him of my intention. Sir George could not get things ready for the voyage so soon as he hoped to do. Meanwhile, my father, Dafydd Cadwaladyr, arrived, upon a Saturday, in the third week in June. His antipathy to all navigable water was so strong, that in coming to Liverpool he always went twenty-four miles round, through Warrington on foot, to avoid it.

He had an interview with Sir George, and told him that he could not consent to my going to India, as he had already one daughter there, of whom he seldom heard anything, and that he did not want to lose another. In consequence of this conversation, Sir George told me that he was sincerely sorry, but he could not take me with him against my father's will; that he was a father himself, and should think it hard to have his children enticed away from him. I entreated my mistress to let me go, but she answered me as Sir George had done. I stayed at their house, and my father stayed at my cousin's house, until Sir George's family went away.

They embarked in the beginning of July, 1816. I saw them all on board, and I almost broke my heart. My father was vexed and thought that I loved Sir George and my lady better than I loved him.

I was from infancy so spirited, that my father and my pious friends used often to fear I should get into mischief. He was always more anxious for me, than for all his other children, who had quieter dispositions, and therefore gave me more frequent cautions and advice. I became much more thoughtful and steady after Harris died and the _____ family went away. These were great griefs; but in the midst of my gayest pranks, I had long had the root of right-doing within me.

Chapter 5

> – London, opulent, enlarged, and still
> Increasing London. Babylon of old
> Not more the glory of the earth than she,
> A more accomplished world's chief glory now.
>
> Cowper's *Task* – The Sofa.

London

A new Engagement – Flight from Chester to London – Mr David Charles – Mr Bellingham – Miss O'Neill – Rebellious Conduct in a Second London Service.

My father took me with him to the house of my aunt at Chester, and we remained there for a month – my father being occupied with preaching, and a ministerial charge there.

James B availed himself of the opportunity of following up his courtship. He was a good and pious man, as well as a prosperous tradesman; my aunt had so high an opinion of him, that she pressed me to marry him, and promised if I did so, that she would give us five hundred pounds. I had no inclination for him, but he would not let me alone, and I was thus prevailed upon to allow him to fix a day for our marriage. He spoke of our engagement to some of his friends, but I kept it a secret from mine, and even from my aunt, who had influenced me to make it.

I accompanied my father to Bala, where my second sister was still keeping house for him. Mrs Lloyd was very glad to see me again, and treated me in a very friendly manner. She wanted me to re-enter her service, but I declined it. I left home again in August, 1816, and returned to Chester. I did not go to my aunt's house, but I hired lodgings at Mrs Robinson's, in John Street. James B called on me, and asked me to go out and take a walk with him in the groves. We went there and the place was full of company, all walking about for their pleasure. James B wanted to talk to me about household arrangements, and asked me to come into another path where our conversation would not be overhead. I refused; he urged it, and said, jestingly, "I shall be your master in eight-andforty hours," at the same time drawing me towards the way he wished to go. The ground was very steep – I was very angry – and I gave him so violent a push, that he tumbled headlong down the bank. I instantly ran away, jumped over the wall into the churchyard, and out of it over the tall railings into John Street. I went to Mrs Robinson's, rushed upstairs to my own room, locked the door, and sat on the bed all that evening and all that night. He followed me to the house, and inquired after me; but I refused to see him, and he left word that he would be there again very early in the morning. I resented indignantly his having said that he would be my master, and, resolving to avoid him, at about four o'clock in the morning, I left the house, and walked over the canal bridge to Park Gate, the seaport[1] . I was hungry when I got there, and found that I had left my money behind me. I would have gone to Flint, but the ferryman demanded twopence for my passage, and I had only one penny to offer him. I therefore turned back and walked towards Chester.

About four miles from thence, I met Mr Lloyd, the minister, who told me that all Chester was up in arms for me.

[1] Twenty miles from Chester.

I told him that I was very hungry, and he took me with him to the farmhouse where he was going to preach, and there I had plenty to eat and drink.

As soon as I was thus refreshed, without waiting to hear the sermon, I set off again for Chester. As I passed along Watergate Street, I saw several ministers and others, who were friends of mine, standing talking together. Among them was Mr Parry, the publisher, whom I knew that James B had asked to give me away. It was past nine o'clock at night, and another Mr Lloyd took us home to sup with him at his house, in Deansgate Street, where his niece lived with him, and headed his table. Mr Parry mentioned my intended marriage. This was Tuesday, and it was fixed for Thursday.

Mr Parry and Mr Lloyd spoke very highly of James B as a good Christian, and a man who was doing well in the world.

When the party separated, and as soon as I had said 'Good night', the thought struck me that I would go to London, and get effectually out of James B's way. I went at once and booked my place by the mail, and then returned to Mrs Robinson's for my boxes. I was told that James B had been watching and searching about for me all day long. I took a person to carry my luggage, went to the inn, and seated myself upon the top of the coach.

I know that I used James B very ill, and that I had no just cause for thus breaking my promise to one who truly and faithfully loved me. I cannot even now quite account for my conduct, and cannot excuse it, yet I believe we can love but once; often, after having been in James B's company by day, Harris would come back to my mind .at night, and, comparing the two men, I used to think that I never could like James B well enough to be happy through life with him. This made me the more readily take offence at him. Before I had got very far on my journey, I repented of what I had done, and watched every coach that I saw, in the hope of finding one that would take me back again. However I met with none until it was too late.

Between five and six o'clock on the second morning, I reached the Golden Cross, Charing Cross, weary, and wet through with heavy rain, having remained with the coach until it stopped at its last inn, because I knew not where to go.

The landlady received me with real hospitality, and took me to the bar parlour to dry my dripping clothes. She gave me a good breakfast, and pressed me much to go to bed, inquiring very anxiously what friends I had in London, and where I wished to go. I named a cousin of mine, who was a shoemaker in Maiden Lane. She told me he was her own shoemaker, and that she thought him a very worthy man, adding, that she could not say as much for his wife.

As I could not be persuaded to take a bed at the Golden Cross, the landlady sent a man with me to guide me to my cousin's house, and to carry my boxes thither. It was then between seven and eight o'clock in the morning. There was a man in the shop, and I was shown into the parlour. My cousin soon came down, recognized and welcomed me, and said that Jane would be down shortly, and we should have our breakfast. In the course of ten minutes she came in, and he introduced me to her as his cousin from Bala.

"Yes," she said, tossing her head, "one of your friends. They are all cousins!"

I declined taking any breakfast, and said that I would rather go and lie down to rest.

She sent a maid to conduct me to a garret, in which there

was no other article of furniture than an old mattress with a rug spread upon the floor. The girl locked me in. I laid down and cried myself to sleep. I slept, and awoke, and tried the door. I found it was still fast locked, and I lay down again. I could hear the workmen busy at their trade in the adjoining room. It was past ten o'clock on Saturday night, when I tried the door again, and found that it had been unlocked. I went down the three flights of stairs to the kitchen where I saw one of the maids, and told her that I had not eaten anything since Friday morning, and that I was cold and famishing. She replied that she must not give me either victuals or drink. However, she lent me a pint jug, and I went out and bought some bread and cheese and beer close by. At my entreaty she permitted me to warm the beer over the kitchen fire, expressing much fear lest her mistress should know that she had thus disobeyed her orders. I took these provisions up stairs to the garret, and being afraid that I should again be made a prisoner, I dragged the wretched mattress partly through the doorway before I again lay down upon it, and slept with my head out of the room where my feet and body were. At four o'clock, on Sunday morning, while all were asleep, I arose and left the house. I walked by Charing Cross and St James's Street, and on further and further, until I got into Sloane Street, without meeting with any human creature excepting the watchmen. There I met a grave looking young man, whom I judged by his dress to be a Wesleyan going to teach in a Sunday school. I inquired of him where the chapel of the Welsh Calvinistic Methodists was. He said he did not know of any Welsh chapel nearer than the Borough, four or five miles off. At his request, I turned back, and walked with him until we had passed through Temple Bar, and turned into Chancery Lane. There we met another Wesleyan teacher, who was on his way to Bow. My first acquaintance asked the second about the Welsh chapel. He answered that there was a chapel of the Welsh Independents in Guildford Street. I explained to him the one I was in search of, and he recollected that it stood in Wilderness Row. I accompanied him as far as the Old Bailey, and from thence he directed me across Smithfield to the place. Attending to his directions, I readily found it, but the gate was shut. I walked up and down until the people assembled, and I went in among them; but saw not a creature that I knew. When the service was over, I came out and walked about again until two o'clock. I was very melancholy, weary, and hungry, for I had not eaten since the night before. Shops were open, and I had money in my pocket, but I never even thought of the possibility of buying anything on a Sunday. I went into the chapel again with the afternoon congregation, and presently I observed my old school-fellow, David Charles, the doctor, in the opposite gallery. He recognized me, and came, after service was over, to speak to me. I told him that I was desolate and hungry, and he took me with him to the King's Head, where the landlord, John Jones, gave me plenty of everything. He was a noted man, and a great poet. He first established the Cymreigyddion in London. His bardic name was 'Glangors'. He was a distant kinsman of mine. Dr Charles went to visit some patients, and left me with him, telling me to go again to chapel in the evening, and that his housekeeper would be there, and should afterwards bring me to stay at his house at No. 11, Camberwell Grove. I did so, and met his housekeeper. I had known her before at Bala. She grumbled and was much displeased about my going to her master's house. We walked together to the Elephant and Castle, and there she purposely lost me in the crowd.

I was in sad trouble, not knowing my way, nor what to do. A coachman asked me where I wanted to go, and I stepped into his coach and he took me there. The housekeeper had arrived before me. Dr Charles gave me a most hospitable reception, took me to sit in the parlour, and ordered that I should have the best of everything. He desired me to consider that house my home as long as it suited my convenience.

I stayed there that night, and the next day until about two o'clock, when the Doctor being out, the jealous housekeeper informed me that she was going into the city, and that I had better accompany her part of the way to look out for a situation as a servant.

When we came to the Bricklayers' Arms, she directed me to Bermondsey, and told me to go into shops and inquire. Instead of so doing, I went to Mr Jones, of the Waterman's Arms, and asked after my brother John, who was captain of a ship; and I learned there that he had not yet returned from India. Having no alternative left, I then entered a shop in Tooley Street, and saw two men there, and asked if they knew of any family in want of a servant. They said, "No", but told me if I called again, they would let me know should they hear of anything.

Before I had got as far as London Bridge, one of them came running after me without his hat to say that his master wanted to speak with me. I went back and found Mr Tyler and his family at their tea. He talked with me, and asked whether I had a relation at sea. I said that my brother, John Davis, commanded the *Susanna.* Mr Tyler knew him well, and was accustomed to do business with him. He had remarked the likeness, and conjectured the relationship.

Mr Tyler and his wife agreed that I was likely to suit her

sister, Mrs Bellingham, and he sent the porter for a coach, and paid three shillings for my fare to Russell Square, sending by me a note of recommendation. Mrs Bellingham hired me in the capacity of plain cook, and I agreed to enter upon my duties the next day. I went back that night to sleep at Camberwell Grove.

Mr Bellingham was a tailor in great business, and had a country house at Highgate. The day after the Princess Charlotte died, there were forty-eight carriages at his door in London, besides orders by letters and messages.

I sent a porter from Mr Bellingham's to fetch my boxes from Maiden Lane; on the following Sunday, my cousin and his wife had the impudence to call on me, and I shut the door in their faces.

Miss O'Neill, the great tragic actress, lived on the opposite side of our street; and, as she employed my master, she would sometimes call to me and send me to him on business. She had a very fine, graceful figure; but was not pretty in the face, and had light hair.

She often spoke to me, and always kindly; and several times she gave me a ticket for Drury Lane Theatre. Once, when she had done so, I gave the ticket to my master's eldest daughter, who wished so much to go, that her father bought another ticket for me to go with her.

This happened on the very night that Cook had pawned himself for the sum of thirteen pounds, knowing that Mr C Kemble, the manager, must pay the money or stop the play, as Cook was to perform one of his best parts. I think it was *Shylock*. I never cared for comedies; but I liked the grave noble acting in tragedies, though my father would not have suffered me to attend either the one or the other.

I think there is much to be learned from a good play.

Mr Bellingham made some of Miss O'Neill's wedding clothes when she married Sir Wrixon Becher. I remember especially one white cashmere pelisse, trimmed with lavender-coloured satin.[2]

I lived three years with Mrs Bellingham, and I might have been there much longer but for the jealousy of an old nurse who used to scold and beat the children. They would come to me to complain of her and be comforted. I used, when my work was done, to dress myself and go with them when she took them out to walk; I liked to carry them, and to do anything for them, but I never went to the nursery. The old nurse told our mistress that she felt herself to be of no use, as the children were so much with me. Mrs Bellingham assured me that she would send her away and pension her, but I preferred going myself to being the cause of her going. I had also at that time an intention of marrying H_____, the draper, of the firm of H_____ and H_____, in Bishopsgate Street. I therefore left my place and took lodgings with Mrs James, in the Barbican.

He took a house for our residence in Shepherd's Walk.

One day I read in the *Times* newspaper an advertisement for a laundry maid, and I went at the day and hour appointed to offer myself, at the house of Mr R_____, in Pullings Row, Islington. There were sixty or more young women crowding the two parlours on the same business. I was the tallest, and Mrs R_____ asked me several questions over the heads of those who stood in front of me, and hired me at the rate of eighteen pounds a year.

She was a Wiltshire lady, daughter of Sir Thomas T____,

---

[2] According to Burke, Miss O'Neill's marriage took place on December 18, 1819.

and second wife of Mr Samuel R_____, the cow keeper. He always kept nine hundred and ninety-nine cows – he never could keep a thousand, for one always died directly he made up that number. My place was a hard one, for I had to wash, iron and mangle for five gentlemen and seven ladies, besides the house linen, and only the housemaid to help me every Monday. My master had two brothers: Thomas a cowkeeper in the Edgeware and Hampstead Roads, and William, a brickmaker. They were all wealthy people. My master's eldest daughter married a son of Winston, the great auctioneer. All my master's children were by his first marriage. I did not like my mistress; she knew nothing of domestic management, and I thought her very silly. She came to the laundry one day, and expressed her wish to learn how to iron the fine things. She took her first lesson with a pair of old, greasy kid gloves on her hands, and dirtied at least two dozen articles that day.

Afterwards, she came again several times, and did no better. I had to wash and iron all she touched, for they were unfit for use; and thus my work, which was too heavy before, was greatly increased. One day in particular, she came in new tan gloves, and made a worse mess than ever. I grew desperate, and resolved to put a stop to such folly, at the risk of being turned away from my place. The next time, in she came, as she always used to do, jumping along as if she were hung on a string. I had contrived to summon her only a few minutes before two o'clock, the parlour-dinner hour; and as soon as she had set to work, I left her, and went to the room where all the children and the French governess were assembled, and, to their great amazement, I seated myself at the head of the table.

Miss R_____ said, "You won't stay there until papa

comes?"

I said, "You shall see that I will."

The dishes were brought in by the footman, and the old gentleman came with his spectacles on. He looked extremely surprised, and said, good-naturedly, "Elizabeth, what are you doing here?" I replied, "I am not Elizabeth today; I am Mrs R_____. As she has taken my place in the laundry, I am come to take hers in the dining-room."

He went immediately, and fetched Mrs R_____, who came and stood, laughing, behind the chair on which I was seated. I expected to have been discharged forthwith, but I was not even scolded; every time that I gave warning to quit, Mrs R_____ entreated me to stay, and raised my wages at the rate of two pounds a time. She never again troubled me in the laundry. It was a liberal house, but the mistress trusted to the cook; her domestic arrangements were so bad, that on two successive Sundays no dinner was provided for the servants, and we were obliged to send out and get something to eat from a cook's shop.

One day, after I had given one of my many notices to quit, Mrs Sharrick, an old midwife, who had often heard me say that I should like to go abroad, came and told me of a sudden opportunity of gratifying that wish. She had two daughters, and one of them had bound herself under a forfeiture of one hundred pounds to go to the West Indies. She changed her mind, and would not fulfil her engagement; and the mother requested me to go instead. If this had not occurred, I should probably have stayed on again with Mrs R_____, who at last consented to have a man to turn the mangle, and objected strongly to my leaving her.

As to my proposed marriage, it ended as my former

engagement had done.

One day, H_____ asked me whether I had told my sister Bridget that I had consented to marry him. She was then living in London, in a place which I had procured for her. I answered, "No." We had a dispute about it, and quarrelled, and broke off the match.

He wrote to me afterwards, and sent a friend to me to try and make it up again; but I refused to have anything more to say to him.

I left Mrs R_____ on a Thursday, and went that same evening to Queen's Terrace, Brompton; and there, at the house of a French count, I agreed with his sister-in-law, Mrs S_____, to enter her service, and to wait upon her and her child to the West Indies and back again.

On Friday, Mrs R_____ sent after me; and, although my rate of wages had reached thirty pounds a year, she said she would not hesitate to give as much more as I chose to ask, if I would only return to her.

This it was no longer in my power to do.

In November, 1820, I sailed for the West Indies, on board the merchant ship *Iris,* my master, Captain S_____, being her commander and joint owner.

Chapter 6

Where first his drooping sail Columbus furled,
And sweetly rested in another world,
Amidst the heaven-reflecting ocean, smiles
A constellation of Elysian isles;
Fair as Orion, when he mounts on high
Sparkling with midnight splendour from the sky;
They bask beneath the sun's meridian rays,
When not a shadow breaks the boundless blaze;
The breath of ocean wanders through their vales
In morning breezes and in evening gales;
Earth from her lap perennial verdure pours,
Ambrosial fruits and amaranthine flowers;
O'er the wild mountains and luxuriant plains
Nature in all the pomp of beauty reigns.

Montgomery's *West Indies*, Part i

The West Indies
**The Captain of the *Iris* and his Family – Realization of
Early Visions – St Vincent's – Sins carried to Trinidad for
Absolution – Visits to various Islands and to the Mainland
– Return to England – Engagement with Captain and Mrs
Foreman – Visit to Dafydd Cadwaladyr at Bala.**

Captain S_____ was a very fine-looking man, with a fair
complexion, large blue eyes and light curling hair. He was a
native of the West Indies, and second son of old Dr S_____ of
St Vincent's, and of his Creole wife. Captain S_____ had

served as a Lieutenant in the Royal Navy, under his kinsman and namesake, the celebrated Sir Sydney Smith. He married a sister of the well-known law-stationer of Norfolk Street. They had one child, a boy of a few months old, and his name was Orlando Furioso Stanislaus Francescal Sydney. One of the first orders the Captain ever gave me was never to leave the child with its mother. He was very fond of it and of her; but he never seemed to have any confidence in her. She was a pretty little woman, but quite a dumpling in figure. He was a good man, and a Protestant, as all his family were. My mistress was a Roman Catholic, and very superstitious. The child was very handsome, and of a good disposition. He soon showed a strong affection for his father, and for his nurse; but he never was fond of his mother.

We reached the West Indies after a voyage of five weeks. Sailing from Barbadoes to St Vincent's, we touched on our way at the little island, or peninsula, of Calique, and went ashore there. Words cannot tell my surprise, my amazement and horror, at beholding there for the first time in my life, cocoa nut trees bearing fruit – the very trees, the very same big nuts, which I had imagined to myself as strange impossibilities of my own invention, when I used to sit alone in the hole of the rock at Pen Rhiw. The sight of these trees, and of the negroes, caused me to think that the wicked spirit, who had power to show all the kingdoms of the world and their glory, had previously made an exhibition of these wonders to me.

At St Vincent's, my master and his wife made their home at his father's house, while I was sent every night to sleep on board the *Iris*. When we first arrived, there was hard work to get a bedstead for them to sleep on. There was only one in the house; it was a huge four-post bedstead, and ten people slept in it. At last, a tent-bedstead was procured, and put up in the breakfast-room, for my master and mistress.

One of the windows, which looked into the garden, used to be left open at night because of the heat; and, for the first three weeks, a large snake used to come in every night, and lie coiled up on the bed at the captain's feet. In the morning, when I went to the room to fetch the child out of the little crib by the bedside, I used to see the snake. The first time I caught sight of it, I was just going to call out, but my master raised his finger to silence me, lest his wife should be frightened. She never knew of it, I believe. My entering disturbed the snake, and it used to lift up its head, and gape, and slowly unwind itself, and crawl away out at the window. It had a nest under the sour-sop tree[1] in the yard. It was rather a light coloured snake, of a harmless sort. Such visits were put an end to by its being killed.

These creatures were very numerous in the West Indies. For the bite of venomous snakes the negroes used to make a plaster, composed of a native oil spread on the bark of the soap-wood tree.[2] One negro was bitten by a black snake, which he killed before it had torn the flesh out. He applied to

---

[1] *Annona Muricata,* a species of custard apple, indigenous to the West Indies. The taste and smell of the fruit, and of the whole sour-sop tree, resemble the black currant. The properties of the natural order are strongly aromatic.

[2] *Sapindus Saponaria,* the soap-berry tree, is also indigenous to the West Indies. The pulp of its fruit, being a strong abstergent, is used for washing linen, and is said to be more efficacious than sixty times its weight of common soap. The embryo of the soap-worts is generally either twisted spirally or curved. A remarkable instance of this formation has obtained for a Demerara species of the name of snake-nut. The properties of the order are poisonous.

the wound the bark and leaves of the sour-sop, which soon cured him. That fruit is the favourite food of the black snake.

Captain S_____ had freighted the ship for a voyage of mercantile speculation, and when he took her round to the islands, the child and I used to go with him, as well as some friends of his, while Mrs S_____ remained with his father's family at St Vincent's.

The people in the West Indies had no life and cheerfulness in them. They were a languid, slothful race, both men and women; and in proportion to the population, I never saw so many bad persons in my life, of both sexes. Husbands thought nothing of keeping a harem in the home of the lawful wife, and mere children, boys and girls, were dissipated and profligate. The habits and manners even of the innocent were so strange and bold, that at first, I really thought there were only wicked women at St Vincent's.

My mistress sent me once to Martinique, to buy finery for a ball at Kingstown, St Vincent's – white satin with green leaves and roses – to trim her lace dress. Captain S_____ and his mother and sisters went with her to the ball. They returned home about eleven o'clock at night. After I had put my mistress to bed, I went down to the beach and stood waiting for the boat to come and fetch me on board to sleep, when I heard the sound of groaning and sobbing, and discovered Lady C_____'s maid sitting forlorn, without shawl or bonnet, upon a piece of timber. She explained her sad condition by telling me that having unfortunately forgotten to place the Lady's night clothes on the usual chair, her ladyship had beaten her, dragged her by the hair of her head, and turned her out of doors at midnight.

This maid was a particular acquaintance of mine, as we

had often met in our morning walks with the children of our respective mistresses. I made her accompany me on board the ship, and left her there, when I went on shore to my business early the next morning. Many gentlemen were clustering together in the town as I passed through, and talking very earnestly together. Mr Cox, a merchant, came from among them and spoke to me, remarking upon the great care I took of the child which I had in my arms. He told me that Lady C_____'s maid was lost, and it was feared that she had drowned herself. The Governor, Sir Thomas Brisbane, and his sons were walking towards the other gentlemen. I went into a shop to buy some tobacco, as I had promised for a sailor, and the tradesman, mentioning that the maid was lost, I hinted that I knew where she was. This information was quickly conveyed to the gentlemen, among whom was Lady C_____'s husband. I related the cruel treatment which the maid had received from her mistress, and declared that this being the third time of her having been turned out of doors, she would never re-appear until she was set free from her engagement. I also demanded that her three years' wages, and twenty guineas for her passage home to England should be paid into the hands of her friend the Wesleyan minister. After some contention, Sir Thomas took up the matter, insisting on all this being done, and Mr C_____ submitted to release her from her contract, and to pay the money.

The family being Protestants, my mistress had some difficulty in managing her diet for fast days; when there chanced to be beef or fowl for dinner on Friday, she would take her portion and pass it through water, and, after this process, would declare it to have become fish. Sometimes she ventured to ask me if I did not perceive the change, and on my answering, "No", she would shake her head, and say, "Oh! you have no faith."

One evening she put into my hands an unsealed paper and ten doubloons,[3] and ordered me to leave the baby at home, and embark immediately on board a draager[4] for Trinidad, to deliver the paper to the bishop, to pay whatever he might require, and return on board the draager as soon as the business was settled. There was no bed for me on board, so I sat all night in the cabin, and amused myself with reading the paper of which I was the bearer. I found it to be a catalogue of my mistress's sins for the last seven weeks, which she was sending for absolution to the 'holy father', as she called him.

It was a terrible night, and the wind blew a hurricane. The captain of the draager came in and out of the cabin, looking at his charts, and seeming very uneasy. He told me he had been employed for ten years in carrying sugar between the islands, and never was out in such a night before; that he had reefed all the sails, and done his best. He seemed very gloomy, and to cheer him up I said, "You never before had so heavy a cargo."

He looked surprised, and replied, "I have none at all. What do you mean?"

"Well, you have got me on board, and all my sins; and, as that is not enough, I have another person's sins of some weeks in my pocket."

"This is no time for jesting," he said, "don't joke."

---

[3] The American doubloon is worth £3:5s. in English money; the Spanish doubloon, £3:6s.

[4] A sort of 'clipper' used for traffic between the islands. The local term for such a vessel is 'drogher', or 'draager', a carrier, from the Dutch verb 'draagen', to carry.

He was a Spanish Creole. I asked him if he believed in almighty God. He assented, and I inquired whether he remembered who said to the sea, 'Thus far shalt thou go and no farther, and here shall thy proud waves be stayed,' and who declared that he holdeth, 'the sea in the hollow of his hand?'

He said, "In such a night it is almost impossible to believe it." He then spoke more about the heavy load I carried to the Bishop of Trinidad, and said that had he known of it before, he would not have brought me.

"Never mind," I replied, "no harm will come of it. The wind will go down at daybreak." It did so, and we arrived in safety. I took my breakfast on board, and then went on shore and called at the bishop's house. A black servant told me that the bishop was gone to give the viaticum to a dying man, and conducted me to a room to await his return. About ten o'clock he came, shook hands with me, and called me 'daughter'. He took down three books from a shelf and laid them before him. Having asked if I was from Europe, and some other questions, he then said "Well, daughter, are thy sins great, or middling, or small? If great, lay a doubloon on this book; if middling, lay half a doubloon on this book; if small lay two bits (8d.) on this book. Come near, kneel down and confess."

"Toot!" I exclaimed, "I am not a Roman Catholic. I am no such fool!" He put his hand on the bell to have me shown out, but I stopped him from ringing it, and pulling out my mistress's list, laid it before him, saying, "Please to look at that before you send me away."

On seeing the paper his countenance cleared and brightened; he read it slowly, and crossed himself now and then – I suppose when he came to the rump-steak and the chicken. He next began to write. I told him that I knew my mistress had not set down her greatest sin – that of burning her husband's Bible. He intimated that he did not regard that action as a sin. He summoned the black man, who now moved about the room burning incense, and six boys walked in the thick smoke round the table, bearing candles, and tinkling little bells and singing, while the bishop knelt and prayed aloud in Latin to some images, which he handled and turned about, and then set again upon the table. When he arose, the boys chaunted and left the room. The bishop then produced three little tapers of different colours, folded and sealed them up in the paper on which he had written, and directed it to my mistress. He put the packet into my hand, and asked whether my mistress had entrusted me with money to place upon the book. I said that she had not known what it would cost, and had sent ten doubloons. He ordered me to place seven (£23:2:0) on the big book. I did so, and asked why he would not himself receive the money. He answered,

"It does not belong to me, but to the saints."

I said, "I am surprised that an old gentleman like you can believe such foolery."

He observed, "You call yourself a Protestant. You have no faith."

I retorted, "You don't believe the Gospel and the Bible."

"We are the Gospel," he replied, and crossed himself.

I said, "I can tell you what the Gospel is. The sum and substance of the Gospel lie in two things – an empty sinner and a full Saviour. We don't want so much mummery and mockery."

He replied, "You have been brought up a Protestant. I have been brought up a Catholic. I know there are many things in our church which are not founded on the word of God. As long as we are in the church of Rome, we must obey her laws. I approve of many of Luther's doings." He then mentioned several passages of Scripture on which individual Roman Catholics put different constructions.

I said, "If you wanted to do me any good, why did you not pray so that I might understand you?"

"Well," he rejoined, "we cannot convince one another. I ought by rights to turn you out."

He did not shake hands with me at parting, I suppose because I was a heretic; he, however, sent the black man to request me to come back and have some dinner, but I refused the invitation. I walked about and saw the town, and found my way to a plantation belonging to Mr Shum, of Liverpool, where I made acquaintance with the manager, a young man named Charles Griffith, from Brecknockshire. I stayed that night at his house, and went the next morning to the town, to make inquiries about my passage back to St Vincent's. I met the captain of the draager, who had brought me and said to him, "Well, captain, will you take me back? I am not near so heavy now, having delivered the load of sins to the bishop. "

I settled to embark with him at five o'clock that afternoon. I amused myself until that hour, went accordingly, and reached St Vincent's between three and four the next morning. I duly delivered the bishop's packet, and returned the three spare doubloons to my mistress.

Though I never was sent again to Trinidad, this was not the first nor the last errand of the kind with which my mistress entrusted me.

One day, at St Vincent's, I took the little boy, Orlando Furioso, for a walk, and two black girls went with me. We meant to go up to the flag-staff, on the top of the hill just above Kingstown. As we passed on our way behind Dr French's plantation, we heard a noise like the baying of hounds, and, looking towards Calique, beheld horsemen and dogs in full chase.

As we stood watching them, one of the negresses suddenly cried out, "Oh! Missy Betsy, Missy Betsy, lie down flat!" I could see nothing to be afraid of, until I looked about and perceived in the hollow space between the two hills, a huge serpent. We all lay down flat on our faces, until this strange creature with all the horsemen and dogs after it had gone past us; and then we got up and went on to the top of the hill where the flag-staff stood.

The monster went towards the Botanic Gardens. Several gentlemen were walking in those gardens at the time. A row of six pounders was set in the niches of the garden-wall; and, when the serpent approached, old Mr Rogers – a Welshman from Montgomeryshire, who had the care of them – drew out one of these guns, and shot the creature twice – one ball passed through its open mouth, and the other through its heart. [5]

The next day all the people of the town, and people from Martinique and Dominique, and other places, both far and near, came to see the creature. I was there, and saw it too. This serpent had a head like a shark, with holes for ears, six wings, and twelve feet, besides a row of feet across the widest part below. The colour was green, mixed with white above, and the colour of oyster-shells beneath. The front part looked like feathers, and the hinder parts shelly.

[5] 'Can this be true?' an arch observer cries.
    'Yes,' (rather moved) 'I saw it with these eyes.'
    'Sir, I believe you on that ground alone,
    I could not, had I seen it with my own.'
    (Cowper's *Conversation*)

It was thought by the best informed persons to have escaped from some passing ship, as foreign birds, and monkeys, and other strange creatures often did.[6]

My master sailed with the child and me and two young ladies from St Vincent's to Kingston, in Jamaica, and round to all the ports of that island. Wherever I was, I attended church or chapel; and I used to go and teach in the Sunday School at Port Royal.

From Jamaica we went to St George's, in Demerara, and there Mr Porland, a cousin of the Captain's, received us at his house. Mrs Porland was a mulatto – a very nice lady. They made the Captain send for his wife and sisters. They came, and we all stayed three months in that house – the Captain going about the while with his ship on short trading voyages.

Mr Porland had 1450 slaves on his plantation. I did not think their state was slavery at all, excepting in two particulars: they were not treated as if they had immortal souls; and they were subject to be sold. These things were horrible; but all the rest appeared very well. They were not over-worked. From half-past six to nine, from half-past nine to eleven, and from three to five, were the hours of labour; and they had Saturday and Sunday wholly to themselves. Ground was assigned them to cultivate for their own profit, and they sold the surplus produce at the Sunday market. I was at Demerara during the commotion about Smith the Missionary; but I left before it was finished. I used to go every

---

[6] It is not easy to determine the true species, or even the genus of the reptile thus described; but most probably it was a python, observed under the influence of astonishment, and remembered with supernumerary attributes.

Sunday from Mr Porland's house to Joseph's Town to teach the black children in the Mission school. There was a little pious black boy there, who wanted much to go home with me to England, because, he said, there was a bigger door from thence to Heaven than from those islands. He died not long afterwards very happily.

The captain, with the child and me, went from Demerara, leaving Mrs and the Miss S_____ there while we made a five weeks' voyage to the Havannah, Martinique, and Trinidad. Having sold all his merchandize, we returned to St Vincent's, and sugar was brought from his own and his father's plantations in several islands on board the draagers to load the *Iris* for England.

After our return to Dr S_____'s house at St Vincent's, I used to take the child out very early every morning for a walk. On returning one day, my mistress asked me where I had been. I answered that we had been to Mr Fraser's plantation, that he had wished to detain us to breakfast, but I would not stay, as I had not her permission to do so. She said, "It is a pity you did not stay. You may stay any morning."

I thanked her, and replied that I would stay some cloudy morning, when the heat of the sun was not too great. Accordingly, soon afterwards I did so, and, in consequence, was a little later than usual in arriving at home; though I had set out so early that the difference was not much. As soon as I came in sight, there stood outside the door my mistress, her mother-in-law, and her two sisters-in-law. They all exclaimed against me; and my mistress, snatching the child from my arms, cried out, "You good-for-nothing wretch! you want to kill my child. I will make George," (a slave), "tie you to a tree, and give you a good horse-whipping."

The old lady and the young ladies reproached me with having stopped out too late in the heat. I explained that my mistress had given me leave to stay to breakfast at Mr Fraser's plantation. The child screamed at being kept from me, and they passed him from one to the other to try and comfort him. He lisped out that he wanted to go to Sissy, and would not be pacified. They took him away, and I went to the gallery. I got home at a quarter past nine, and the child cried incessantly until two o'clock, when my mistress brought him in her arms to me, and said, "Take this little wretch!"

I refused, and told her to have me flogged, as she had threatened. She took the child away again, but none of them could pacify him. My master was out, spending the day at Dominique. Miss Eliza entreated me to take the child, declaring that it would break her brother's heart to see the little boy in that state. I could not bear the sight of his distress myself, and kept out of the way in the gallery. He could not be soothed to sleep; he would not eat, and about four o'clock he fell into a fit. My mistress rushed into the gallery, and fell on her knees at my feet, sobbing out, "For God's sake, come and take my child!"

Without a word, I ran to the baby, who was lying, insensible, across his grandfather's knees. The old doctor thought that he would die. I asked how long he had been in the fit. At the sound of my voice he opened his eyes, and threw his arms around my neck, saying, "My Sissy." I took him, and soothed him, fed him, washed him, and put him to bed, and he was fast asleep before his father came home – though he sobbed in his sleep all through that evening. I did not like to make mischief between husband and wife, so I never told my master of my mistress's unjust conduct and cruel threat.

In a few weeks from that occurrence, the *Iris* being loaded, we embarked for England. One night at sea. my master called me up to my mistress. None of the family had expected her confinement, and she had not made any sort of preparation for it. I found her very ill, and having tried hot flannels, hot salt, and other things in vain, I began to recollect that I had formerly seen a person in that state before. I also thought over what I had read in Dr Buchan's book, and became quite certain about the case. I gave her a cup of green tea, which had wonderful effects, and about two in the morning, a fine boy was born – I being the sole attendant upon her and the infant.

I wrapped it in some of the elder child's clothes, and soon stitched up some little shirts and flannels, as there were abundant materials on board. This was my first experience in such matters. The Captain christened the child Alexander Crichton Archibald Johnston. He was a beautiful baby, and likely to live and thrive, but his mother was the death of him. Nothing would persuade her to allow the newborn infant to be placed in the same bed with her. By day I made up a little bed on the top of a box, and put all the warm things I could around him, but I could not put many for fear of crushing him. At night, I took him and his brother to my own bed. The captain took the little one in his arms to his wife, and entreated her with tears to let him lay it beside her; but she would not. She used to say, when I begged and prayed her to do so, "Take the little wretch away. It will give me the fever." On the fifth day at noon the child died. The mother declared it was a good thing the poor little wretch was gone. The father wept bitterly. He had three coffins made, two of wood, and one of lead. He wrote the name of the child, the date, and the name and position of the ship on a piece of parchment, and enclosed it in a phial, which he placed in the shell with the corpse.

At midnight, twelve hours after the death, the ship's muffled bell was rung, and the captain and his crew, with four ladies, who were passengers, and myself, assembled on the deck. It was very solemn. The captain read the service for the burial of the dead, and the mate made the responses as clerk. All was so silent, that a pin might have been heard to fall. The coffin was lowered very softly, as if into a grave. There was no splash until the men drew away the ropes.

The mother knew nothing of the funeral – she was lying fast asleep in her cabin. Next morning she gave me a sealed phial and twopence, and told me to put them into the child's coffin, supposing that he would be buried that day. She was well and on deck in a fortnight after the birth.

We got safe to the port of London. They took lodgings in Poplar, and I stayed a fortnight with them there. Mr Elliott, the captain's partner, came, and the *Iris* was immediately unloaded, and freighted directly with mercantile goods.

One day the captain appointed me to meet him on some business in the city. On my way thither, I called upon a friend of mine, Captain Horshaw's wife, and she asked me to leave a parcel for Malta in the London Docks. I went there, and inquired of the gatekeeper where the *Albion* lay. As we talked he remarked to me, "You are a West Indian." I said, "No, I am a Welshwoman." I was as yellow as a tawney, and my black eyes made me look as if I was not a European. "I am just come from the West Indies, and I want to go to the East."

"You do?" he said.

"Yes," I answered, firmly; but the thought had only just come into my head. He told me that he knew a lady who wanted a maid to go with her to Van Diemen's Land and New South Wales, and perhaps to the East Indies, directing me to call that evening, about six o'clock, at No. 4, Broad Street, and inquire for Mrs Foreman. After having done my master's business, I called at the place, and found that the gatekeeper had already mentioned me to Mrs Foreman. She engaged with me at once to go to her on the following Tuesday.

The engagement with Mrs S_____ terminated on my return to England. The captain and my mistress wanted me to go again with them to the West Indies; and my fondness for the sweet child, whom I had nursed so long, would have led me to do so, had I not still remembered the threatened flogging with resentment. On Saturday, I informed my mistress that I had hired myself to Captain and Mrs Foreman. That day the Captain and his family went to Brompton on a visit, and I had a holiday during my short remaining sojourn at their lodgings in Poplar. On Sunday I was to dine by invitation with Mrs Foote, for whom I had brought a parcel from Jamaica. She lived in Queen Anne's old house, Church Street, Spitalfields. Her husband was a prosperous manufacturer there. The daughter of the lodging-housekeeper at Poplar, assisted to dress me up in a white gown, which I used to wear in the West Indies, and, being proud of her skill as a tire-woman, she led me to a glass that I might see how well I looked. I believe that I had not seen my face since I sailed for the West Indies. I could not believe I saw myself I was shocked at such an ugly thing – but the good natured young woman, who had not known me before, persisted in declaring that I looked very handsome.

As I went along the streets, men, women, and children stared at me, and flocked after me. Some said, "What a beautiful foreigner!" Others said, "What a fine-looking woman!" In the

Commercial Road, a gentleman came up to me, and said, in French, "You are a stranger here? Can I be of any service to you?"

I had picked up a little of that language in the West Indies, therefore understood his words very readily; but I was afraid of him, and made no answer. He walked by my side, and addressed me a second time, speaking Italian, and offering to show me the way to any place where I might wish to go. Still I did not utter a word. At last he said aloud to himself in English, "Poor soul! I can make nothing of her. I can be of no use to her. She cannot understand me." He then walked away. Soon afterwards I met the mate of the *Iris,* who had promised to come and show me the way to Mrs Foote's. He took me there, and left me on his own affairs. I remained with Mrs Foote all day, and as pouring rain came on, I stayed all night.

On Tuesday, I entered upon my new duties with Captain, and Mrs Foreman. Their ship was not ready to sail as soon as they had expected, and they allowed me to go into Wales on a visit to my father. I was very glad to see him again, and I desired no better company when he was at home, but when he was absent on his ministerial duties, I found Pen Rhiw rather dull, and spent a great deal of my time at Plâs yn Drêf with my old and kind friends, the Lloyds.

At their house, I had the pleasure of seeing again, and of shaking hands with Judge Barrow, who was in the habit of making his home there at the time of the assizes. He had become quite blind, and I had some difficulty in making him recollect me. He lived in Bedford Row, and was succeeded on the North Wales' Circuit, by Baron Richards.

I related the circumstances of the two Liverpool robberies, and reminded him of his wish to be acquainted with my parents, which was now as far as possible fulfilled, my father being there, and my mother being dead. Mr Lloyd kindly told him that I had lived four or five years in his house when I was a child, and that he had never known me tell a falsehood.

Mr and Mrs Lloyd pressed me very much to stay and live altogether with them in any capacity I chose, and on my own terms; but I was bent on seeing more of the world. At the end of three weeks came my summons to rejoin Captain, and Mrs Foreman. In travelling into Wales, I had carefully avoided Chester, and in leaving Wales, I likewise chose the Shrewsbury road, and spent three days in that town at the house of Mr Colley, the banker. I got safe to London, and was soon busily employed in preparing for the voyage.

Chapter 7

Bards tell of many women valorous,
Which have full many feats adventurous
Performed in paragon of proudest men.

Spenser's *Fairy Queen*, Book Hi, Canto 3, Stanza 54

London to Hobart Town
Captain and Mrs Foreman, and the Denmark Hill – Mrs
Fitzherbert – Storm at Sea – The Thetis – Isle of Marsevan
– Dishonest Steward – Van Dieman's Land.

Captain Foreman was sole owner of the ship – he called her the *Denmark Hill,* after the name of a house which belonged to him, and in which he allowed his mother-in-law to live. He had commanded the ship for many years, was an aged man, and very skilful in navigation; being also very careful, he was considered by good judges to be one of the safest commanders in the merchant service. He was, upon the whole, a good man, and would suffer no evil doings and no bad language among his crew. He was a very kind husband, and his concern for his wife, who always accompanied him, seemed to add to his watchful attention to the management of the ship. He was rich, but anxious to acquire more and more; and he did not scruple to enforce his orders by very rough and abusive language.

He did not employ any London agents, and being particular in the choice of sailors, was long in getting a crew. I had the charge of letting the berths, and of making arrangements for the passengers, and also of taking in stores.

The *Denmark Hill* lay in the London Docks. I lived on board, but went on shore daily to cook for my master and mistress at their lodgings; and he used to come three or four times a day to see what passengers had engaged with me. Mrs Foreman's brother was for many years foreman to Mr Apsley Pellatt, the great porcelain manufacturer.

We embarked one hundred and eighty passengers, of whom forty-eight were children. Sir George M_____, who was going out to fill a high post in the Colony, was on board, with Lady M_____, their five children, and whole establishment – forty persons in all. He paid two thousand pounds to Captain Foreman for the five months' passage: that sum included wine and all other necessaries; and the confinement of Lady M_____ took place on board. After the ship had been taken out, contrary winds drove us into Brighton. Mr Malcolm, who was going out with us to take an official appointment in Van Diemen's Land, was acquainted with Mrs Fitzherbert, the reputed wife of King George the Fourth, then Prince Regent. She was at Brighton; and to please Mr Malcolm, she had given him leave to bring Mrs Foreman and the lady passengers to see the Pavilion. He took me with them, where we found luncheon prepared for us, and Mrs Fitzherbert herself sat at the head of the table. Mr Malcolm used to be very ill at sea; and, to secure my good nursing, he took the opportunity of showing me this great civility, and treating me as if I had been a lady instead of a servant.

From Brighton we went to Portsmouth, where the last of the passengers joined us. We set sail from Portsmouth, and got down the channel, but the wind turned us back from the Scilly Islands; and we put into Plymouth harbour, and took in fresh provisions and water, our stock having been diminished by the long delay. We purchased ten slaughtered oxen, about a score of sheep, and two calves, and hung them all up in the rigging, which is a ship's larder in cold countries.

The meat becomes salt there without any trouble; to take off the incrustation and make it fit for cooking, we used to put pieces into a net, and dip them into the sea, over the ship's side.

We had stormy weather in crossing the Bay of Biscay, and afterwards, when we came to the place where the four seas meet, the waves, and wind, and thunder, and lightning, were awful. It was the dead of night, and dreadfully dark, the glaring blue lightning flashed incessantly across the ship; she was going at a rapid rate, all sails set, when she was taken aback and went under water as far as the mainmast. The surgeon rushed down the cabin stairs, crying out, "We are sinking!" Men, women, and children, rushed from their berths with horrible shrieks, and crowded the quarter-deck in their nightclothes. Mr Pringle, a passenger, took the helm, in his shirt. The screaming still rings in my ears of those two hundred people in despair. The captain stood upon the cuddy, until the water washed him off. He bade me take the passengers from the quarter-deck. They were standing half naked in the water. The hatches had been opened, and the sea poured in; there was no leak, the waves came over the ship. We got the passengers into the cuddy, crowding one over the other in the utmost confusion.

The foremast and foresail were set on fire by the lightning. The captain had ordered all hands aloft to take in the sails; there was great difficulty in doing it, and several of the sailors were struck blind by the lightning. One man called from aloft in a desperate manner for a certain rope to be let go; I did not know one rope from another, but rushed about the deck, up to my neck in water in some places, and let go every rope that I could get hold of. Down came rushing heavily, all the sails at once, bringing many sailors with them like lead upon the deck, while the crush of the canvas and the violent rain put out the flames.

The ship righted instantly, and Captain Foreman exclaimed, "Thank God! The *Denmark Hill* is saved!"

The ship was laid to, one little sail was stuck up, and the rudder tied; she rocked a little, but lay very still. The captain then summoned everybody to the quarter deck, just as they were. All fell upon their knees, and all wept, even the hardest sailor, while the old man read with fervent thankfulness the whole of the thanksgiving service, from the book of Common Prayer, for deliverance from a storm at sea. The psalms and prayers went to our very hearts. He concluded with Farmer's prayer, and said as the sailors rose to disperse, "Now, my boys, never forget the mercies of this night."

This duty being done, we applied ourselves to comfort the passengers, who were all mixed together shaking like aspen leaves with chill and terror. We took them below, got dry clothes for them, put them to bed and gave them warm brandy and water. The steward's wife, Maria, had charge of the children. My mistress lay fainting in the state cabin; the seamen were lading the water out of the lower cabins; the passengers' servants were worse than useless, and could only cry and shriek; the attendance therefore fell chiefly upon me. When, at last, all were served, I took something myself, and heard meanwhile the captain asking the mate, "Marshall, who slackened the ropes? It was a quick thing, and saved the ship."

Marshall said, "I do not know. The sails took me with them

into the long-boat." Pringle interposed a remark, that he believed Elizabeth had done it.

"Hu!" said the captain, "old faggot! God bless you, Betsy, you saved my old ship!"

After daybreak the weather improved – the thunder ceased and the wind and sea went down.

We touched at Madeira for wine; and at Tenerife for wine and Canary birds. We also took on board at St Jago twelve birds of paradise, some macaws, and a great many more canary birds. All these were used to be kept in cages; and I had upwards of two hundred birds, of all sorts, under my care. This bird speculation was Mrs Foreman's venture; and it answered well, as she intended that it should, by supplying Van Diemen's Land with breeding cages. Only three of the birds of paradise lived through the voyage. Seven of those that died were stuffed by a sailor on board. They felt small in the hand, though they looked large in their feathers.

We afterwards stood out to sea, and made for the Cape of Good Hope. Fourteen women were confined during the voyage, and I assisted the surgeon in attending them.

Within the tropics, and especially near the equinoctial line, I used to catch a sort of fish which the sailors called 'sun's eyes'. They came into the pails which I let down for sea-water. This creature had a head like a lion, with long, green, silky hair spreading round it – no body – and nothing below the head but bubble.

When we were very near to the Cape, a dreadful tempest of wind and rain came on, and the sea rose tremendously. The three masts, with a man and a boy, were carried overboard. The captain had a jury mast set up; but we were in a miserable state, expecting every instant that the ship would go down.

About three or four miles off we could see a ship on fire. She was in a storm of thunder and lightning, without high wind or rain. The lightning set her on fire, and she burned to the water's edge. That ship was the *Thetis,* East Indiaman, homeward bound. Between six and seven o'clock in the morning, the boats of the *Thetis,* crowded with people, and the captain among them, came alongside of the *Denmark Hill,* begging to be taken on board. Captain Foreman answered, "You see the state we are in. I cannot answer for your safety, nor for my own either. If you choose to risk sharing our fate, come on board." There were about four hundred and thirty persons; and, having no better chance of escape, they all came on board, for the boats were in danger of being swamped.

A sailor of the *Thetis* had saved an infant from the wreck, not knowing to whom it belonged; he put it into my arms, saying, "You can take better care of it than I can." I took it to the state cabin, where Mrs Foreman was lying ill in bed, and placed it beside her, and she welcomed the innocent baby as gladly as if it brought a promise of deliverance from danger. When I returned to the deck I saw a lady, who had come on board in another boat from the *Thetis.* She was running distracted about the deck, raving about her lost baby, and tearing her hair, believing it to have perished. She proved to be the mother of the child whom the sailor had brought to me.

At Cape Town, the whole population was out of doors watching the ship; but the sea ran so high, that a crew could not be got to man a boat to tow her into the harbour. At last, Mr Cook the missionary, jumped into the life-boat, saying, that come what might, he would try to save the ship, for he could not bear to see so many of his fellow creatures perish before his eyes. Encouraged by his example, the seamen belonging to the life-boat, followed, and put out. With extreme difficulty, it was brought within reach of the ship, received a rope, and took the *Denmark Hill* in tow; but the surf ran so high, that it caught the boat when returning towards the shore, hurled it over the pier, and dashed it against a warehouse, killing one man and breaking the arm of another. Everybody wondered that the ship had stood the storm. She was a narrow-bottomed ship, and rode the sea so well that the waves could not get hold of her. We immediately landed all the people from the *Thetis,* and went ashore ourselves, that the masts might be replaced. A subscription was raised for the sufferers of the *Thetis,* who were without clothes to their backs – nothing having been saved from the burning wreck, but one small box, which the seamen who rescued it mistook for the captain's desk. It proved to belong to the lady who had lost and found her infant, and contained its clothes and some money. The ship's papers had been destroyed, and everything else besides. The grateful mother gave ten pounds to the man who had saved her child, and five pounds to me for having preserved it. She also gave a card to him, and one to me, bearing her name and address. I lost mine, and forget the name; but I think her place of residence was Hendon. She was an officer's wife, had stayed in India for her confinement, and was following him back to England. She gave also one hundred pounds among her fellow passengers, and fifty among the crew of the *Thetis.*

Many persons at the Cape proposed to give Captain Foreman a testimonial, but he made them give the money to the *Thetis* people.

On leaving the Cape of Good Hope, we had fair weather, but the sea rose so high that we were obliged to put in at the little island of Marsevan to take water for our use, from the hold – not being able to open the hatches without taking the ship into shelter in the bay. There were three waterfalls which came into the bay, from three islets which formed a group. I went on shore to look about me, with the carpenter and a sailor. Thinking the place to be desert, they cautioned me not to go far inland, lest I might meet with some danger.

I walked along the sand and having caught sight of cultivated land, called to my companions saying, "Come, here is a field of Welsh wheat." I went on, and they followed me. Having seen the wheat, I expected to meet with a human habitation, to which I soon found an approach through a bowered avenue of trained vines about forty yards in length. Passing through a little gate, I came to a dwelling-place composed partly of a cave in a rock, enlarged by a wattled structure covered over with goat skins. It was the home of two Scotchmen, who received us very kindly, and told us their history.

They had been shipwrecked in that bay, twenty-eight years before, the only survivors of their crew, and they had saved nothing from their ship but a few pieces of timber, the carpenter's box of tools, and a few handfuls of wheat and oats. The island abounded with goats, which supplied them with milk and meat. They made clothes of the goat-skins, sowed their grain, and in due time reaped it; built themselves a house, and lived without seeing another human being for twenty-five years. At the end of that time the produce of their ground had so greatly increased that they thought it would be well to barter it for some other commodities. They, therefore, set up a signal which soon attracted the notice of passing ships, and for the last three years they had been in the habit of supplying such with corn and fresh meat, and of receiving, in exchange, agricultural and other implements, clothes, and various articles.

They gave us three slaughtered goats, and we gave them potatoes for seed, clothing, salt, and rum. They begged for an old flag, and Captain Foreman presented them with a new Union Jack to hoist as a signal. They were very contented, and did not seem to have a wish to leave the island, or to have the number of settlers increased.

We touched next at another island, for the same purpose as we had visited Marsevan.

One day, while at sea, I unfortunately scalded my hand, and was forced to allow Maria, the steward's wife, to attend upon some of the ladies whom I had been accustomed to dress and undress. The first evening on which she performed this part of my duty, I was in the ship's pantry with her husband, the carpenter, and the steward's mate, and when she returned, she sat down with us, and began to slander the character of one of the ladies. Crib, the steward, confirmed what she said, and added several infamous fabrications, as if from his own knowledge. I contradicted their assertions, vindicated the lady's fame, and related her real history, which was a very simple and guiltless one.

After this conversation, I found, to my great surprise, and sorrow, that Mrs Foreman was completely and suddenly estranged from me; and for several following weeks I felt that I was shunned by the passengers. At last a hint was given me of the true state of affairs, and I came to an explanation with my mistress, who informed me that I was charged with having defamed the lady whom I had, in reality, vindicated; and, moreover, with being myself a wicked woman, and behaving shamefully ill. I declared that I would have justice. The captain came in, and Mrs Foreman said to him, "I do not think Betsy is guilty."

He replied, "I have watched her everywhere, and, never saw anything wrong."

The captain mentioned this subject to some of the passengers, and Mr Malcolm came to me, and promised to investigate the matter. He did so that very evening, and held a sort of court of justice, swearing in a jury, and sitting as judge. I was put upon my oath, and I related the facts of the case, and my conversation in the pantry with the Cribs. The carpenter and the cabin-boy bore witness to the truth; the passengers, against whom I was said to have offended, completely freed me from the charge, and gave the strongest possible testimony to my upright and proper conduct. Crib and Maria refused to give evidence upon oath, and Mr Malcolm refused to take it without an oath. I was most honourably acquitted; and all the passengers and crew, excepting Crib and Maria, rejoiced to acknowledge that they had not been disappointed in me.

I subsequently returned good for evil, by nursing Maria in her confinement on board. There was an attempt at destroying the child, in order to conceal its birth; but I insisted on seeing it; and the child lived and throve, until we came, many weeks afterwards, to land. On the second day afterwards it died, under its mother's care.

She was a very wicked woman, and had no scruples of conscience, and her husband was as bad. He pretended, while at sea, that provisions had been consumed by the passengers, which I knew could not fairly have disappeared in the given time. He wanted me to supply him with more, and I would not do it, and proved to the captain by my account book that there must be foul play. One day, by accident, I saw the inside of the steward's cabin, and noticed there a locker partly open, and seaweed hanging out. My suspicion was excited, and I pushed back the slide, removed a board, and found a secret hiding-place, in which were stowed away bladders full of lard, reindeer's tongues, bacon hams, flour, butter, wine, and spirits besides quantities of china and glass, which were patterns sent from the London warehouses for choice, entrusted to the steward, to be returned, and fraudulently detained by him on starting. I spread these things out upon the floor, and immediately fetched Captain and Mrs Foreman to look at them, and they sent for Crib and Maria, and told them their dishonest practices were detected.

Those people had thirty corded boxes on board, which proved, on examination, to be all empty; and were, doubtless, intended to contain the stolen articles.

When our ship reached Van Diemen's Land, I admired the scenery very much, and more especially in going up the Derwent to Hobart Town – the Derwent being ten miles across, with a tiny island in the midst of it, parting the stream.

Chapter 8

There is a kind of character in thy life,
That, to the observer, doth thy history
Fully unfold.

Shakespeare's
Measure for Measure Act i. s. 1.

**Lands and Seas of the South and the East
Hobart Town – The Poison Bush – Quarrel with Mrs
Foreman – Singapore – Calcutta – Mrs Nelson – Hunting
the Kangaroo – Jericho – William Taylor**

Lists of the passengers were sent to the Colonial Office at
Hobart Town, and they were not allowed to land until their
names had been three times published in the local gazette.

One day I was sent on shore to buy bread from a baker's
shop in Liverpool Street. I had not been made acquainted with
the habits of the place, and was very much astonished at being
seized hold of by two constables, who said to me, "Free or
bond?" I did not know what they meant, and they threatened
to lock me up in the cage, for not answering the question. At
last, they took me before Captain Waddy. He had been on
board the *Denmark Hill,* remembered that he had seen me
there, and ordered the men to let me go about my business.

As soon as I was released, I set out once more for the baker's
but, before I could get back to the ship, I was again arrested.
Happily, the high constable, who knew me, was at hand, and
immediately desired the under constables to let me go.

While the greater number of the passengers still continued on board the *Denmark Hill,* three weddings took place there. Mr White, the clergyman performed the ceremony. The brides had come out with us under engagements to the bridegrooms, who were settlers at Hobart Town; and the ladies would not land until they were married. We had a very merry day on the occasion. Within a week afterwards, three ladies' maids were married to settlers, who each paid one hundred pounds to the mistress of his wife, as forfeit money for the breach of their contract of service for five years.

My courage being known to those who had come out with me, and robberies being frequent at Hobart Town, I used, soon after our arrival, to sleep often at the house of Mr and Mrs East, who had come out in the *Denmark Hill.* Mrs East's maid soon found a husband, who thought that he also must pay the hundred pounds penalty. On reading her agreement, however, I discovered that it did not contain any clause forbidding marriage. A lawyer was consulted who confirmed my opinion that the penalty could not be exacted. The maids who had previously been married, regretted very sincerely that they had not also consulted me, and thus saved their husbands' money.

I had several offers myself about that time, but I did not wish to marry. Among my suitors were two tailors, Batty and Smith, and Mr Malcolm, the surveyor. He was a very nice gentleman and a godly man, but I preferred seeing more of the world, to going with him into the bush.

Captain Foreman did not bring the Cribs to trial for their crimes, but as soon as we were allowed to set anyone on shore at Hobart Town, he dismissed them without giving them any wages. They asked the passengers to give them something for their services on board, and they being chiefly rich and generous persons, marked their opinion of Crib and Maria by subscribing between them all the sum of twopence, However, they did not leave the ship without money, for the purse of a lady passenger disappeared the very morning that the Cribs left the ship, and that purse contained forty-five pounds.

After their dismissal, Captain Foreman had several stewards one after another on board the *Denmark Hill;* but he did not replace Maria, and I was henceforth the only woman, excepting Mrs Foreman, who belonged to the ship's company.

There was then at Hobart Town, a very disagreeable and decrepid old man about ninety years of age, who used to hobble about on two sticks. He was called Paddy Millar. He and his first wife were among the earliest convicts ever sent to that colony. He had gained immense riches under some government regulations which were afterwards altered, but he could not legally be deprived of the profits they had brought to him. He had married seven wives in succession, portioning off one to make room for another; and the women thus enriched by him had readily found new husbands.

One day as I was passing his door he entered into conversation with me, and proposed to marry me; I did not for a moment think the poor old creature could be in earnest, and was foolish enough to joke with him on what I should require, naming a brown-bodied coach with two grey horses, several thousand pounds a year, two houses, and other extravagancies. To my great surprise, the next day, he sent Mr Murray, a lawyer, to me on board the *Denmark Hill.* Mr Murray who once lived at Brecon, had been transported for bigamy; his business with me was to draw my marriage settlements with the old convict, on the terms which I had jestingly made. I told him that he either must be mad, or suppose me to be so. Mrs Foreman was as much surprised by this proceeding as myself; and we endeavoured to make him ashamed of his errand.

From Hobart Town, the ship took us to Sydney, where any woman might marry that wished so to do, for the proportion of men to women was less than one to thirty. Mrs Foreman took me with her from Sydney on a visit to Paramatta, and from thence to Liverpool, to visit Mr Cartwright, the magistrate, and Mr Bell, his assistant.

One day, three maid-servants and I went out to bathe in the lake below Mr Bell's house. When we came out of the water, being full of life and spirits, we ran about to dry the bathing-gowns upon our backs, chasing each other among the brushwood. Mary cautioned me against going near some bushes which she said were poisonous, but when Harriet was pursuing me, I thought only of avoiding being caught, and heedlessly jumped into a poison bush. A large leaf instantly struck me with a smart, flat stroke upon the leg, and before I could retreat, the whole limb swelled frightfully. Mary ran to look for help, and found Mr Edward Bell, the assistant's son, not far off. He had his gig with him, and being aware of the necessity for prompt surgical aid, he at once took me up, just as I was, with bare head and feet, and no clothes but the bathing gown, and drove off at full speed. Without stopping at his father's house, or at Paramatta, or anywhere else, he made a short cut, along a bad road, and never drew bridle until he reached the door of Dr Bland's surgery at Sydney. I was in dreadful agony. Dr Bland cut a hole in my leg, and poured in a liquid which, I believe, was spirits of wine. It burned like fire as a quantity of blackish green fluid ran out, and the swelling sunk as it flowed. He then put an issue where he had made the incision. I soon recovered, but ever since have found a peculiar insensibility to pressure or pricking in the part affected, which was a few inches above the instep. I never heard any other name for the shrub which had hurt me, excepting that of the poison-bush. The leaf was flat and wide, and the stalks had bunches which looked white, and curled something like endive.[1] I spent one day at the doctor's house, and the next I went on board the *Denmark Hill.*

Mr Edward Bell had saved my life, but I had no inclination to reward him, as he wished, by becoming his wife.

A few weeks afterwards, the *Denmark Hill* removed to Piper's Point. I was on shore there, one day, taking a walk to see the country, when I met with a convict, servant to Captain Piper, who asked me to walk with him to a neighbouring wood.

I feared the man, and refused; on which he tried to persuade me, saying it was a very pretty place. Finding he could not prevail, he seized hold of my arm to make me go. I caught up a broken bough of a tree, knocked him down, beat him severely about his legs and arms, left him on the ground, and ran away. I met Mrs Foreman, Captain Piper and his wife, and told them what had happened.

The convict, after this occurrence, threatened to waylay and murder me; and Captain and Mrs Foreman, fearing the villain might keep his word, went back with me to the ship at Sydney harbour.

---

[1] This shrub appears to have belonged to Lindley's natural order, *Loganiaceae*, of which a few species are found in Australia. "It would be difficult," says that distinguished botanist, "to name a more venomous order."

The vessel was soon chartered for China by Mr Jones, a tea broker; and, while she was loading, Mrs Foreman took it into her head to invite a lady to dinner one day, and to make a plum pudding for her, with her own hands. I saw that she had not put sufficient flour to bind the fruit and other rich things together, and warned her that, when turned out of the shape, the pudding would fall to pieces. She scorned my caution, and, when it was brought to table in fragments, flew into a passion with me, and bade me go over the ship's side, and never show my unlucky face to her again. I took her at her word, and went on shore directly. I chanced to meet with a gentleman whom I knew. He was about to commence housekeeping, and invited me to enter at once into his service, and to prepare that day's late dinner in his new abode. He had already one servant there, so I went and set to work.

Meantime, Captain and Mrs Foreman, wanting their tea, had discovered that I was gone. They had not supposed that I should so readily have left them in a place where all was strange to me. The Captain came to look for me, and finding me employed at Mr James Cobb's, gave me a volley of angry words, and ugly names. I explained the matter. He urged me to return with him to the ship, reminded me that my clothes were on board, and threatened not to pay me my wages unless I came back; and then he went away without me. Mrs Foreman next sent several ladies and gentlemen to persuade me, and they stayed talking in vain until after midnight. About one o'clock she came herself, and trying to carry things with a high hand, addressed me with, "How foolish you were, Betsy, to run away."

This provoked me to the utmost, and I declared that I would never return to the ship until Mrs Foreman had begged my pardon, on her knees. Some of the ladies expressed much indignation at my pride, and exclaimed, "The idea!"

However, they all quitted the room together; and when they came in again, Mrs Foreman approached me very quietly, and said in a low voice, "Come, Betsy, it *was* my fault," slightly bending her knee upon a chair, as she spoke.

I was pacified by this submission, and returned with her on board the *Denmark Hill.*

We took a cargo of wool, bark, and mercantile goods, and cedar wood for ballast. We had also many passengers on board when we sailed from Sydney to Whampoa, and Macao. After having unloaded the ship between these ports, we loaded her from them with tea, fancy goods, silk and crapes, and went to the Custom House at Singapore. The Foremans had many friends there, and especially Mr Thomson, the missionary, and they went often on shore, and took me with them. I got many a ride on the elephants and camels, and enjoyed the new exercise, vastly. One day I mounted a camel, set out, and trotted about all day long, for I could not guide him, nor get him to turn homeward. At last, night came on, I met some Indians, and let them know my distress as well as I could by signs and gestures. They soon understood me, and turned the camel, who took me back to the place from whence I had started in the morning.

From Singapore, we took the ship to Bombay, and from thence returned with passengers to Hobart Town and Sydney, having rather a stormy voyage.

When we reached Sydney, Captain Bunster spoke to Captain Foreman about chartering the *Denmark Hill* for Calcutta and back again. We, therefore, unloaded her as quickly as possible, and took her to Hobart Town, where we loaded her with potatoes, wheat, bark, staves, and mercantile goods for Calcutta. Captain Foreman also took many passengers. At Calcutta we unloaded, and re-loaded the ship with sugar, rice, coffee, and other things.

While this business was going on, I went about to see the place. One day I went to Mr Ferguson's counting-house, to inquire for Mr Henry Fleming, who had told me to call there, if ever I should visit the East Indies. He was not at home; but Mr and Mrs Ferguson gave me a kind reception, remembering that he had often mentioned my name, related the services I had done, and the good advice I had given him, when he was a wild schoolboy, and used to spend his holidays with his school-fellow, young Henry Bellingham.

Another day I went to see the view from Fort William: it is one of the most beautiful my eyes ever beheld. As I passed through the fort with Major Marley, an officer and lady were walking together there, and the major remarked to me, that he should not care how soon he was married, if he were sure of being as happy as Captain Nelson and his wife. He then talked with them, and asked after their four little boys, and introduced me as a person who had been attentive to him when he was seasick on the voyage. Mrs Nelson was rather a little woman, and had a pleasant look.

I did not observe her particularly, nor did I feel any interest in her; yet, many years afterwards, I learned that she was my eldest sister. Captain Nelson was in the East India Company's service; and some years before, when recruiting in Wales, he came to Bala to look after his party. Standing at the window of the Lion Inn, he saw my sister Mary pass by. She was then about fifteen years of age. He watched for her; and as she was going after her father to chapel, he caught her up, thrust her

into a post-chaise, and ran away with her to Dolgellau. He had
seen her only once before and, until then, had never spoken
with her. That same night, about eleven o'clock, he brought
her home again to Pen Rhiw, and sent her into the house while
he waited outside. She came with her marriage certificate in
her hand to take leave of the family, as she was on the point
of setting out at one the next morning, with her husband and
the soldiers, to make a journey, and to embark for India.

Years after this accidental meeting at Calcutta, I saw her
again at Pen Rhiw, when we recognized each other.

From Calcutta I returned with the ship to Hobart Town.

While the *Denmark Hill* lay at Hobart Town, a gentleman
named Cheritree made a large party of his friends – among
whom were Captain and Mrs Foreman – to go to a farm of
his, called 'Nonsuch Cordon', which was kept by his bailiff or
steward – Mr Bennett. There were altogether about a hundred
guests, and the object of our visit was to hunt the kangaroo. It
rained so hard that first night, that the party could not go out,
and sleeping accommodation being scarce, I had only a
kitchen for a bedroom, where a good fire of four trees was
burning on the hearth, and I lay in front of it with a carpet and
comfortable bedding. I had taken my first nap, and was lying
awake staring at the log-fire and the wide chimney, when I
saw a foot and leg coming down. I jumped from my bed, and
calling out, "Stop, stop, I'll help you!" I seized hold of the leg,
which, being hastily taken up out of my reach, left a piece of
the corduroy trowsers in my grasp. I was not frightened, and
thought the man must belong to the house, and have a right to
come into it. I therefore lay down again and watched the
chimney. Down came the leg again, with the same shoe and
blue stocking, and torn corduroy. I called out, "Stop!" and in

a moment the leg was out of sight again.

There were many dogs about the house, and just then I heard them bark furiously; I went to the door, opened it, and stood looking out. I saw a man leading a horse, which had a sack across its back, and I heard the dogs raving as if they would burst their chains. I said to the nearest of them, "Foolish dog, to bark at a man going to the mill!" I shut the door and went back to the kitchen, and distinctly heard the step of a man, and the fresh burst of rage among the dogs; then I was convinced that thieves were about the premises, and I went to the passage and bedroom doors and called, "Murder!" to arouse all the sleepers. Ladies answered in faint, puny voices, and at last Mr Bennett awoke, reached his gun, and came out. He had slept in the storeroom, that visitors might occupy his usual chamber; and as the goods had a strong smell, he left the window open when he went to bed. He soon discovered that thieves had been in and out at it, and carried off large quantities of convicts' clothes, provisions, wheat, barley, and other stores. He gave the alarm through the house, which was all on one floor, and all the gentlemen in their shirts, rushed out armed with swords, and guns, and sticks, and went round the different farm buildings. All the servants were convicts, and they slept in a hut by themselves, quite apart from the master's dwelling-house. When morning came, Mr Bennett missed his pony from the field where he had left it the night before. Suspecting the servants, Mr Bennett took the whole band that day before the magistrates at Jericho, which was fifteen miles from Nonsuch Cordon, but nothing could be proved against any of them.

That night was fine, and we all went out to hunt the kangaroo. This hunting was a dangerous sport, for brush-wood and moss covered swamps and precipices, and many of our party had some very bad falls; I had a terrible tumble myself, but happily escaped without broken limbs. We had sixty dogs out, and yet, such is the fleetness of the kangaroo, that only one was killed – a noble fellow, and a heavy burden for the three men who carried him. His tail was an enormous weight. I wish we had it here to make soup of – there is none better anywhere.

Getting an opportunity of talking with me concerning the robbery, seeing the piece of corduroy, and hearing my description of the dress of the man who led the horse, Mr Bennett consulted with Mr Cheritree, and the Jericho magistrates, who thought it right to examine the servants a second time, and to send me a summons to appear as a witness. I had returned to Hobart Town on the morning after the kangaroo hunt, and had therefore a long and hasty journey to make in order to attend this trial. I rode on horseback forty miles from Hobart Town to Nonsuch Cordon, and walked from thence with Mr Bennett, and his forty or fifty convict servants, fifteen miles through the bush, to Jericho. We had to wait there in court while several other trials went on, and I noticed a man who appeared desirous of avoiding my eyes. He was brought up and accused of various offences, which were proved against him. At last, our cause came on, and I was desired to pick out such a man as I had seen, from among Mr Bennett's servants. I answered that he was not one of them; but taller than either. I was then desired to point him out, if I could see him anywhere in the court, and I immediately said that I believed the tall man with a broad hat on, who had been found guilty upon other charges, was the person I had seen leading away the horse with a sack from

Nonsuch Cordon. The rogue instantly owned the fact, saying to the magistrates, "Yes, I did it. You have given me a sentence of eighty lashes already, and what more can you do to me?"

After this business was over, I had to set out on my journey again, for I knew the *Denmark Hill* was to set sail the next day but one. Mr Bennett was obliged to go off somewhere on horseback. I was afraid to go without him with his servants through the bush, so I waited until they had set out, and then I followed them alone through the bush to Nonsuch Cordon. I expected to be murdered by some of them for the evidence which I had given against the tall man, with whom I thought it likely they might have been accomplices. It was night, and I had a dreary walk of fifteen miles, starting at every sudden noise, and almost scared to death in passing through a wood by the screams of thousands of cockatoos.

At last, I reached Mr Bennett's house, where I had something to eat and drink, and started without more delay in the dead of the night, in a bullock cart, which was guided by a convict servant, whom Mr Bennett considered to be the most trustworthy person in his set. We had forty miles to go, and three rivers to cross. There was straw in the cart, I was very tired, and fell fast asleep. I was awakened by the driver jumping into the cart.

"What do you want?" I cried out.

"Come, we'll have a comfortable snooze together," he said.

I was very much frightened, and the more so as the oxen suddenly stopped.

"Why do they stand still?" I inquired.

"To drink," he replied.

I never thought of the river, nor of anything else in the

world, but of escaping from my companion; and I jumped clear over the front of the cart into the stream. I did not care at the moment whether I got drowned or not; but, somehow or other, I scrambled out.

There was a blacksmith's forge on the bank, but I feared the people there might be as bad as the man I fled from, and I plunged along through the bushes and briars, until I was almost flayed alive. The driver followed me with the bullock cart, declaring that he meant no harm, that he only intended to ride through the water and to rest a little, and promising that he would not again attempt to get in, if I would but take my place in the cart again.

He talked for a long time in vain; but, after I had walked a considerable distance my strength failed, and I was obliged to yield. I got into the cart – he sat on the shaft – we entered into conversation, and he told me his history. He seemed to be so sorry for having frightened me, and so willing to do all he could to make amends for it, that I thought he must deserve his master's good opinion, and I listened with interest to what he told me of his misfortunes – I really believe that he spoke the truth. He was a Cornish man, of the name of William Taylor, and had once been a groom in the service of Lord Carew.[2] There was a servants' ball in the neighbourhood, which he attended in company with several other men of his lordship's household. The ball was kept up until after midnight, and Taylor attended to her home a young housemaid, with whom he was in love. In entering her master's premises, they passed through a shrubbery in front of the dwelling-house; and, the

[2]   Query – Mr Pole Carew?

gentleman hearing footsteps, threw up a window, pointed a gun at him, and bade him surrender. A few hours afterwards, he was taken before the magistrates, and the housemaid swearing that she knew nothing of him, and had never seen him before, his account of himself was discredited, and he was committed to Exeter Gaol to take his trial as a burglar.

Meanwhile Lord Carew and his family thought he was lost, and could not in any way account for his disappearance, until some weeks afterwards, when the butler accidentally read in a newspaper an account of William Taylor's trial and condemnation to fourteen years' transportation. The butler, and some of the other servants who had been at the ball, set off directly for Exeter, to tell what they knew of him; but it was too late, and the poor man was shipped off to Van Diemen's Land.

Our tedious journey ended between ten and eleven o'clock in the forenoon; and I reached Hobart Town, soaking wet, scratched, and torn.

Sometime afterwards, I had the pleasure of hearing that Lord Carew had succeeded in obtaining William Taylor's liberty; and two years and a half after his arrival in Van Diemen's Land, he returned a free man to England.

The housemaid died mad, and spoke of him in her ravings.

Chapter 9

Bear me through regions where gay fancy dwells,
But mould to truth's fair form what memory tells.

Bloomfield's Farmer's Boy, Spring.

Australia, the Mauritius, India, and China
Port Phillip – India – Suttees – Bishop Heber – Juggernaut
– Mauritius – Canton.

The next day the *Denmark Hill* removed to Port Phillip. The
captain always would set sail on a Sunday, often repeating
the adage, 'Sunday sailing never failing'. He had only one
eye, and was certainly a little crazy in the weak time of the
moon.

We spent two days at Port Phillip; and I went on shore to
see the place, Mr Peel – Sir Robert Peel's kinsman – was
there, having obtained a government grant of 100,000 acres
of land; and he had brought out two hundred emigrants to
cultivate it; among them I found some Welshmen from
Cardiganshire. Returning from Port Phillip, we went to see
Botany Bay village – a very beautiful place, as far as the
country goes. We then went to Sydney. Mr Parker, a sail-
maker, took the ship to carry sail-cloth to India. We went
from Sydney to Bombay, and thence to Madras, where I
called at the register office to ask for Sir George and his
family. Unluckily, I could not recollect the name of the place
where his property lay, so I could not learn anything about
them.

I had friends at Madras among the missionaries; and I went one day in company with Mr Elliott, Mr Cook, and Mr Benini, to see a suttee. The widow was only eighteen years of age. The pile of wood and everything was ready, and a multitude of people came to look on.

The widow, in the midst of her numerous relations, was walking towards the pile, when Mr Cook and Mr Elliott met her, and asked her quietly whether it was her own will to be burned. She answered, "No". They next asked whether she would escape, if the opportunity were given her; and she answered, "Yes". The missionaries contrived to free a path for her, and she got off; but the English sentries stopped her. To avoid their bayonets, she threw herself into the river. The missionaries rescued her, and made an application to the governor; so that she was saved at last.

From Madras we took the remainder of our cargo of sails to Calcutta. As the ship went up the Ganges, I was surprised and enraged to see the bodies of infants floating round her. I wanted the captain to stop the ship that she might not touch them, but he would not. I counted thirty-two little corpses, and I saw five mothers throw in their babies. The women knelt down at the water's edge, and each took her child by a leg and arm, and uttering a horrible howl, threw it in and left the place. One poor little thing, being older and stronger than the others, struggled so long that I begged hard to have the boat put out to save it, but it was not done. I saw those little drowning babies in my thoughts for many nights afterwards. I never saw anything more dreadful, nor anything that troubled me more. I witnessed at Calcutta another suttee, where an old widow insisted on being burned with her dead husband, in spite of good Dr Carey's expostulations.

Dr Carey[1] was then staying for a while at Calcutta, and one Sunday he took me to church to hear Bishop Heber[2] preach.

The text was: "When my father and my mother forsake me, then the Lord will take me up."

He spoke very well, and among other things which struck me very much was the remark, that when the thoughtless children of pious parents strayed away like the prodigal son into far countries, even there the prayer of a godly father might overtake them in blessings from our God, who is always ready to pardon. After the service was over, Dr Carey introduced me to the bishop, as the daughter of Dafydd Cadwaladyr, and his lordship asked me to come and dine with him the next day, as he wished to talk with me about North Wales. He also invited Mrs Foreman, who was with me at church. We went accordingly about two o'clock, and dined at the same table with two or three Indian gentlemen, Mrs Heber, the Bishop and their two little girls; the youngest was dressed as an Indian boy, and I mistook her for a boy. Mrs Heber had not the look of a godly woman.

Dinner being over, the bishop took us to his museum, and showed us a great many curious things, which he had collected on his travels through the country.[3] There were writings upon

---

[1] Dr William Carey, the eminent Baptist missionary and linguist arrived in Bengal in the year 1794, settled at Serampore in 1799, and died in 1834.

[2] Reginald Heber was born at Malpas in Cheshire, April 2nd 1783. When travelling abroad in the year 1805, he visited the Crimea. In 1822 he was appointed Bishop of Calcutta. He left England for India, June 16th 1823, and died at Triehinopoly on the April 3rd 1826.

[3] Bishop Heber having visited the upper provinces of his vast diocese in the year 1824, it appears that Elizabeth Cadwaladyr must have seen him at Calcutta between that time and 1826, when he resumed his visitation.

stone, upon shells, and upon leaves of trees; and there were all sorts of idols worshipped in different parts of his diocese.

Among these idols was a tiny bit of a fly's wing. The bishop held it up before me, and said, "Can you learn a lesson from this?"

I answered, "I think I can, my lord. Everything in God's creation keeps its place excepting man, and nothing goes so low as he does."

"How do you account for that?" said the bishop.

I told him that I supposed it was because of the fall. He assented.

He talked to me about Dolgellau, and Llyn Tegid and Bala, and other places in my native country; asked me if I knew Rowland Hill, and what I thought of him; adding, that all the Hills were old acquaintances of his. He asked what I called the Holy Spirit in Welsh, and I said, "Ysbryd Glan". He remarked that Rowland Hill had taught him that – and that the expression was very beautiful. He was then studying the Welsh language. He told me that the Chaldaic and the Syriac were branches of the Welsh, and that Abraham was a Welshman before he went to Canaan, and afterwards the languages got mixed. He told me he had heard that there was a Welsh tribe among the Indian mountains, and that he intended to go there and ascertain whether the report was true. He inquired whether I had known Charles of Bala? I said that he was my old neighbour at home. He inquired whether I knew Griffith of Nefern? I said he was my cousin. He repeated a monody,[4] in Welsh, on the death of Charles of Bala, and

---

[4] Marwnad y Parch Thomas Charles, A.B. o'r Bala, gan Dafydd Cadwaladyr.

asked if I knew that pious and heavenly-minded brother of his, who was the author of those beautiful and very original verses? I said, "He is my father."

"Give us your hand!" he cried out, quite delighted.

He told me there was one of the finest ideas in that monody of any he had met within poetry.

The bishop had a fine, heavenly-looking countenance, and was fit to be a missionary – making friends with everybody, and associating with Christians of all denominations.

The verses in my father's poem, which he particularly admired, and read to me, were the following:

> Nawr'r wy'n colli'm golwg arnat,
> Dwy'n nabod dim o honot fry;
> Nid wyt ti swm yr un o'r tywod,
> Nid wyt ti bwysau'r un o'r plu;
> Nid tebyg wyt i un creadur,
> A welwyd mewn daearol fyd,
> Does arnat liw, na dull, na mesur,
> Er hyny sylwedd wyt i gyd.

> A wyt ti'n gweled peth yr awrhon,
> O ddwfyn ddirgelion Tri yn Un?
> Pa fath olwg sy'n y nefoedd,
> Ar a gym'rodd natur dyn?
> A ydyw rhyfeddodau'r Duwdod.
> Yndod i'th olwg heb ddim rhi'
> Neu ynte wyt yn gwel'd efengyl,
> Yn llenwi conglau'n daear ni?

TRANSLATION BY G. G.

Now is thy sight lost to me!
No knowledge have I of thee in higher spheres;
Thou art not the size of a grain of sand,
Thou art not the weight of a feather,
Thou art not like to any creature,
That has been beheld in this earthly world;
Thou has neither colour, form, or measure,
Yet thou art altogether reality.

Art thou now beholding
The profound mysteries of the Three in One?
What sight is there in Heaven
Of Him who took once the nature of man?
Do the wonders of the Godhead
Come unnumbered to thy sight,
Or dost thou see the Gospel
Filling every corner of our earth?

While the ship remained at Calcutta, I went, with Dr Carey and his son, and some of the other missionaries, to see the procession of Juggernaut. Bishop Heber and many clergymen went also. We had a carriage part of the way, and alighted on a common, when we met the procession several miles from the city.

I never in my life, before or since, saw such thronging multitudes of people. Three hundred or more little gods were carried first, and about fifty little gods were carried after the great idol. The car was drawn by several hundred men. The procession went straight on. There was a terrible rush among the people, and many threw themselves on the road just in front of the wheels, and were crushed to death. Hundreds of men and women, uttering joyful shouts, sacrificed, themselves in this way as the car rolled heavily along. They must have died instantly, for 1 heard no screams or groans. When 'the car reached the outskirts of Calcutta, there was a. platform set up, and priests, or some such persons, mounted upon it in bands of twenty-four, or more, at a time, who prayed and figured about with weapons like large carving knives in their hands, with which they pricked the great idol, and then made a show of throwing blessings from him among the people who crowded round. There was a *tommen* (mound) of fine white dust, which had been brought and put down close by the platform; and as each band left the platform, the priests rolled themselves in that dust, and threw handfuls of it among the people.

I climbed on the steps of the platform, and got a good view of the beautiful dresses.

For whole weeks after this dreadful sight, 1 lost my sleep, and lay awake at night, thinking how low man had fallen.

At Calcutta, a Portuguese merchant took the ship for three years and a half. His name was Andrea Antonio Benjamin Barbosa, and he was principal of the firm of Barbosa, Martin, and Burke, general merchants of Macao, Sydney, Lima, Rio de Janeiro, and Calcutta.

His father was brother to King John the Eighth of Portugal. Barbosa was sent when a youth to study at the University of Oxford. He there became a Protestant, and, on returning to his own country, was disinherited on account of the change in his religion. Being thus cast out by his family, he took the surname of his mother, and became a merchant, although he was first cousin to Don Pedro, Emperor of the Brazils.

Mr Barbosa loaded the *Denmark Hill* with tea and other things, came on board to act as his own supercargo, and sailed with us from Calcutta to Ceylon. On entering the harbour of Trincomalee, we came at once upon the city. It seemed to be a fair day, or a market day, for great numbers of people were assembled together with all sorts of things for sale. But what surprised and amused me above all was a row of some hundreds of elephants, quite 'even and dressed' as the soldiers would say, in a line, all having their trunks turned up, and a black man seated on the back of each. They stood as still as if they had grown there under the hill, and the sun shone bright upon them. I quite forgot my business, and stared at them with admiration, until Captain Foreman raved at me, and reminded me of the cabin passengers. I was only once on shore during our stay of twenty-one days there.

We discharged our cargo, re-loaded the ship, and sailed back to Calcutta. The good Bishop Heber had died since my last visit to that place. We loaded the ship from thence with calico, and a general cargo for China.

We had the monsoons and very bad weather.

We touched at Macao, and stayed several days there. The wind, being contrary, prevented us from getting up the river to Canton, so we anchored about a mile from the city, between the English factory, and Cock Lane, which is inhabited by Jews. The cargo was soon sold, and we moved to the English factory, and there loaded the ship with tea and silk fabrics, for Port Elliot, in Bengal.

There I had a holiday allowed me, to go and see the country. I spent the day roving about by myself, and was so well amused, that I never thought how fast the time was passing. I was very busy picking leaves and little flowers which I had never seen before; and, pushing my way among the tall grass and reeds, I found some little shells upon the ground. The sun had set, and I was reminded of it by hearing wild beasts begin to roar. Suddenly I came upon two panthers lying together. Happily they did not see me; and being then really frightened, I made the best of my way back to the ship. From Port Elliot we sailed to the Mauritius.

At Port Louis, in the Mauritius, I saw the two missionaries, Mr Griffiths and Mr Jones, and the Christian converts from Madagascar. I was much with these good people, and found nothing besides in the island half so interesting.

The missionaries showed me the tomb of Paul and Virginia. It had a long inscription, and the effigies of a man with a rope round his waist, and of a young woman. The tomb was arched, like a camel's back, and had four busts on the four columns. Across the end of that tomb at the foot, there was a grave with two busts of a negro man and woman. I never read their history. Mr Jones had owned it once; but it was lost before I met him there.

I saw in the Mauritius two Welshmen from Pembrokeshire. The name of one of them was Philips. I forget the name of the other.

From the Mauritius we sailed to Siam, and loaded there with goods for Madras and F_____. There we loaded a general cargo, with fine woods and ivory for Canton. On reaching that city, we anchored in Cock Lane to discharge the cargo, and then went up to the East India Company's Factory, and loaded the ship with tea. The foreman there was an old Chinaman, who had been thirty years in the factory. He used often to come on board the *Denmark Hill* for a meal of beef, biscuit and grog; and I made a joke of asking him to take me to see the city. One day I told him that I would give him no more beef and grog until he did take me. I thought the thing impossible, and only said it to teaze him. The old man looked very hard at me, as much as to say, "Are you in earnest?" He went on shore, and I thought no more about it. He spoke English very well.

The next morning, about nine o'clock, I was very much surprised to see a grand native boat come alongside our ship. This great boat was of all the colours of the rainbow, with the union-jack and the Company's flag flying together at the stern. The rowers were ten Chinamen, dressed all in white, with green sashes. The boatswain wore a pink robe, with a red sash, and had a white and green cap on his head with a very large green and red feather. They all wore satin slippers, with wooden soles to them, and very narrow, turned-up toes.

At the same time the old foreman, Fa Pooh, came on board the *Denmark Hill* from the factory, bringing a passport in his hand for my mistress and me to see the city. She was afraid, and would not go; but I would not lose such a chance, so I dressed myself up in a pink gingham dress, and went alone in the barge in the care of the little boatswain. Neither he, nor any of the crew could speak English, and when I talked English to them, they stared foolishly at me; but when I spoke Welsh to them, they pointed out the different places that came in sight as we went along the river, and I never will believe but they knew what I said.

They took me as near as the barge could go to the gates of Canton, and I landed and had to take care afterwards of myself. Fa Pooh had taught me what I was to do. I gave in my passport, expecting that it would be looked at, and returned to me, but instead of that, I was kept waiting so long that I grew very uneasy, for the Tartar sentinels were staring fiercely at me all the time. The gatekeeper at last gave me a new passport, which he had been writing out while I stood there. The same thing was done at all the other gates which I passed through that day. I think that I had twelve in going through the city.

Being let in, I wandered about and saw a great many craftsmen at all sorts of works. Some were weaving; and others making cabinets; others turning with a lathe. Everyone was busy that I saw, and they were all gentle and civil in their manner towards me; but they eyed me, I thought, as if they misdoubted me. There was not a woman among them. I felt uneasy, and was sorry that I had come. None of them uttered a word to me, nor did I speak to them. Not knowing where I went, I came at length into the Royal Square, where I found a great number of women all very industrious and working in sets at all kind of things: some were at embroidery; some were weaving silk or camels' hair textures; some were turning ivory; and others making fans, and pretty toys. I was very much pleased to see them. I should think there were five hundred there. They all seemed by their manners to be ladies. They were beautiful creatures, very fair and had a delicate pink colour on their cheeks. I do not know whether it was paint or not. Their eyes were some dark and some light in colour; but too small to have life enough in them. They were very silent, but looked pleased at me.

I was told afterwards that this was the Emperor's harem.

I began to talk Welsh to them; and the leader of them, who seemed to act as foreman in their works, took me round, up-stairs and down-stairs, and showed me everything. I think she understood what I said. I am sure there is come connection between the Welsh and Chinese languages.

This old princess looked at my dress, and smiled, and patted my face, and stroked me down, and we were very good friends. I stayed some hours with these kind ladies; and, when I was coming away, the old princess fetched a small parcel, folded up in a China silk-gauze handkerchief. I did not examine what was in it; but I felt very thankful for her kindness, and I offered to shake hands with her, saying, "Diolch yn fawr i chwi," and making a curtsey. She kissed my hand, and I went away.

I did not know where I was going; and got into a gallery, and passed along it for some distance. It skirted the Royal Square, but all ways seeming the same to me, I stopped short at a door which I saw in it, and passed into the longest room I ever beheld in my life. The walls were bare, and there was no furniture, excepting two images, with a great deal of Chinese writing about them. In the further end of the room several men were sitting together in a group upon the ground.

I had scarcely time to notice these particulars, when a gentleman came rushing after me, saying, "For God's sake, don't go there! It's as much as your life is worth."

I was frightened, and asked, "What have I done?"

He answered, "Do you know where you are? Down on your knees and stop so until I tell you!"

I sat down on the floor, and he fell on his knees, and raised his joined hands, as if he had been praying.

One of the men from the other end of the room now got up. He wore a long robe, glittering with precious stones, and had in his hand a sceptre, about three yards long, with a sort of crown on the top of it. With that he came towards us, and measured from the spot where Mr Cruikshanks knelt, thrice its length along the ground. Mr Cruikshanks then walked that distance on his knees, with his hands lifted up as they were. The man measured a second distance, and Mr Cruikshanks passed it in the same way. When he reached the party, they made him sit down cross-legged, and gave him a pipe to smoke, and talked with him. By and by, he was brought back again with the same ceremonies to the spot where I was sitting on my heels. He told me to do everything as he had done; and that he had explained about me. The way was then measured for me, as it had been for him, but I found great difficulty in getting along, for my petticoats hindered me, and I was obliged to tuck the princess's parcel across the back of my legs, to have both my hands free for holding up. When I got to the group of gentlemen, I sat down cross-legged, as Mr Cruikshanks had done. They all looked at me and laughed; the youngest and most plainly dressed of them handed me a pipe. I never thought that they could intend me to smoke it, but supposed they wished me to see how pretty it was, so I took it all to pieces, and looked at it bit by bit, and gave the biggest branch back again to the young emperor who had passed it to me. At this they were more amused than ever, and laughed very heartily.

Thinking it was time to go, I arose and stood upon my feet, but in an instant the chamberlain who had measured the ground, and was sitting cross-legged with the rest, planted his fingers so firmly in the palm of my hand that he pulled me down again. My hand was black and blue for days after that pinching gripe. He measured the ground again, and I tried to imitate the way in which Mr Cruikshanks had walked backwards on his knees with his hands lifted up together. I scrambled and crawled some how or other along the first distance, but when the chamberlain measured the next I lost all patience, for the party all shrieked out, and the old man shook me with angry looks for not going in the right posture, so I suddenly started to my feet and ran out of the room face foremost. and down a flight of many hundred marble steps, and into a fine chapel, and through it to the river's bank. I could go no further in that direction, so I recrossed the chapel – it was inlaid with dazzling stones, and there were no idols in it. In going up the marble steps, I met Mr Cruikshanks coming towards me. He said it was a mercy he had seen me, or I never should have come out of that room alive. The young emperor had only arrived at Canton the day before. and was sitting in council when I went in upon him.

Mr Cruikshanks was a Scotch merchant, who had lived twenty eight years at Canton. He took me to his house in the square, and there I saw his wife, who was a Scotch woman, and their children. They were very much surprised to see me there. I took tea with them. and that being over. Mr Cruikshanks walked with me through the city to the last gate, where the boat was waiting for me.

About eight o'clock in the evening I got safe back to the ship. My friends there feared I was lost for ever, and Fa Pooh had been several times on board showing great anxiety for my safety.

The next morning I opened the princess's parcel, and found in it a fine camel-hair dress. of a yellow and white striped pattern, the white being like open needlework. It had hanging sleeves, and strings with tassels to draw it into shape. I thought it was too short for me so I gave it to Mrs Foreman, who asked me for it. I heard afterwards that she was offered eighty pounds for it.

Many years afterwards I met and talked with Mr Cruikshanks in London.

Chapter 10

Wanderer, whither dost thou roam?

James Montgomery

Excursions from Singapore
The Burmese Ladies – Visit to an Old Friend – Hindoo Convert.

We sailed from Canton to Singapore, and were detained there six weeks by the Custom House. We brought a cargo of tea from Canton, and a great number of passengers: among them were three Burmese ladies, who landed at Singapore. They did not understand a word of English, and Mr Norwood, a merchant on board who spoke their language, acted as interpreter, and transacted business for them with Captain and Mrs Foreman. They were going to the interior of the country and they proposed to Mrs Foreman that I should attend them on their journey home, and then return to the ship. I had no objection to this plan, and embarked with them in a passage-boat on a sort of canal. which took us, I supposed, one hundred and sixty miles to F_____. [1]

We there took leave of the boat, and went to an inn, and I walked about to see the place. Not seeing the ladies, I went in

[1]   The heroine's uncertainty concerning the names of the places which she visited in this expedition, and her want of sufficient geographical knowledge to distinguish between straits, canals, and rivers, have hitherto baffled the writer's efforts to identify the scenes of the adventures related in the present chapter.

search of them, and found them in a pagoda sacrificing to their fire-idol – which was a sort of golden grate, like two faces, between which the fire was burning. I stood to look on among a crowd of people.

The three ladies stood on one side of the altar, and six priests on the other side. Each of the ladies had a golden cup in her hand, with which she took up certain things, and threw them into the fire. At one time they threw perfumes into the fire, which made a very sweet smell; and they threw a great deal of rice and Indian corn, not only into the fire, but all over the floor. While the ladies did this, the priests were praying; then the three ladies took each other by the hand, and made a kind of jumping dance together round the fire-idol, which was set in the middle of the floor; and as they danced, they kept saying something. When they had done this, the priests began all to join hands together, and they danced round the idol as the ladies had done. One of them climbed upon the altar, and threw something into the very top of the idol's open head. At last the ladies took three china bowls, and put a great number of rupees into them, and held them up as offerings to the fire-idol, and knelt down and laid them down before him. This being done, they arose, and made bows towards the fire-idol, and clasped their hands, and moved backwards out of the temple – all the priests and the people chanting, and making loud and doleful noises with gongs and other instruments, sounding altogether like the roar of a bull with a squeak in it. The clamour must have been heard for miles and miles around.

I had no one to explain these things to me, for I could neither understand nor be understood there by a single creature: but I fancied that the ladies went through all these

expensive ceremonies to regain their caste; for when they
were on board the ship, they used to eat of our food, and to
receive my help in dressing and undressing, which, after this
visit to the pagoda, they never did. I never was allowed to
touch them again. We could not talk to each other, but they
used to look pleasantly at me. On returning to the inn, we had
a plentiful dinner of coffee, rice, and fish. As soon as it was
over, two elephants were led by two Indians to the mounting
block. They had no howdahs or furniture of any sort upon their
backs. The three Burmese ladies placed themselves upon one
elephant, and I was directed by signs to seat myself upon the
other. This being done, the Indians whispered some words into
the ears of the elephants,[2] and off they set side by side, going
over the ground very fast and very steadily. We had no driver,
or guide, or attendant; the three ladies and I were quite alone
with the elephants. I felt as if perched on a crow's nest on the
top of a tree. The elephants trotted on without slackening their
pace, or changing their step, or stopping, through all the rest
of the day, and all night long. It was bright star-light, and I
saw that we were passing over a fine level country. At

---

[2]   In Sir John Bowrings "Kingdom and People of Siam", there is a
      curious account of the manner in which elephants are honoured and
      trusted: "When the king of Siam sent three elephants to Louis XIV –
      animals, let it be said, treated in Siam as reasonable beings – he
      whispered in their ears: 'Go, depart cheerfully. You will indeed be
      slaves, but slaves to the greatest monarch in the world, whose sway
      is as gentle as it is glorious.'" *Athenaeum.* No.1533., p.335, March
      14th, 1857. Those persons who have known the habits of elephants
      at Moulmein and other places. where their sagacity has been
      heightened by human notice, without the counteracting depression
      of ungenial climate, can believe much more than is here related of
      their wonderful performances.

daybreak we crossed a hill, and came into another plain, and travelled across it, until, about twenty-four hours after we had set out, we came to an indigo plantation, and saw a good many huts and a comfortable looking dwelling house. The elephants, of their own accord, stood still at the door. A number of people came out to welcome the ladies, and four men brought a palanquin and lifted it up to assist them to alight. The ladies went into the house, and the men took me down also with the palanquin. I saw no women and only one girl. The Burmese people showed me into an outer room; one of them brought me some raw rice in a metal cup, another brought me a calabash full of water, and a third brought a calabash of some sour liquid. I knew by their signs that they meant me to prepare the rice for cooking. I did so, and they carried the things away, and by and by they came back again with boiled rice in a china bowl with sugar and sour sauce, and a china spoon for me to eat with. They brought me afterwards a mess of green stuff with black spots in it, which I was afraid to touch, and some cakes, like cheesecake or custard, of which there were four or five on a china dish. I was in the act of taking one of them, when the man who stood watching me cried out, "Woo, woo, woo!" and made me take them all at once. I was supplied with a calabash full of a clear white, cordial liquor, which had a fresh sharp taste and yet was sweet. I found it very pleasant and refreshing after my long fast day. When I had finished eating and drinking, a door was set open, and a man, after pointing towards it, moved his fingers about on the floor at my feet. This I took to be an invitation to go out and look about me, and he seemed much pleased when I did so. The house was of one storey, well finished and ornamented, and a pagoda stood near it. There were many men about the place, and I caught sight of two little girls, who were peeping at me.

On returning into the eating-room I saw the chief-waiter again. He gabbled something at me, opened an inner door, and repeated his sign for me to walk.

I followed him into a hall, and noticed that he made an obeisance in passing an image. He led me through many vacant rooms, into a little chamber, pointed to a bed, walked away, and shut the door.

There was no lock or fastening upon any of the doors, which were made of fine wood, and inlaid with mother-of-pearl. All the tables, ottomans, and ornaments, were of china; and the mattresses and cushions were of silk. The windows were like the horn used in lanterns, with a whiter and more silky look. I was very tired, and glad to lie down and sleep.

At daybreak, I was awakened by the same man, who was standing beside my bed and babbling something to me. He went away as soon as I opened my eyes; and, supposing that he meant me to get up, I did so at once, for I had not undressed, and there was no water in the room for me to wash with. I found my way back to the eating-room, and two men immediately set about preparing for my breakfast. They laid a skin upon the table instead of a cloth, and set a china basin and spoon upon it. They brought me coffee and bowls full of rice, of stuff like lobster sauce, and of green and red vegetables, mixed in stripes. I ate up everything, not knowing how long it might be before I should have a chance of eating again. Presently, came the chief waiter, making many bows, and showing me to the door, where I found the three Burmese ladies mounted upon one elephant, and another elephant waiting for me. Four men raised me in a palanquin to my seat on his bare back. Men whispered in their ears, and off they trotted, side by side.

The little Burmese ladies grinned at me sometimes in a friendly manner; but we did not, and could not, exchange a word; and the only sound that broke the stillness of my journey, was a snort now and then from an elephant.

We travelled, as before, across the country, without going through any towns or villages. We saw several at a distance, and one stood near, under a high mountain at our left.

That evening, about six o'clock, we reached a large plantation, with upwards of two hundred huts, a large handsome dwelling house, and two pagodas. The elephants went opposite to the house door and stood still. This was the end of our journey, and the home of the three Burmese ladies.

A whole fleet of people, old and young, men and women, boys and girls, came out to receive the ladies, and to help us with a palanquin to alight from the elephants. Immediately on arriving, the three ladies went into the great pagoda to worship. I have often felt shame and guilt as a Christian, at being convicted of my slow thankfulness by the zeal of the heathen.

I went at once into the house, and was served with plenty of dishes, and very good food. I had two men to wait upon me, and one of them was a Lascar, who could speak a few words of English. When I had eaten enough, he took me out to see the place. We went into the great pagoda, and he threw about rice and Indian corn there. The outside of it was very showy with gold and coloured ornaments. The other pagoda was smaller and plainer. I suppose it was meant for the use of the servants. The Lascar went back with me to the house, and took me to a spacious sleeping room. As soon as he had shut the door behind him and was gone, I undressed myself and lay down to sleep on the fine silk mattresses with a fur coverlet over me. The next morning, at daybreak, I was called up. and found a good breakfast of coffee, rice, and fruits provided for me in the eating-room. The Lascar told me that the elephants were ready. I never saw the ladies after our arrival. I asked the Lascar's leave to pick a flower; and, with that in my hand. was hoisted again upon an elephant. A man was placed upon the other, words were whispered in the elephants' ears, and off we trotted.

The man who was my fellow-traveller spoke not one word to me, nor I to him all the way to the Parsee-house, where I had halted with the ladies. I was treated there with the same civility and attention as before; and I occupied the same little chamber that night which I had previously slept in. At daybreak, the head-waiter aroused me, and I found my breakfast ready. I saw the man, who had come thus far with me, set out with two elephants to return to the home of the Burmese ladies. Two other elephants were brought to the door for me. Four men brought the palanquin, and lifted me into my perch. The second elephant had nothing on his back. Words were whispered in their ears, the elephants said, "Pha!" and off they trotted one under me and one by my side. Not a creature in either of the two Parsee-houses had touched even my fingers' ends or the hem of my garment. and none but the Lascar had spoken a word to me; but I did not feel quite so lonely there, or in the former stages of this journey, as in the last, when, all day and all night long. I travelled quite alone with two elephants.

At five o'clock in the morning. the elephants stood still at the block beside the boat-house inn, from which I had started a few days before. The passage-boat did not go from thence that day. The people of the inn spoke English. I talked over my strange journey with them, slept at their house that night, and embarked the next day on board the passage-boat. Many loaded boats carried on a brisk traffic up and down that canal.

On reaching Singapore. my friends welcomed me with great joy having had many fears for my safety.

The sailing of the *Denmark Hill* was still delayed. and I found Mrs Foreman on a visit to a friend on shore. She told me that she wished she had not sent me with the Burmese ladies, because a missionary was going from Singapore to B_____, and his wife was in such delicate health, that he was anxious to obtain a European attendant for her on the journey, which he meant to begin the next day. I said to my mistress that she need not regret my having gone with the Burmese ladies, as I felt both willing and able to set off with Mr and Mrs Winckworth. Indeed, that I should take it as a favour, her giving me such a holiday, as I had an old friend at B_____ whom I wished very much to visit. She was a Miss Dale, daughter of Captain Dale, of the merchant service. She had inherited a large fortune from him, had come out to India for the purpose of establishing schools among the natives, and was married to a missionary named Sands.

I left Singapore with Mr and Mrs Winckworth, by a passage-boat, on the same canal which I had passed along with the Burmese ladies, but now we stopped, and disembarked at a much shorter distance from Singapore. We travelled the remainder of our journey upon camels. Mrs Winckworth was in very ill health, and needed great care and attention to enable her to get through her fatigue. I sat behind her on her camel, and supported her.

The place we went to was near a very high mountain, which was called Mount Ararat.

Mr and Mrs Sands received me into their house at B_____, and were very kind to me. They had four children; and a Welsh clergyman, named Hughes, whom I had known at Liverpool, was their inmate at that time, on a visit from his own station at Malacca. Mrs Sands had the charge of sixty schools, which were distributed round that neighbourhood. She was a very godly woman, and had always a placid, heavenly look. Her husband told me that he had then been married nine years to her, and had never seen either a frown or a smile upon her face – not even with the children. They took me about to see the people and the schools, and, in seeing them, I saw the country. Mrs Sands used to ride a dromedary, and I had another to go with her, and Mr Sands walked after us with Mr Winckworth and Mr Hughes.

One day, we left our dromedaries at a schoolhouse, and joined the missionaries to go on foot along the slope of the mountains, to visit another school about three miles distant. We soon perceived a wild elephant walking slowly up a steep place which layout of our track. The gentlemen thought that he was going to a shady place for water.

As he stepped quietly up, a lion came running down, and, as soon as he caught sight of the elephant, he rushed at him furiously. We all stood still to watch the wild beasts fighting, wondering which of them would gain the victory. The lion attacked the elephant's legs. The elephant, after a struggle, released his foot.

Mr Winckworth said, "The lion is called the 'king of the forest'; he ought to beat the elephant."

Mr Sands answered, "I think the elephant will gain the

battle, this time."

The elephant lifted the lion on his trunk and tossed him in the air; then, before the lion could recover himself, the elephant set his foot upon him as he lay, and beat him with his trunk. We could hear their snorting, and could see the lion's tail and haunches struggling and writhing. At length, the lion lay still, and the elephant stood awhile with his foot upon his neck, looking at him; then lifted the carcase on his trunk, tossed it down the cliff, and walked quietly away up the steep, just as if nothing had happened. Mr Sands sent an Indian to flay the lion, and he brought the large skin and showed it to us.

I spent a fortnight at B_____, and liked the country and my friends and their way of life there so much, that, if I had had my box of clothes with me, I believe I should have stayed there altogether. However, the time came for me to return, and Mr Sands lent me a dromedary to ride upon, and sent an Indian servant with me to the house of a clergyman named White, where I rested for the night. Mr White told me that he had business at Calcutta, and that, if I would spend that day with his family, he would, on the next, accompany me as far as Singapore on his way. This I did, but he was unable to fulfil his promise; for his eldest child, a fine boy, was taken ill that second night of my stay, and died early the following morning. I was, therefore, forced to set out alone with the dromedary and, after travelling all day, I stopped for the night, by Mr White's direction, at the house of a converted Hindoo.

This man had, I think, been a priest, and he seemed to me to be the Christian pastor of the people around. He showed me quantities of gods, which he had collected from converted natives, and was packing up to send to England: these were ugly dolls, and stones, and snakes, and insects, and all sorts of contemptible things. He and his family were very kind to me. Speaking of England, he said to me, "No bad people at home!" This I thought was proof of the good conduct of the missionaries, which had given him such a notion of their countrymen. I embarked in the canal passage-boat, and got safe back to Singapore.[3]

---

[3] Endeavouring to trace the persons mentioned as missionaries in the course of this narrative, the writer has applied to several societies for copies of their reports, and lists of stations and labourers, for the ten years which would include the most important references. To the secretary of the London Missionary Society the writer is indebted for his prompt and exact compliance with the request. The secretary of the Church Missionary Society did not even reply to the letter of inquiry.

Chapter 11

The immense Pacific smiles
Round ten thousand little isles.
Haunts of violence and wiles.

But the powers of darkness yield,
For the Cross is in the field,
And the Light of Life revealed.

James Montgomery's *Voyage round the World*

The South Sea
**Mr Mills of Bathurst – A Comet – New Zealand – Otaheite
– Owhyhee – The Pamperos – Lima – Valparaiso – Beunos
Ayres.**

Soon after my return to Singapore, we sailed for Sydney. On
arriving there we unloaded the *Denmark Hill,* and she was sent
to the cove to be examined and cleaned, to have a new keel and
new lining, and a thorough repair and fresh painting. This was
the first time of her being turned up and refitted since we left
England. While she was in dock we lived thirteen months at
our leisure; visiting our friends and going about from one place
to another, making Sydney our headquarters, as the captain was
obliged to be often there to see after the ship.

In company with some of the missionaries from the South
Sea Islands. my mistress took me to Bathurst. where we were
received at the house of Mr Mills, the builder, and principal
proprietor of the town. He and his wife were very much

respected there. I went with Mr and Mrs Mills and some other persons into the country. and passed a month very agreeably in their company.

Mills had once been a journeyman tailor in London. and with six of his companions was thrown out of work for eighteen months. Having spent their all and being in much distress, they took to robbery for a maintenance. They used to fill a carpet-bag with stones, order a dinner at a tavern, eat it, and if they found no opportunity of slipping away unseen, they would even pay the bill, but they made a practice of carrying away all the spoons, forks, and other silver articles.

In this way they went on for a long time, until at last Mills grew tired of this wicked course of life, and resolved to put an end to it. Dining one day at the London Tavern, he sent his gang away with the bag full of plate, and put a fish-slice into his own pocket in such a manner that the waiter could not help seeing it. Mills being apprehended, his accomplices were soon discovered, and they were all tried and convicted at the Old Bailey. Two-hundred-and fifty pawnbrokers' tickets were found upon them; for Mills told me, that although they took the plate, they never had it melted down – always consoling themselves with the thought that some day they should get into honest employment again, and be able to redeem it, and to restore the various articles to the tavern-keepers whom they had robbed. Mills was sentenced to transportation for life; and by skill and industry during nearly twenty years, had become a very prosperous man.

On returning with my mistress to Sydney, I used to go every Sunday with Mr Hill, the chaplain, to teach the adult school held on board the convict hulk, *Delaford*, an old East Indiaman. The convicts there were all such desperate ruffians, that when they attended divine service in the ship's chapel, each man had an iron collar put round his neck.

After the *Denmark Hill* left the cove and went to the harbour, I taught a Sunday School under Mr Thomas at Windmill Hill.

About this time, I had offers of marriage from several settlers,[1] and from Mr Richards of the Observatory, but I cared for none of them. It was I who first mentioned to Mr Richards the comet which I had seen for several nights from the deck of the *Denmark Hill*. I told him it was just over the governor's house, and he found it as soon as he sought it. He said it was not visible in Europe, and had not been seen in Asia for three hundred years.

This comet looked like a lion, having bright fiery eyes, and a light feathery crown, and the tail of a fish.[2]

We loaded the ship at Sydney, for Rio de Janeiro, taking two hundred and twenty passengers and their goods, and a dead weight of cedar wood to ballast the ship. We called at Hobart Town, where Mr Nott and Mr Platt, missionaries to the South Sea Islands came on board with two chiefs of the Sandwich Islands returning home; The Rev Samual Marsden[3] and his wife

---

[1] It is well known that Australian settlers are pre-eminently considered as increasing their goods by the acquisition of a wife, to work harder and more faithfully than could be expected from a hired servant. Cadwaladyr's superior strength, activity and sagacity must therefore have rendered her a prize well worth contending for, to say nothing of her other attractions.

[2] This description would astonish Alexander Von Humboldt, who holds that the nucleus of comets has generally no definite outline. Vide *Cosmos* vol. 1.

[3] The well known clergyman of Paramatta, near Sydney, and first missionary to the New Zealanders – a most excellent and devoted man.

for New Zealand; and some ticket-of-leave convicts. In the South Sea, we met with a great many whales and sea calves.

Arriving at New Zealand, we put into Port Elliot; I think it is now called Auckland.

There we set Mr and Mrs Marsden on shore. The natives came flocking to welcome him, and received him as if they worshipped him. He was a good and godly man.

We took in water and potatoes; and in clearing the island met with a waterspout, which caused us to stand out to sea to avoid it.

We touched at several of the Society Islands, and landed Harris, the mission school-master, at Aramanqua, and Mr Platt at Borabora.

We then sailed for the Georgian Islands; and, arriving at Otaheite, touched at Haweis Town, where Mr Smith and Miss Davis were to land; but, very early in the morning, before their friends in the island knew of the arrival of the *Denmark Hill,* I got the carpenter and Ted, a sailor, to put me on shore. I felt very glad to see hay fields and Welsh wheat fields there. I know there are plenty of wheat fields in England, but I always thought of my own country when I met with wheat fields beyond the seas.

As I was walking along, I saw no hedges. A group of houses stood a little way off, and people were coming down the hill towards one which stood apart, and was a chapel. A native woman came crouching to me, and stroked my knees, and pointed to the hill, and led me towards the chapel. I should think there were as many as six or seven hundred natives assembled for worship.

The old woman placed a bamboo stool for me, close to the chapel door, outside. A native young man gave out a hymn, and the people sung it so beautifully, that I looked about me to see whether I was in Heaven or on earth.

When the singing was over, the same young man read a chapter from St Matthew's Gospel, and prayed, and the people cried. After that, a tall, thin man went up into the pulpit, and lectured from the seventh chapter of St Matthew. He prayed, and then the young native gave out another hymn, and the people sung again.

The voices of negroes are very sweet, but not to be compared with those of these islanders. I never heard such heavenly singing. The hymns, chapters, prayers, and lectures, were all in the native language. I learned the subjects afterwards.

After the service was over, the tall, thin minister came to meet me as I went into the chapel, where a school was being held in classes. Rice and coffee were provided there, and I partook of them. When the minister was speaking with me, I said to him,

"Are you a native here?"

He answered, "No."

"Are you an Englishman?"

"No."

"You are a Welshman then!"

He was a Welshman, and I had often heard and seen his letters to his friend, the Rev. John Hughes, of Pont Robert.

We had spoken English to begin, but after we knew that we were of the same country, we talked Welsh together. He asked many questions about the people and ministers of Bala, and when he named Dafydd Cadwaladyr, and I said that he was my father, he seemed very much pleased. His name was John Davis, and he had, in his youth, served an apprenticeship to a grocer in the town of Bala.

He said in English to the young native who had read, "This is a daughter of an old friend of mine," and to me, "Now I will introduce you to a king."

That young man then shook hands with me. He was King Pomaré, the ward and pupil of Mr Davis, the missionary. King Pomaré took me aside and spoke to me. He said that when he was of age, Mr Davis would take him *home* to England, and he wanted to know whether I thought him good enough to talk with his brother George. I did not then know that he meant the King of England, but thought he had a real brother there, and so I said, "Yes, to be sure."

Mr Davis came with me to the ship, to meet his daughter, and the young king came also. Mrs Foreman scolded me very much for having stayed out so long.

We went from Otaheite to Eimeo to land a gentleman belonging to the government. From thence we sailed to the Sandwich Islands, to take home the two chiefs. They made Mrs Foreman a present of two human heads, tattooed and dried, with grinning teeth. She presented them afterwards to the British Museum. I went on shore at Owhyhee, and stood upon the spot where Captain Cook was killed.

We had very bad weather on this voyage, for we met with the pamperos, which are the monsoons of the South Sea. They came on very suddenly, the sky being dear and bright one minute, and dark as pitch the next. On the evening of Sunday the 13th of March, I was getting my mistress's supper when I noticed clouds such as my father used to say 'betokened a bad storm' I told the captain so, and he answered in his rudest way, "Your father was a fool."

He did not, however, neglect the caution, for I heard him give orders to reef the sails. About an hour before midnight the sea rose tremendously with a violent gale of wind, so that for twenty minutes or more the ship was caught and driven along at the rate of twenty-four miles an hour. I was undressed for bed and had only my dressing-gown around me, when a sailor came to the cabin to fetch the captain's speaking-trumpet, pea-jacket, and south-wester hat. I ran upon deck: there was a horrible shock, and a heavy surge knocked in the dead lights and half of the ship's stern.

I heard and felt the strong roaring waves under me in the vessel, and rushed downstairs to try to save the passengers from drowning. The cabins were flooded – there was dreadful confusion – people shrieking, wading, and struggling, and ladies floating about on their beds in the water. Sailors and gentlemen were striving to thrust beds, bedding, and everything they could put their hands upon, to stop the gaping leak; they laded the water out in buckets, and carried it on deck and threw it overboard. The sails were all reefed, and the ship laid to. No hope was left; and the captain told the people so. They uttered a great cry; and then, by prayer, prepared themselves for death. All the passengers were on deck. The captain went to his cabin, that he might go down with his wife whenever the ship might sink.

I said to the old boatswain, "The ship lies very still."

He said, "It will lie stiller soon. I have been sixty years at sea, and I never thought till now the sea would be my grave."

A sailor, named Frank, was praying to images with a book. I told him to throw them overboard, and pray to God. All the sailors were praying. At dawn the sea sunk. and the waters whirled, leaving no current of waves to uphold the ship. I entreated the men to put her about. I thought I felt her going down under me. They made a last effort, got into safe water, and rescued the ship from the sucking well that was drawing her down.[5]

Anderson, the boatswain, said afterwards, that he never saw such a look as I had when I brought the people up from the flooded cabin – that I was like a wild Ethiopian, with my hands raised together, my fierce eyes flashing, and my black hair streaming in the wind.

We lay to in still water to repair the ship. Besides the stern being half stove in, the rudder was shifted from its place and partly broken. That ship was so well built that she never sprung a leak in her timbers.

We sailed for Peru, and drew near to Lima, where we had to land Mrs Martin, and her young family.

A pilot boat came off to us with the government mails; for the new ship, the *Prince Regent,* which had set out with them, had run aground. and was taken into dock at Valparaiso. Captain Foreman was not at liberty to refuse, so he took charge of the mails, with an understanding that he was either to carry them on board the *Denmark Hill,* or to forward them by any ship he might meet with that might be going quicker to England.

Mrs Foreman and I went ashore at Lima with Mr and Mrs Martin and their eleven children, and made a visit of several days at their house, in one of the squares. There was war at

---

[4]　It is difficult to identify this "King". He was probably Terouru, Chief of the island of Taravai, who was brought to Haweis' Town by Captain Ebrill, in the year 1832, and received by Mr Davis, as a pupil. – *See the 39th Report of the London Missionary Society; and Ellis's Polynesian Researches, 1830.*

[5]　A sailor, who has been exposed to similar danger vouches for the exact truth of this description.

that time between the Patriots and the Spaniards. One day when I was taking a walk with the children, I found all the thoroughfares blocked up. Mr Martin was on board the ship unloading his goods, and could not get back to his own house for seven days. I saw the Patriot army going to meet the Spaniards, and I fancied the men were about to have some games of sport, they went so merrily to battle. The Patriots beat the Spaniards. The second day after the fight. an earthquake took place between the city and the mountains. Forty thousand houses were destroyed. We felt the awful shock at Mr Martin's house, and watched the falling buildings.

From Lima we went to Valparaiso, in Chili, where we landed Mr and Mrs Law. I went on shore there one day, and visited their daughter's house, where they were staying. I saw nothing remarkable in Chili, excepting rattlesnakes. I was just going into a wood, when a rattle-snake came whistling along the ground towards me. I took to my heels, and escaped from him. I had been warned of the danger; but I did not believe such dreadful creatures were there until I saw one.

We had a stormy voyage along the south-western coast of America, and were obliged to stand out to sea to avoid the icebergs before we rounded Cape Horn. Passing up along the south western coast, we touched at the port of Beunos Ayres, and left Mr Reid there. I did not go on shore, but it seemed a pretty place.

Chapter 12

In Memory's land waves never a leaf,
There never a summer breeze blows,
But some long smothered thought of joy or grief
Starts up from its long repose;
And forms are living and visible there,
Which vanished long since from our earthly sphere.

Holford

Rio De Janeiro
The Old Count – Mr Stone – The Royal Chapel – An Enforced Excursion.

Our next port was Rio de Janeiro; it was tedious work to get there, for it was guarded by ten forts, and we were obliged to drop anchor at each, one after another. Boats came out to meet us, in which were people calling broken English to the sailors.

In one boat, rowed by negroes, there was an old Portuguese count, who said, "Anybody want a cook?" I laughed at him, and talked to him. Mr Barbosa was uneasy, and begged of me not to joke with his countrymen, as their tempers would not bear it.

The sailors were very busy warping the ship. The old count came on board to speak with us, and hindered our work. He was asked to go away, and refused to do so unless I went with him. When he saw that I was only making fun of him, he drew his dagger, and swore that he would either have me or my heart's blood. Finding him to be in such a rage, and not knowing how else to get rid of him, I threw a noose of rope over him, and made the sailors put him in a chair, hoist him to the yard-arm, and dip him three times in the sea. This they did very heartily, and then dropped him into his own boat. He looked furiously mad with rage when the negroes rowed him away.

We had a great deal of trouble with the government officers, who came on board to seal up everything that was in the ship only allowing us to keep what was necessary for immediate use, and for a day or two's subsistence. At last we cast anchor in the harbour. Mr Barbosa warned me of the danger of going on shore, as he thought that the old count would surely seek to be revenged upon me. Nevertheless, I had no fear. My mistress sent me to market, and I went one morning ashore, and crossed the royal square to the place where such things as I wanted were sold. Coming back through a narrow street, which led from the square towards the harbour, I chanced to turn round, and saw the old count pursuing me with a drawn sword in his hand. I ran as fast as my feet could carry me, and he ran after me. I gained the boat, and hurried headlong into it, tossing my basket before me. The meat flew out of it hither and thither, and one piece went into the sea. The sailors were in the act of pushing off when I rushed into the boat, and the old count was so close behind me, that he struck and cut the heel of my shoe and stocking as I got away. When at a safe distance, I could see him raving foaming, and flourishing his sword, and I was even so daring as to mock at him. On several mornings, afterwards, he followed me with a dagger; but I always contrived to escape from him. My chief fear was the he would get a pistol.

One Sunday, Captain White, R.N., who commanded the British frigate, which was then upon that station, asked me to go on shore to see the old monastery. The captain went first on shore, and I followed with his friend, Lieutenant Stone, R.N., who had once been in the naval service of the Brazils. As Lieutenant Stone and I were walking together past the Emperor Don Pedro's palace, he suddenly started and changed colour at the sight of a Portuguese officer who was coming to meet us. Mr Stone remarked to me that the Portuguese officer had been a shipmate of his, and that they were not good friends when they last parted. He had no time to relate particulars, for the Portuguese officer came quickly forward looking glad to see him. I stood still, staring at some ladies who were smoking cigars in a balcony, while the officers met and shook hands, and after the fashion of the country, the Portuguese at the same moment patted Mr Stone on the side of the chest with his other hand. There was a dagger in it, and turning, I saw Mr Stone falling dead at my feet. I got away instantly, and took refuge in another street, at the house of Mr Briscoe, an English merchant. He advised me not to speak of the murder, but to keep quietly on board the ship, as the murderer would certainly be brought to justice, and the powerful relations and friends of the murderer would undoubtedly assassinate me. I returned to the ship, and according to his advice did not again come on shore until the trial was over.

I heard that the Portuguese officer was apprehended on the spot. The British Admiral demanded that justice should be done. The deed having been perpetrated in the open street had many witnesses, although the woman who was with Lieutenant Stone, had disappeared.

He was brought to a speedy trial, and publicly executed upon the rack three days after the murder had been committed.

The court of execution was in the square of the White Sisters at the top of the town.

The rack was a machine like a brewer's dray, but with two wheels working round it. The criminal was stretched upon his back and made fast by strong nails driven through his hands and feet. The surface of the dray was set with spikes, and the wheels being put in motion, the wretched man was whirled round and round, and torn to pieces.

The sailors who saw the execution, said he soon died. I attempted to witness it myself, but could not bear it.

The cause of this horrid business was stated by the murderer to have been simply this. Being on board the same ship with Lieutenant Stone, it was his duty as an inferior officer, to report the events of his watch to him. Instead of taking him apart to receive this report, Lieutenant Stone, without the slightest ill will, or ill humour, asked him for it on the quarter-deck in the presence of other officers. This was deemed by the Portuguese to be a deadly affront, and from the moment when it took place, he watched for an opportunity of revenge.

After this dreadful incident, the Portuguese Count ceased to pursue me, being probably, frightened by the example of the awful punishment set before him.

On Good Friday, I went on shore with Mr Barbosa, and Dr Ersby, to see the royal chapel.

Friars held gold and silver salvers at the doors. On the gold salvers were silver cups, and on the silver salvers were gold cups, all containing holy water. One aisle of the chapel was covered, floor and all, with white satin. Large images very finely dressed, stood in a row below the altar, and everything was decked out to look showy.

The empress came first into the chapel. As soon as she got within the door, she threw herself down upon the ground, made a noise like a dying dog, and crawled along. All the court ladies followed her, and did the same. When the empress reached the front of the high altar, she kissed the hem of the garments of those tall images of saints; then stood upon her feet, and made bows and curtsies to them, and subsequently went into her pew. All her ladies came after, and did all that she had done. Mr Barbosa had taken Dr Ersby and me to his brother's seat, which was beside, and a little back from the high altar. I stood up and had a perfect view of all that passed in the chapel. By and bye came the emperor – he fell down and made a noise, and crawled and kissed the saints' garments, and made respectful bows just as the empress had done; all his court gentlemen followed him in the same way; then the emperor went to the royal pew where the empress sat, and his attendants took their places. All the two parties had white satin shoes on.

Then there was beautiful music – twelve priests and twenty-four boys chanting very low, and carrying candles, passed round the altar, and as they moved there was a sound of the ringing of little bells, which must, I think, have been sown to their surplices. Then an old friar got a thing like the head of an eight-day clock, and played bo peep with it on all sides at the altar: the chanting and music going on and the congregation standing the while, moving their elbows and striking their breasts with clenched hands. Then the cross was held up by a priest, and there was prayer, and all the people shrieked out as if they really saw the Saviour pierced, and the boys went tinkling round the altar. Then a Capuchin preached a short sermon; when it ended, music struck up, the empress came out of the royal pew, made obeisances to the saints at the altar, and walked backwards from it out of the chapel; and her court ladies did the same. Then the emperor came out of the royal pew, and made obeisances to the saints at the altar, and walked backwards out of the chapel, and his court gentlemen did the same.

They were all going to the play, and all the congregation, and the priests. My friends went also; they wished me to accompany them, but as Mr Barbosa told me that the funeral of a friar would afterwards be performed in the chapel, I chose rather to wait there. Being left alone, I walked about the chapel, and looked at the various things in the box upon the altar – thinking how Christianity and Heathenism were mixed together in such ceremonies as I had just witnessed; the largest part belonging to Heathenism.

In walking across the raised platform in front of the altar, I chanced to put my foot upon a secret spring; it opened a trap-door, which, flying up, struck me on the forehead, and knocked me down backwards. On getting up again, and, recovering from my surprise, I heard the gurgling of a plentiful stream of water. I peeped down, but it was all darkness there; so I fetched one of the big candles from the altar to light me. Leaning over the opening in the floor, I saw the water flowing, and beheld a sort of stage, like a shelf, on which images were set in a row; but the candle tipped over out of the candlestick which I was holding in my hand, and fell plump into the water. I took the candlestick back to its place on the altar, and was afraid to reach another, lest I should again have an accident; so I peeped down in the dark, and caught an image by the robe, meaning to bring it to the light, and to have a better look at it; the thing slipped out of my hand, and fell down into the water. I was frightened at the mischief I had done; I shut the trap-door, and went to another part of the chapel. I found that although the images were dressed so richly to the eye, and had silk and satin fronts to their clothes, the parts out of sight were only of cotton.

I went into the pew where the emperor and empress had sat; it was lined with white satin, and ornamented with curious little lamps, of very fine wire, interwoven to make one great light. I unhooked this lamp holder, and took it down to examine how it was managed, but I failed to hang it up again properly; and during the rest of my stay in the chapel, I felt continual fear that I should hear it fall down, and see some mischief done by it.

Having done all these clumsy things, I was dreadfully afraid of being found out, and punished for my meddlesome irreverence, and thinking it would be best to get out of sight, I went back to the seat of Mr Barbosa's brother, and lay along the cushions there, until all the people came back from the play to see the friar's funeral. The emperor and empress acted as chief mourners. The coffin was set down in the choir. It was covered with a pall of pink silk, embroidered with precious stones. It was wrapped close round the coffin, and did not hang loose from it. Mr Barbosa told me that it was worth five thousand pounds.

An old man, with a black cowl over his head, stood saying prayers with his face to the altar, and his back towards the people, and then preached a very short sermon. There were many other ceremonies, and there was a great deal of bowing and kneeling, and crossing, and making postures. Very solemn music was performed; one piece I thought to be the Dead March in Saul. At length, four friars moved a sliding panel near the high altar, and set the coffin upright on its end in the cupboard, and drew the sliding panel to its place again. Then there was loud howling through all the congregation; after which, everybody sat down as still as possible, while friars went round to all the seats with collecting plates. This ended the service, and the people immediately afterwards dispersed.

I was on the point of returning to the ship, when Mr Barbosa and Dr Ersby told me that Europeans were not allowed to walk through the streets after a certain hour in the evening, and that hour being past, I must be content to spend the night at the hotel, where many of our ship's passengers, both ladies and gentlemen, were staying. I had some coffee, and went up stairs to my bedroom, desiring the chambermaid to call me very early, that I might lose no time in getting back to the *Denmark Hill*. I drew the chest of drawers across the door, piled up the chairs for a barricade, and then, being full of the thought of rising soon, lay down in my clothes on the bed, and slept and dreamed very uneasily. .

About five o'clock in the morning I heard a tapping at my door. I said, "Who's there?" and Barbosa's voice said, very gently, "Betsy, it is time to get up."

I was surprised that he should come to call me, instead of the chambermaid, and I answered roughly, that I would be down stairs presently.

He went away, and by-and-by, I got up, cleared away the furniture, opened the door, and went down stairs to the coffee room. There I saw two or three Portuguese slumbering on benches with their pipes beside them, and there I found, Mr Barbosa, Dr Ersby, and Mr Martin – one of Mr Barbosa's partners in business, an elderly man, who was married and had a family. I knew by their clothes and by their looks, that they had been up all night. They had coffee ready for me. I said, I was very anxious to go back at once to the ship, and the three gentlemen came with me to the house door. There, to my astonishment, I saw a carriage and four standing. Mr Martin said that Europeans were not allowed to walk through the streets so early in the morning, and therefore the carriage was to take me to the quay.

I said it would be nonsense to get into it for so short a distance, but he urged me so much, that I did get in, and Mr Martin and Mr Barbosa came in after me. I soon perceived that the carriage did not take the road to the quay, and began to be very uneasy; but I thought it was most prudent to conceal my fears. We went on and on, until, having passed out of the city, we were travelling rapidly along a high road between two hedges. I asked over, and over again, where they were going, but I could get no answer. I became very much frightened; but I still tried to conceal my fears. At length, Mr Martin answered, that they were taking me to see Mr Edward Lord, whom we had brought on board the *Denmark Hill* from New South Wales. I said, "He only went into the country last Wednesday, I don't want to see him again so soon." In asking Barbosa about it, I chanced to touch him, and I felt that he trembled very much. This made me tremble too, for I thought that he must have some wicked purpose towards me, and I resolved inwardly upon the instant, that I would escape, if I killed them both in getting away from them. Having thus made up my mind, I tried to joke with them, and said to Barbosa, "What do you mean to do with me? Do you mean to marry me? I won't marry you unless you make me Duchess of Braganza."

He burst out then with great feeling and answered, "That is what I mean to do. I knew you would not think it a lawful marriage unless a Protestant clergyman performed it. There is not one at Rio, but Mr Lord is now staying with one who will marry us."

I said that I was not a fit person for him, and that he ought to marry a lady.

He answered, "No. I never saw one that I could trust. I love you, and will marry you, I can trust you. I have kept my eye upon you ever since I came on board the ship. I have seen you in the midst of many temptations, and I have seen you resist them all. I know that I can trust you in absence as well as in my presence. I am of a very jealous disposition, and could kill any woman who was unfaithful. I might have married ladies, but I would not; I will only marry you."

Mr Martin said, that I need not have any anxiety about my dress, as Mr Barbosa had provided everything that was necessary.

The carriage stopped at last at an inn belonging to a village, in which there was a Protestant church. We alighted, and had our breakfast at the inn, and found that Mr Lord had been sent here a few days before on purpose to arrange about the marriage, with Mr Rees, the clergyman, who was to perform the ceremony. Mrs Rees was to attend instead of a bridesmaid, and Mr Lord was to give me away. As soon as breakfast was over, Mr Barbosa and Mr Martin went and sat under the verandah, and smoked their cigars, while they waited for Mr Lord and Mr and Mrs Rees to arrive. I saw a nursemaid with some children in a field just below, and I said to the gentlemen that I would go and talk with them. Mr Martin said, "Do, and we will keep you in sight."

In the field I had the pleasure of meeting with a Welsh nurse-maid and Welsh children. I soon made their acquaintance, and we talked Welsh together. The nurse-maid said to me, "There is to be a grand wedding here today, and my mistress, Mrs Rees, is now dressing herself to go to it."

At a little distance off, I saw two gentlemen walking together, and I crossed to join them. One of them I soon saw was Mr Lord – the other I found to be a Protestant clergyman, and a countryman of mine. Mr Lord introduced me to the Rev. Mr Rees as the intended bride, and began to joke, saying, "Is she not a fine Briton?" I begged that they would inform me which was the nearest way back to Rio, and told them that I would not be married. They laughed at me at first; and then Mr Lord tried to reason with me, reminding me of my old acquaintance with Barbosa, and the advantage of having a worthy and wealthy gentleman for a husband. I told them all about my coming, and that I was resolute to die rather than be married.

Mr Rees was much surprised at this, yielded, and took my part against Mr Lord, who said I was a great fool. Mr Rees walked a few steps with me, and pointed out a way across the country to Rio Grande. As soon as he had done so, I started, without taking time to say 'good-morning' and ran off as fast as my feet would carry me. When my breath failed, I stood for a moment to draw it, and then ran off again at full speed; and this I did all the way to Rio Grande.

At Rio Grande I began to feel safe and abated my speed; there I met a man, the first creature I had noticed in my flight; I pointed to a road and asked him whether it led to Rio de Janeiro; he signified that it did, and off I went walking along it. The ground had not felt much of me before, I not having found time to walk so long as I thought that I might be pursued and overtaken. Avoiding the city, I went to the quay, where I found the boat of the *Porcupine* just pushing off. I got into it and was taken safe to the *Denmark Hill*. My mistress was on a visit to Rio Grande, but as soon as she came back I told her all that had happened. Before that time Mr Barbosa had always treated me with great consideration and kindness, noticing when I looked worn with over work, offering me a glass of his mother's old wine, cautioning me against running into danger, and acting as a friend, without professing or showing any particular attachment to me. Mrs Foreman was very much surprised at Mr Barbosa having carried me off, and much displeased at his wanting to marry me, for I was a useful servant to her, and it would have been inconvenient to part with me; and besides she did not approve of my marrying a gentleman.

Just before this business, Mr Barbosa's term of holding the *Denmark Hill* having expired, he had made an agreement with Captain Foreman to renew it. In a few days after the run away business, Mr Barbosa returned to the ship, looking in very bad spirits. When I saw him he was quite cast down, and said to me, "Oh, you cruel girl!" He accused me of liking the ship's carpenter better than him. This I denied, and declared that I respected him as a religious young man, but otherwise cared no more for him than for others. Mr Barbosa regretted that he had taken the ship again, and said he would not have done it, had he thought how I should behave towards him. He spoke to Mrs Foreman, and tried to make her take his part, but she told him that I, being a servant, was not a proper match for him, and that he ought to marry a lady.

The passengers were so well satisfied with Captain Foreman's attention to their comfort on board his own ship, and with his arrangements for their passage on board other ships from Rio de Janeiro to England, that they clubbed together to purchase a handsome present for Mrs Foreman, knowing that such an attention to his wife would be the most gratifying way of showing their esteem for the captain. They gave her two silver tankards, one holding a quart, and the other a pint. At the same time, Mr Lord delivered a parcel to me, directed in the following words: 'From the Passengers on board the *Denmark Hill,* to their kind Betsy.'

I opened it, and found that it contained a diamond necklace, a pair of diamond bracelets, a diamond girdle, and two little bunches of diamonds with little chains to hang over the ears. The clasps of the girdle had little pictures of the emperor and empress, and the clasps of the necklace and bracelets had little pictures of their children. I showed these jewels to Mrs Foreman, and said that such things were useless and unfit for me. She said, "Give them to me." This I refused. I packed them up, and sent them back by the mate, saying that I could do nothing with them, and would much rather have received a watch, or something useful.

Soon afterwards another parcel was delivered to me. It contained a gold watch, with a chain, locket, seal, and key, worth altogether fifty guineas.

While I was at Rio, a miniature picture of me was taken by a Portuguese artist. I suppose Barbosa has it now.

PART 2

Chapter 1

Auspicious Hope! in thy sweet garden grow
Wreaths for each toil, a charm for every woe.

Angel of Life! thy glittering wings explore
Earth's loneliest bounds and ocean's wildest shore.

Campbell

The Cape of Good Hope
Visits to African Missionary Stations – Australia – India.

From Rio de Janeiro we sailed for the Cape of Good Hope, with almonds, rice, wine, and a general cargo.

We went on shore at the Cape, and while the ship lay there, I obtained leave from Mrs Foreman to go to the Paarl beyond Elizabeth Town, to visit an old friend of my father's, who was a missionary there.

I set out by the public conveyance for travellers – a cart drawn by eight bullocks. I had ten or twelve companions, and another cart followed with our luggage. We left Cape Town at three o'clock in the afternoon, and the pace was so slow, that we had not got very far on our way among the dreary hills when the sun set, and we heard dismal howlings, and saw droves of wolves coming down towards us.

The drivers at this sight instantly unhooked the bullocks, and leaving the carts upon the spot, drivers, bullocks and passengers (I among them), took to our heels, and made the best of our way back again to Cape Town.

Hearing that a party of Dutch missionaries were going off very early the next morning to the same settlement, I arranged to accompany them. We travelled only from sunrise to sunset, and thus escaped the ravenous wolves. We reached Elizabeth Town that evening. We continued our journey the next day, skirting the sea-coast, and turning off across a plain where there were many farm-houses. From thence we travelled to a Moravian missionary station, where we rested for the night.

The next day we reached the Paarl, and there I was received at the house of my father's old friend, Mr Evans, who had joined the Dutch Mission. I had known him long before, when he was a bookseller at Bala, and he used to be my teacher in the Sunday school. I spent ten days with him and his wife, and their thirteen children, going about to visit the Dutch and English settlers, and seeing the schools of the country.

On leaving the Paarl, Mr Evans walked part of the way with me, lending me his horse to ride, and sending his black servant with me as far as the Moravian station, to take the horse home again. I stayed that night with the Moravians, and was much pleased with what I saw of their way of life. I had much religious conversation with them, but we disagreed about the manner in which Sunday ought to be spent. Their time was chiefly occupied with teaching, and they did not read much. I attended evening service in their chapel, where a scattered population from the hills, of about three hundred converted natives, were assembled.

The Africans have fine voices, and the singing was delightful.

One of the brethren, a widower named Robinson, an Englishman, from Northampton, asked me to stay among them, and to become his wife. I gave him the same answer as

I always did, sooner or later, to my lovers, saying, "No," at once, for I could never have borne to spend my days in that dull place.

The next day, two of the sisters were going on business to Elizabeth Town, and they took me with them in their little four wheel carriage, which was drawn by two zebras. These animals, together with a young creature, which they called a unicorn, had been sent from a relation as a present to one of the sisters. I saw the unicorn[1], tethered in a field near the buildings, and the Moravians petted him. He had one horn, small and straight in the middle of his forehead. Behind his head there was a sort of natural collar and strap which passed under one shoulder, and to this the iron chain was fastened. His legs were thin, something like those of a horse. I never saw another animal anywhere that was like him altogether.

The sisters took me to a Moravian house at Elizabeth Town, and I was for some little time, at a loss how to get on to Cape Town.

At last, a Scotch brother suggested that I might go by water, in a little trading boat which would sail in a few hours. I went on board at the time appointed, and had a safe, though slow, passage. The crew were Englishmen, and would not accept of any pay from me.

At the Cape, we loaded the *Denmark Hill* with a general cargo, and sailed from thence to Hobart Town, where we

---

[1] This animal was probably a rhinoceros. The heraldic unicorn, if not a conventional configuration of a real animal, must have a similar origin as the centaur. A horse with a spear held over his head, seen from the front, and the rider being thus concealed, affords a lively image of the unicorn. A vignette in Rogers' *Poems*, vol. I, p. 156 Ed. 1852, unintentionally illustrates this subject.

landed passengers, and on to Sydney, where we unloaded the ship, which was afterwards taken to the cove for repair, while Captain and Mrs Foreman and the rest of our company lived on shore.

One morning, as I was going to market, Barbosa met me on the rocks. He asked me to go with him a little way to a point from which the view was very fine. I said, "It looks beautiful." We fell into discourse, and he soon got back to the old subject. He knew that I liked Sydney, and he offered, if I would marry him, to make his home there, and to send Burke about with the ship. He said he was convinced that I had no confidence in him, and to prove how sincere he was, he proposed to free me from my contract with Captain Foreman, to pay my passage home to England, by any ship I chose, to take his own passage by another, and on arriving, to marry me in the presence of my friends, and to live with me there or anywhere else that I might prefer – as one part of the world was just the same to him as another.

I asked him to give me time to consider this proposal. He pressed me to let him have it there, at the same hour the next day. I said that would be impossible, as I was going to Paramatta with Captain and Mrs Foreman; and I turned away, and left him without naming any time for giving him an answer.

I went that same day to Paramatta with Captain and Mrs Foreman; and, about five o'clock in the afternoon, I saw Mr Barbosa and two or three other gentlemen riding on horseback past the window of the house in which I was staying. I instantly ran off to the farm, to be out of his way; so, when he called upon Mrs Foreman, I was not to be found, and he had to return to Sydney without seeing me.

I went with Captain and Mrs Foreman from Paramatta to Liverpool, and from thence with Mrs Foreman to Bathurst, where I saw Mr Mills and his family again. We next visited Mr Bates, at Rock House, beyond the Blue Mountains, and stopped there some weeks. On our return, Mr Bates lent us horses to carry us to Bathurst. We spent three days there, and three more at Liverpool with Mr Cartwright. He sent us back in his carriage to Sydney.

I went on board the *Denmark Hill* to take in stores, and Mr Barbosa was there. The first day, he kept quite aloof from me.

On the evening of the second day, he came to me, and inquired whether I had made up my mind.

Instead of giving him a serious answer, I made a jest of the business, and said, "What? to go with the ship to India?"

He very gravely and earnestly replied, "To accept of my proposal – to go to England?"

"Oh!" I went on, "I can't bear to part with you long enough for that. I am going to India with you. I have no time for thinking of anything else."

One day on board, he showed me, privately, the white satin dress which he had prepared for my wedding at Rio. He always carried it about with him in a flat box; and, in the same box, I caught sight of the set of diamonds which I had returned by the mate to the gentlemen.

Mr Barbosa always looked, and walked, and did everything like a perfect gentleman. He was in the prime of life, and very handsome. I never saw or heard of the least levity in his conduct or conversation. He showed, on all occasions, a deep, sincere, and durable attachment to me. He would often stand by me, or walk the deck beside me, in a quiet, friendly way, which showed real affection; yet I could scarcely believe he was in earnest in proposing to make me his lawful wife, and I did suspect that he was still at heart a Roman Catholic. These doubts, joined to my usual dislike to the thought of marrying, and my want of any particular love for him, were, as far as I can understand, the reasons why I could not make up my mind to accept his offer, although I have since had good cause to wish that I had done so.

One day I chanced to overhear a conversation between Mr Martin and Dr Ersby, about myself. The Doctor said that I had lively spirits, and doubtless was not so prudent as I was thought to be. Mr Martin took the opposite side, and said, "You had better take care. I never saw man or beast look so fierce when she is angry." Dr Ersby did not take the warning, and had afterwards the daring to ask me to give him a kiss. I had a bason of suds in my hand at the time, and in my sudden rage at this affront, I emptied it over him, and spoiled his new jacket – to the great amusement of the other gentlemen who were standing by, and especially of Mr Barbosa.

Mr Martin said, "There, I told you so!"

He must have remembered how I looked, when they ran away with me.

We had a safe voyage to Calcutta, and there we unloaded some of the mercantile goods.

I paid a visit to Mr and Mrs Ferguson, and Mr Henry Fleming, and made my home at their house while the ship remained at Calcutta.

In Bengal, an Indian prince offered Captain Foreman one thousand five hundred rupees for his passage with two servants to the Mauritius. Captain Foreman agreed, and they came on board. Not long afterwards, at sea, the Indian gentleman asked me whether I would nurse him if he should be ill on board. I told him that I would. He spoke English very well.

One afternoon, I was going to fish, as I used to do very often for amusement, and had already got my rod and line, when the Indian beckoned me to follow him to his cabin. He bade me be secret, and not mention to anyone that he was ill. I noticed that his finger nails, and the tips of his fingers had turned black. He reached a bottle, and gave me out of it half a glass of some sweet stuff like treacle. He then lay down in bed, and ordered me to cover him up with quantities of beautiful furs which belonged to him. It was then three o'clock, and he told me not to come to him again until nine the next morning. He desired me to carry the bottle away with me, and to swallow another dose of the contents before, and only just before, coming into his cabin the next day.

I obeyed his directions exactly; but when I knocked at his cabins door the next morning, and heard no answer, I feared he might be dead; so I opened the door, and went in. He then spoke in a low voice, and desired me to take a dozen of the leopard skins and furs, and throw them overboard, and told me to come to him again in an hour. The cabin smelt very unhealthy, and the furs were soaked with perspiration. At the end of the hour I went, and he bade me take away another dozen, and throw them overboard; and after another short space of time to come to him again. I did so, taking a dose from his bottle every time that I went in. He then ordered me to take the rest of his furs, and throw them overboard. I grudged to do it, for they were very beautiful; but I felt there would be great danger in keeping them on board. Soon afterwards, the Indian came on deck, and took some negus and biscuit. He was very weak, and continued to be so for some time, but had not any return of his complaint. I purified the cabin with burnt vinegar and chloride of lime, and no one on board caught the disease.

On recovering, the Indian told me that the black cholera had attacked his people, and that no captain of a ship, knowing the fact, would run the risk of taking him on board. This caused him to offer so high a price for his passage to Captain Foreman, who accepted it without suspicion.

From Calcutta we went to Madras, and there unloaded the remainder of our cargo. At Madras, a government contract was made for the *Denmark Hill* to carry stores and amunition to the Mauritius.

Arriving there, we set on shore the Indian prince who had had the black cholera on board. We speedily unloaded the ship, and sailed – for the first time without a cargo – for Canton.

We took in a cargo of tea at Canton, and sailed with it to Sydney. There we unloaded, and loaded again, for Madras, with canvas, wheat, potatoes, and other things. At Madras we unloaded the ship, and loaded it with bales of nankeen and cotton, sugar, tea, spices, and preserved fruits for Rio de Janeiro.

Chapter 2

_____ To realms beyond
Yon highway of the world, my fancy flies,
When by her tall and triple mast we know
Some noble voyager, that has to woo
The trade-winds, and to stem th' ecliptic surge:
The coral groves, the shores of conch and pearl
Where she will cast her anchor, and reflect
Her cabin-window lights on warmer waves,
And under planets brighter than our own:
The nights of palmy isles that she will see
Lit boundless by the fire-fly, all the smells
Of tropic fruits that will regale her, all
The pomp of nature, and th' inspiriting
Varieties of life she has to greet.
Come swarming o'er the meditative mind.

Campbell's *View from St Leonard's*.

The Mediterranean, Eastern and Southern Seas Malta – Greece – Egypt – The East Indies – The Brazils – Admiral Sotheron's marine reception of the Emperor Don Pedro and his Court – Australia – Calcutta – China – Farewell to Barbosa.

At Rio de Janeiro Barbosa again pressed me for a final answer. I gave him one, and he then left the *Denmark Hill,* and took up another ship; and Mr Reid, a merchant at Rio, chartered the *Denmark Hill* for the Mediterranean.

We sailed from Rio, passed the straits of Gibraltar and went to Malta.

We had on arriving there some Thames water on board, which we brought many years before from England. People often speak ill of Thames water: I think there is none like it for goodness; I could drink it if it was thirty years old. After having been first put in casks it smells bad very soon. We had to run it off into fresh butts about the third day; and when it smelt badly again, we ran it off again, leaving each time a quantity of sediment behind. After settling the third time, it needed no filtering, but kept perfectly pure, cold and bright for ever. There is no other water in the world will do this, that I know of.

I went to see all that was to be seen at Malta, and admired the buildings very much, particularly the church of St John, whither I went every day. The women who attended there, used to wear hoods which hid their faces. The bazaars at Malta were very pretty. I used to scull myself ashore in the little boat, and to go about looking at everything.

We sailed to Greece, and I went on shore and saw the Piraeus and other places. We proceeded to Constantinople, and there Mr Reid made contracts to sell the remainder of his cargo, and took in Turkish goods, carpets, silks, satins, and other woven fabrics for Alexandria. We sailed thither, and afterwards went to Cairo. I saw the Pyramids and Obelisks, and wanted very much to learn the history of the old places, and the meaning of the things; but I had no tongue to ask of those who could have taught me. In Egypt we unloaded the ship, and loaded her with cotton, cork and bark. That bark would dye four different colours by the use of different processes.

We left the Mediterranean for Bombay, and from thence we sailed to _____[1] in Bengal.

The *Denmark Hill* was there, hired by seven Indian families to convey them and their goods up the river, as far as it was possible for the ship to go. A raft followed close behind, bringing the numerous camels which belonged to the Indian families.

We had to warp the ship nearly all the way. We saw nothing but the two banks of the river and the country here and there between the woods. We met no ships or boats. We had only Indian passengers on board with whom I could not exchange a word, and they could not join in our usual lively games, of the whistle and blindman's buff, nor enjoy our exercises of strength and lithesomeness. It was altogether the dullest time I ever spent on ship, and I often wished myself at home, or anywhere else.

My only amusement was reading Shakespeare's Plays in the cabin, by myself, and trying to look as I fancied the heroes and heroines must have done.

The first crocodile I ever saw was in that river. One night we anchored at a place where large trees hung over the pebbly shore. The crocodile came out of the water to air himself, and a bear came for a walk out of the wood.

They met and there was a fight, the bear attacking the crocodile who after a hard struggle, got back again into the water, and peeped up now and then to look at the bear, who howled with rage.

We went fifty miles up the river with the Indian families, and found the depth of water was not sufficient for the ship to go any

[1] The name of this place the narrator cannot recall.

further. We therefore unloaded on the grass, and left all our Indian passengers with their goods and camels to get up the country as best they might, while we returned very gladly to _____.[2]

From thence we loaded the *Denmark Hill* for Rio de Janeiro, taking also many passengers. We arrived in safety, without meeting with anything remarkable.

While the ship lay there, I used often when I went to market to see the Emperor and Empress going out, or coming back from their morning ride. They had no attendants, not even a groom. They looked like two gentlemen on horsebacks, for the Empress was dressed in dark green clothes as he was, and wore breeches and Hessian boots, and rode astride. The only difference was in their hats: his was plain, and hers was turned up in front and had a feather.

I used often to go to Braganza alone in the ship's gig, with a little sail, which I set when the wind was blowing the right way, and otherwise sculled myself along. Sometimes I went there to fish, and occasionally to gather oranges, lemons, pomegranates, grapes, and other fruit. I ate so many of these, that people used to say the fruit was the means of saving me from the fevers and other diseases of the country. I used to bring back with me my boat full of fruit for the ship's crew and passengers.

One evening, in returning from Braganza with a boatload of oranges, the wind blew so strong against me, that I could neither reach the ship nor the shore.

In this distress, I was nearly run down by the royal barge, which was going to Braganza with the Emperor and Empress and their court on board. Mr Smith, a page, or officer of the

---

[2] The same place in Bengal of which the narrator cannot recall the name.

household. called to me in English from the royal barge, and asked why I got in the way. I told him my condition. The course of the royal barge was checked and changed to avoid me; and I was left to my fate.

It was two o'clock in the morning before I was able to make my way back to the *Denmark Hill*. A few hours afterwards, Mr Smith was sent on board from the Empress to inquire if I was safe.

At this time, the British Admiral, Sitheron[3] gave a grand entertainment on board his flagship.

The captains of the merchant ships were requested to place their ships alongside of each other, so as to form the supports of a bridge of planks with railing on each side of it. A floating pier, covered with green cloth, was hitched on to the wharf on the land side, and to our ship on the side towards to the sea – for the *Denmark Hill* was the outermost of the merchant ships, on account of her being the best finished and having a handsome set of mahogany steps, with a brass balustrade. The men-of-war were too high in their sides, and drew too much water to be put there.

There were perhaps twenty-four or twenty-five merchant ships forming the floating piers for the bridge, which was covered all over with cloth and ornamented with flags. Two Brazilian corvettes were placed between the merchant ships and the admiral's flagship; and all the men-of-war upon the station – English, Spanish, French, American, and the rest, were formed into a crescent at the stern of the flagship. Every ship of every sort, was dressed out with flags and lamps.

---

[3] This distinguished officer died in 1839. He was entrusted by Nelson with the defence of the Bay of Naples.

The Emperor and Empress, and a little prince and princess, their eldest children, crossed the bridge to the admiral's ship with their court, just as I was returning from the shore on board the *Denmark Hill.*

The little Princess was so delighted with the bridge that she continued to run backwards and forwards across it; and could not be persuaded to go back to the royal party, although some of the attendants followed her, and tried their best to make her do so. Meeting me as she ran, the little Princess seized me by the hand, and insisted on my running up and down with her, and lifting her, and swinging her up to see what lay on each side beyond the balustrade. She talked Portuguese to me all the time, and I talked Welsh to her. When a gentleman came to fetch her to dinner, she made me carry her on board the flagship, and would suffer no one else to seat her in her chair at the table. The little Prince was younger and quieter than his sister. She was a very pretty child, of about six years old.

Looking on for a few minutes at the royal ball, I saw the little Princess dancing with the old English admiral. At nine o'clock the royal children were to be taken home, and Mr Smith was sent on board the *Denmark Hill,* to tell me to come and fetch the little princess, as she refused to let anyone else carry her. I went to her, and she immediately allowed me to take her up in my arms, and carry her home across the bridge, and through the Royal Square, to the palace; officers standing with drawn swords, and sentries presenting arms, as we passed by. When I set her down, the little Princess patted my cheeks with both hands, and said some words in Portuguese, which I supposed to mean, "Come again tomorrow."

On my way back, I was very much struck by the beautiful

appearance of the ships. It was a very fine sight to see all the flags, and the lamps lit up across the ships at night.

The Emperor and Empress, and their court, went on shore at twelve o'clock, and the admiral went with them. When they were gone, the officers of all the ships, and their wives and friends assembled on board the flagship, and kept up the ball all night. I was with them, and danced, among others, with Captain White, of the flagship, who was my old acquaintance, and wanted to marry me. Mrs Smith and her two daughters were with us. They, as well as Mr Smith, were English.

The little Princess was afterwards Queen of Portugal, and mother of the present King.[4]

Our next business was to take in a cargo of wine for Hobart Town and Sydney. We had a safe voyage, and when I got to Sydney, my way to the market led past the house where Barbosa lived. I used often to meet him, and sometimes he would come on board the *Denmark Hill,* and stand about or walk up and down.

We left Sydney with Colonel Cotton and his wife, Major Marley, Captain Lane, and many other passengers and soldiers on board, besides mercantile goods, and arrived at Calcutta. While we lay there, some officers on board the *Southampton*

---

[4] Don Pedro I Emperor of Brazil, eldest son of Don John VI, King of Portugal, was born in 1798. He married in 1817, Lepoldine, Archduchess of Austria. She died in 1826, having had five children of whom Donna Maria was one. In 1829 Don Pedro married secondly, Amelia Beauharnais, Princess of Leuchtenberg. He died in 1834. His son, Don Pedro II, became by his father's abdication in 1831, Emperor of Brazil; and his daughter, Donna Maria, was, by her father's victory over Don Miguel, established as sovereign Queen of Portugal.

got up some scenes of plays, and had a grand theatre there, and one night a large assemblage of ladies and gentlemen came to see the acting.

Somebody being wanted to take the ladies' parts, I performed Lady Macbeth in the sleeping scene, and Mrs Foreman performed the waiting maid. I also performed the Indian queen, and sat dressed out in green velvet and gold, upon a throne with a fine footstool, and slaves waiting round me.

I liked playing Lady Macbeth the best, but was very much applauded and praised for my acting in both parts. Everybody said that I played very well; Mr Thomson, the merchant, said it was a pity I did not become a professional actress; and that my eyes looked so vicious in Lady Macbeth, he should be afraid to meet me in the dark.

I did not perform comedy. I always chose the tragic parts, when I read Captain Foreman's Shakespeare alone in the cabin.

From Calcutta we went to Canton, where we took in a cargo of tea, silks, and crapes; and then to Singapore, where, as usual, we had to unload every scrap of the cargo at the custom house.

We had very bad weather for the voyage, and passing close to Shangai and Amoy, were driven near to an island of very dangerous savages, who came off in canoes to the ship. We would not take them on board, but they held on to the ropes' ends which hung from the ship, and the captain could not shake them off. He came down to the cabin in a great passion, saying, "I do not know what to do with the rascals. I cannot get rid of them in any way. They will follow the ship."

I said, "Why don't you shoot them?"

He answered, "Heu! Heu! Shoot them yourself, old faggot!"

I took the rifle, went on deck and fired over their heads. Every rope was let go, and every canoe was off in an instant. The gun was loaded only with powder.

This gun used always to be fired on board at eight o'clock in the evening, when the watch was set; and at twelve at night. It kicked, and used to knock everybody down that fired it, except myself so I was generally called to fire it. I managed to rest it against the side of the ship, and to avoid the rebound it gave.

The weather continued very stormy, but we reached Hobart Town at last, and took in water there, although we had plenty below, to avoid opening the hatches in so high a sea. We had then been for several weeks on an allowance of half a pint of water apiece in the twenty-four hours, from not being able to get at the casks. We used to heat the salt water and collect the steam, and of this we made the best tea I ever tasted.

We lost more sails in this boisterous voyage than in any former one.

At last we got safe to Sydney. Mr Barbosa was there, looking shy and stiff. One day, when I was on shore, he followed me, and asked if I would not speak to him, and what sort of a voyage I had had, and where I was going next time.

The day before the *Denmark Hill* left Sydney again, I went on shore to do my last marketing, and was detained rather late in bidding some of my friends good-bye, not expecting to see them soon again, as the ship was homeward bound.

As I passed Mr Barbosa's house, Mr Burke called after me. Mr Barbosa and some of his friends were sitting in the balcony above, taking coffee, and smoking cigars.

Mr Burke showed me up stairs to the party. The old woman, who was Mr Barbosa's housekeeper, waited there. Mr Burke began to talk to me about taking up the *Denmark Hill* again.

Barbosa had only looked at me without speaking, until I said, in answer to Mr Burke's remark, that we were to sail the next morning for England. Barbosa turned pale, fetched a chair for me, and grasped my hand as he set it down. He then fetched wine, and poured out a glass for me, and begged that I would stay and take tea with them. I did so, and afterwards took leave of the party. I shook hands with Mr Burke, and then with Mr Barbosa, who said that he would walk to the boat with me.

I was forced to hire a boat, having sent back the one which belonged to the ship.

Barbosa walked by my side, looking deadly white. I said something or other to him, and found that he could hardly speak, he was so distressed.

At last he asked whether I should ever return to Sydney.

I answered that I did not know.

He then said, "The carpenter goes with you, does he?"

I told him yes – adding that the carpenter was nothing to me. Before we turned to the wharf, he stepped on, stood before me with his face towards me, stopping me in my way, and said, "If I thought I had any chance, I would sail with you tomorrow."

I gave him no encouragement, but passed on, and called to the black man to bring the boat. He did so, and I said to Mr Barbosa, "Well, good bye, sir."

He said with tears, grasping my hand, "God bless you, Betsy! This is the last happy day I shall ever have in my life."

He stood watching as long as I was in sight. I had a great mind to turn back. When I saw his tears, and heard his pitiful voice, I felt sure that he was sincere, but having once said no, I did not like to alter.

Chapter 3

Now to thee, to thee I fly,
Fairest isle beneath the sky,
To my heart as in mine eye!

While I bid them all be blest,
Britain is my home, my rest,
Mine own land! I love thee best.

James Montgomery's *Voyage round the World*

Homeward Bound and in the London Docks
Loss of the Ship's Port – Clearance Certificate – St Helena
– London – Death of Dafydd Cadwaladyr – Old Friends–
Pecuniary Losses – Separation from the Foremans.

We sailed from Sydney to Hobart Town, having unwarily taken on board several persons, who were the cause of a great deal of trouble and vexation to me, and to all the other people in the ship. Among those troublesome persons were Captain C_____, and a person who called herself Mrs Fowler, and her three little children.

When we reached Hobart Town, Captain Foreman's mate and the ship's cook, both of whom he had hired at Sydney, went on shore, got tipsy, fought with their drinking companions, were put in prison, and detained there for some days.

The captain made inquiries about them, and found that the magistrates had recognized them both to have been convicts.

He then went to the governor and to the colonial secretary,

and proving to their satisfaction that he had been imposed upon by the false accounts which the mate and cook had given of themselves, Captain Foreman obtained the sanction of these authorities for breaking the agreement with the mate and cook, and for leaving them behind him in Hobart Town.

The captain, however, did not do the business well, for he omitted to inform Mr Smith, the deputy colonial secretary, of this arrangement.

The consequence was, that when the *Denmark Hill* got under way, Mr Smith came after her in a boat, bringing with him the mate and cook, and hailing the ship for them to be taken on board.

There was no time to explain the matter, but the captain refused to receive them; and Mr Smith in anger demanded, 'The ship's clearance'.

This demand Captain Foreman knew that he had no right to resist, so he threw the port clearance into the boat, and Mr Smith went away with it.

We were thus made liable to have the *Denmark Hill* seized as a pirate in any harbour she might chance to enter. Captain Foreman ought to have returned to Hobart Town to explain what had happened, and to get the ship's clearance, but he would not do so, and no one could prevail on him to return. He was in such a terrible humour afterwards, that hardly anyone dared to speak to him.

When we reached St Helena, instead of being in his place on deck, he went to the cabin, almost mad with vexation. I was the means of persuading him to put in there, or rather of allowing the ship to be taken in; for he would do nothing, and only suffered it to be done. The new mate had no influence with him, and was afraid to speak to him.

I was on board when the port officer came on board, and asked for the captain.

I answered, "I am the captain."

He said, "What! is the captain dead?"

I told him that he was not, but alive, and below.

The officer went with me to the captain, and asked him for the port clearance.

Captain Foreman, in despair, told him gruffly that he had none.

"No," said I, "but you have what will do as well," and, as I spoke, I put into his hands the government despatches, which the ship was carrying.

This set Captain Foreman at ease again, and satisfied the officer. The thought only came to me just at the moment, for I chanced to catch sight of the parcel of papers.

I went on shore at St Helena with Mrs Foreman and people from the ship. We visited Napoleon's house, and saw the French General, who had been his friend. Sir Hudson Lowe was governor of the island when I was there; and he came on board the *Denmark Hill,* and invited Captain Foreman to dine with him. The captain was known and respected everywhere. I saw Napoleon's tomb, and the willow tree, which some artists have delineated, in the form of his shadow.

I was told in the island that Napoleon had been fishing the last time he was ever out of doors, and that, being taken ill at the water's side, he threw his fishing rod down just where it touched the willow, which afterwards overhung his grave.

After doing a great deal of mischief, of different sorts, during the voyage, and making himself so notorious that none of the passengers would speak to him, Captain C_____landed at the Isle of Wight, and left the ship. He gave information there to the custom house officers of some smuggled goods which he alleged to be on board the *Denmark Hill;* and when we reached London, the ship was on that account very strictly searched.

Once more I found myself safe in the London Docks. From thence, I went with Captain and Mrs Foreman to their house in Broad Street, leaving on board the *Denmark Hill* many valuable things which had been given to me by passengers. Among them were several mattresses, and other articles of furniture, hampers with wine and other things, which, having been purposely left behind by them, became my perquisites as stewardess. Barbosa alone had left on board for me four dozen of the finest wine, and other valuable property.

Soon after my return, I went to see my sister Bridget, who was living in London.

From her, I learned the sorrowful news that I had now no father.

He died on the 9th of September, 1834; more than a year before I came back.

He often used to say to me, and the words were in the last letter that he ever wrote to me, "Try to live as you would wish to die."

He had been Mr Lloyd's tenant at Pen Rhiw for sixty-two years.

My sister Gwen was married long before his death, to a minister of the Connection, who was a widower, and had a house ready prepared for her at Bangor. My sister Sarah and her husband took care of my father in his latter days.

On the Sunday after I reached London, I went to the old Welsh chapel. Mrs Lloyd, of Plâs yn Drêf, my old mistress, happened to be in London, and she attended that day at the chapel. She was old and in bad health, and when she caught sight of me, she knew me in a moment, and fell into a fit from the surprise.

She was a clergyman's wife, but in her early days the Calvinistic Methodists had not divided themselves from the Church, and Mr Lloyd was always a good friend to Mr Charles, of Bala, and to my father.

She was very glad to see me again, and wanted me very much to go back into Wales with her; but I would not, for I intended at that time to go to sea again with Captain and Mrs Foreman.

One day, in the London Docks, 1 noticed a well-dressed, and very respectable-looking man, who was standing and walking about, evidently trying to attract my attention.

At last he passed close beside me, and said, "I have been in Chester once."

"What's that to me? So have I," I said, abruptly.

He stood and said, "Don't you know me, Betsy?"

I then saw that he was James B. He had grown so stout, that 1 did not know him at first.

We talked together, and he told me that Mr Morris, his old master, had left him all he died possessed of; that he had sold the business for a large sum of money, and had come up long ago to London to look for me. He had set up in partnership with a friend, as merchants, in Leadenhall Street, and was successful in trade. Some rumour had reached him that 1 was at the Cape of Good Hope, and he had, therefore, taken a ship and loaded it, and was on the point of sailing for that place.

He tried very hard to persuade me to marry him, and go with him to Gravesend, and there embark with him for the Cape; but I would not do it.

A gentleman, named Sherman, who came with us in the *Denmark Hill* to England, had taken a liking to me upon the voyage, and offered to marry me. He had left a sister of his to take care of his property in Van Diemen's Land, and he went from England to Germany, which was his native country, intending to settle his affairs there and to return and make his home in Van Diemen's Land. He hoped that I would marry him; and I had, at that time, some thoughts of doing so; but the thing came to nothing, for I could not make up my mind to it at last.

Soon after we got to London, Mrs Foreman sent me to the British Museum with the two tattooed heads of the Sandwich Islanders in a basket, as a present to the Museum from her.

Hearing among my friends that Mrs S_____, my former mistress, was in London, I paid her a visit. The captain had made only one voyage after I left them; and, on returning to the Port of London, he died in the prime of life, after only three days' illness. His widow returned with the child to St Vincent's. The guardians sent him back to school in England.

The widow married in the West Indies a surgeon, named W_____, who belonged to the _____th regiment. He was extravagant and drunken, and soon brought her to poverty. She returned with him to England, and, when I saw her, was in tatters, and had only some rice and a few potatoes for dinner.

Orlando Furioso was grown a fine young man. I saw him in the docks just as he was going to embark for the West Indies, where he had a good estate. He was brought up at Eton.

Directly he saw me, he knew me, and said, "My Sissy!" He was very glad to meet me again, and spoke with great concern to me about his mother and her idle husband.

Many years before, and at the time when I first entered

Captain Foreman's service, he was the owner of a parrot, which he had got at Bombay, when it was only six weeks old. Mrs Foreman's mother took care of it while we were abroad, and the bird became very fond of her. One day when the captain was playing with it, the parrot bit his finger, and he scolded and beat it. This the parrot never forgot, but disliked the captain ever after, and used to shrink and tremble when he came near it, calling out, "Old Skipper! Villain! Beat poor Poll!"

At one time, I used to sleep in the kitchen where the parrot was kept in its cage.

As soon as day dawned, it would call out, sometimes "Get up, Betsy! Polly wants her breakfast."

I used to say, "No, no. Don't tell stories."

Then the parrot would laugh, "Ha! ha! ha! Pretty Poll made a fool of Betsy!"

On a Sunday morning, seeing through the window Mr Trimmer, a very large man, passing by, on his way to attend the prayer meeting at the floating chapel, the parrot would call after him, "Ha, little fellow! Where are you going? Going to Wapping, little rogue? Ha! Ha! Ha!"

This parrot was a grey bird. What it said always fitted the time. it knew me when I came back from abroad, and said, "Ha! Betsy, good to pretty Poll." It died of grief at last, for the death of its old mistress.

While I was abroad with Captain Foreman, I used to speculate a little in merchandise myself, with a bag or two of almonds, some chocolate, crapes, and other little things, and in this way I made a good deal of money. My wages were not high, but the passengers gave me handsome presents.

All the time I was away, I never received my wages. They

were paid to me in the lump on my return. I was anxious to layout my earnings to advantage, so as to make a provision against old age and sickness. I had talked with Mrs Foreman about buying a little schooner, which was for sale at Hobart Town, and we agreed to have her between us, to call her the Eliza Elizabeth, after our own christian names, and to employ her in trading about Van Diemen's Land and Australia; but the captain and Mr Hall – an old West Indian planter – persuaded Mrs Foreman and me to give up this plan, telling us that house property in London would be a much safer investment. They recommended us to layout our money in purchasing some houses, which Captain T_____ had for sale in Stepney Square, and in Cold Harbour Square, Commercial Road. Mrs Foreman and I took their advice, and we each of us bought separately a certain number of these houses. Mr Hall also bought more of them than we did.

He laid out £4,000; Mrs Foreman laid out £2,000; and I laid out £1,283 10s. 4½d. I paid the money to Captain T_____, and received from him the conveyance deeds of sixty small houses for mechanics. Several of these houses being in an unfinished state, I reserved a part of my earnings for the purpose of completing them, expecting, when that was done, to let them, and to secure for myself a comfortable little income from the rents.

About three weeks after this bargain had been made, Captain and Mrs Foreman were dining out one day, when Mr Watson, and another respectable looking man came to the house where I was living in Broad Street, and asked me to allow them to look at my title deeds to the houses which I had bought. I showed them the deeds, and Mr Watson showed me other deeds, and proved to me that the stranger – who was a

Mr Smith – had previously bought the whole of the same property from Captain T_____; and that my title-deeds, and those of Mrs Foreman and Mr Hall, were worth nothing.

Captain T_____ went off to America, out of the way of justice.

Mr Hall, though a rich man, loved money so much, that the loss drove him out of his senses, and he died of grief for his four thousand pounds. Mrs Foreman was troubled very much by her loss; but she and the captain had plenty of money left. I was the worst off, having lost what I had worked hard and long for, and only my own labour to look to for more.

I lost, also, in another way, a large portion of the sum which I had reserved for completing the houses. Among my seafaring friends, was Captain Robert H_____, a worthy, honest man, to whom it was always a pleasure to render any service. I believed him to be with his ship in North America, when one day a man named P _____, who had married H_____'s sister, came to me at Captain Foreman's, and told me that H_____ had been wrecked on the northern coast of England, and had saved nothing from the ship; that he had written to P_____, and requested him to ask me to lend him ten pounds for H_____, who was a man well off in the world, and to say that H_____ would repay me as soon as he could get at his own money. I never doubted what P_____ told me; and, not having a ten-pound note, I gave a fifty pound to P_____, telling him that I would call at his house the next day for the change. The next day I went after P_____, and could not find him; and I learned from old Mrs H_____, upon whom I called, that P_____ was a bad man, and that Robert was still at Quebec. Sometime afterwards, I found that P_____ was living expensively in lodgings. I went to him, and demanded my money, and he threatened to kick me down stairs.

I had nothing to show in legal proof of my claim, for I had not even asked for a note-of-hand, or acknowledgement; so I lost my fifty pounds, without remedy.

Captain Foreman was busy, preparing the ship to take out passengers to Sydney, and I spent the chief part of every day on board, receiving stores, and answering the persons who came to inquire for cabins.

One morning, the captain was with the carpenter in the little boat close below the ship's stern, when the cabin-boy, who was washing wine-glasses, chanced to throw away some of his rinsings so that they fell over Captain Foreman.

The captain got into a passion, and accused me of having purposely done it. I said I had not.

He answered hotly, "You are a liar."

"If you think that, sir," I said, "it is time for me to go."

I gave notice upon the spot, and left his service the same day, although Mrs Foreman begged of me to stay.

Chapter 4

How soon
Our new-born light
Attains to full-aged noon!
And this how soon to grey-haired night!
We spring, we bud, we blossom, and we blast
Ere we can count our days, our days they flee so fast.

Francis Quarles

**Domestic Service in London: with Country Excursions
Temporary Housekeeping – Lord Brougham – Mr Charles
Kemble – A Service of several Months – A Service of many
Years.**

On leaving Captain and Mrs Foreman's house, I went to Mrs
Colston's and made calls upon several other friends. That very
night I heard of a place likely to suit me.

Mr G_____, a lawyer, living at 26, Birchin Lane, was in
want of a person to act as his housekeeper for a few weeks, his
old one being very ill and expected to die, and his new one
not being able to come to him without delay. Mr G_____ was
a bachelor. He kept twenty-seven clerks, and several of them
lived in the house.

One day, when an important cause was coming on, a parcel
of papers had been sent from Mr G_____'s office to Lord
Brougham, but one was forgotten, and Mr G_____, hastily
recollecting it, bade me run with it instantly, and deliver it
very carefully.

I went, and was shown into a room where I saw a person whom I took to be a clerk. I gave the packet into his hand, and told him to be sure to give it to his master.

He nodded his head, and said quietly, "I dare say I shall."

I was provoked at his taking it so easy, and said to him, "You sulky old fellow, I'll tell your master. Look at the paper, It is of great consequence, Mr G_____ says, and you must look at it." I would not rest until he did so, and then I went away.

Mr G_____ told me afterwards that it was Lord Brougham himself; who was so pleased with my faithfulness about the paper, that he gave Mr G_____ half a sovereign to give me 'for my impudence'.

Mr G_____'s sister was married to a Mr W_____ about this time, and Mr and Mrs W_____ came to London to spend the honeymoon with Mr G_____. The Kembles were old schoolfellows of Mr G_____'s father, and Mr Charles Kemble, to honour the bride and bridegroom, offered to bring some players and to get up private theatricals at Mr G_____'s house for their amusement. He did what he had thus proposed to do, and brought Miss Stephens,[1] Liston, and many others. They sang a great deal, and acted scenes from *Hamlet*, *Douglas* and *Paul Pry*. It was my business to get supper ready for the party, so I had not a moment to spare to go and see the playing; but when I had sent it up and was free, I found Shakespeare's plays on a table in the kitchen. I do not know how they came there.

I opened the book at *Hamlet*, and read, and thought to myself, I can do like this and then I turned to other plays and

---

[1] Miss Stephens was married to the Earl of Essex, April 14, 1838.

read and acted characters. I took the poker for a sword, and was brandishing it about, thinking that I was quite alone, when all of a sudden I caught sight of Mr Charles Kemble standing in the kitchen doorway, looking steadfastly at me. I stood still in a fright.

He said to me, "You have been on the stage?"

I answered, "No, sir."

"Then you have been much at the theatre?"

I answered, "No, sir, very seldom."

"Well," he said, "I have never seen anyone with so great a capacity for tragic acting, since my poor sister!"

He asked me to come and stay at his house, promised that he would teach me for nothing, and then engage me for three nights a week at the theatre, and said that I might earn fifty pounds a night by my acting. He gave me his card, and told me to call on him in Charles Street, Berkeley Square.

I said that I would think of it.

Soon after this, I was going one morning to Covent Garden Market to buy asparagus, when Mr G_____ told me to call at the theatre and deliver some papers there to Mr Charles Kemble, by three o'clock. I went to the theatre before that time, and asked at the door for Mr Charles Kemble. The porter said there was a rehearsal, and showed me the way I was to go. I found one or two hundred people, men, women, and children, assembled – being the full complement of the company belonging to that theatre.

I was obliged to pass very close to them, and I saw that many were poor, untidy-looking creatures, and that some were quite dirty ragamuffins, shoeless, and without stockings, or perhaps shirts.

Mr Charles Kemble came to meet me, and took me to the

green room, and asked me whether I had made up my mind. Mrs Charles Kemble and other ladies were there. She said that I had the eye of an actress.

I said to Mr Charles Kemble, "If I come, must I play with the people I have just seen in the long passage?"

He answered, "Sometimes, with some of them."

I told him they looked dirty and nasty, and I did not like such company, and would never go near them, nor suffer them to come near me; and I, therefore, gave up all idea of accepting his proposal.

He said, "Do you stop with G_____?"

I told him why I could not; he wanted to know where I was going, and seemed very sorry that I would not be an actress; telling me that I should soon have made a fortune on the boards.

The sight of those ragged wretches again, as I left the theatre, made me resolute to have nothing at all to do with them.

Mr G_____'s other sisters came to town after that, and took me once or twice to the play with them. I saw Miss Chester – a fine, tall woman, in a white satin dress. I also saw Miss Stephens, Miss Kelly, and Mr Wood, in the *Beggars' Opera*.

Mr G_____ was very sorry when his new housekeeper came, and wished that he had not hired her. She was spared to him as a favour, by one of his relations, otherwise he would have contrived to pay her for a disappointment, and to let me keep the place. However, my master said, that he was sorry to part with me; and I went to Mrs Colston again.

The Captain and Mrs Foreman had sent after me to her house several times, but I would take no notice; and at last the *Denmark Hill* sailed to Sydney, with a great deal of my property on board, which I thought they ought to have set on shore for me.

One day, in the street, I met a young Irish girl, who asked me whether I could help her to get into service.

I answered, that I wanted a place myself.

She told me that she had just been to offer herself for a place which she was not a sufficiently good cook to take, and that she did not doubt it would suit me. She directed me to the house.

I went there, and was hired by Mrs U_____ at once, for she took a fancy to me; and that very day she talked to me for two hours, and told me all the particulars of her family history. Her husband was a great Darlington merchant. Her maiden name was P_____, and she was the only child and heiress of the Mr P_____ who first began to build about Gower Street and the Regent's Park. She was, when I knew her, eighty-two years of age, and a Roman Catholic. Her husband was an aged man. Their three unmarried sons, a widowed daughter, and that daughter's daughter, all lived in the same house with them.

My business was to cook for them, and I had seven separate little dinners to send up every day, besides one for the servants. It was not hard work, but always messing. She would sometimes ring the parlour bell in order to summon me to take her orders for dinner, and when I answered it, I found her in the act of reading prayers for the other two ladies. Yet, she would not suffer me to leave the room, but went on first with a few words of the prayer, and then with a few words to me about the dinners.

She used to say, "What is in season?"

I answered, "Such and such a thing is in season, but very

dear." This I soon found led her to buy whatever it was that I spoke of as too dear, for she immediately patted her pocked, and said, "Do you know who I am? Mrs U_____, with eight thousand pounds a year pocket-money, that no one can touch!"

I have heard that Dr Bartoloni, the family confessor, received a salary of five hundred pounds a year from them.

I was not easy in her house. She fidgeted me. She was always changing the servants, and I have known seven successive under-housemaids there, in the course of a single week. She frequently hindered me at my work by coming to the kitchen, and was affronted when I had not time to talk to her. She often came as early as eight o'clock, and would have kept me for hours talking of her family troubles. When I did not attend, she would go away and return again; and one morning, I chalked forty eight times that she had come to me down four pairs of stairs.

Her daughter had not married well, and her sons were wild. She was a good woman, although I am sure she was crazy.

She used to take me every night to her bedroom, to assist her in searching for thieves under the chests-of-drawers, and in other places where they could not possibly be. One night she called to me in the midst of her search that she had found a quantity of cobwebs to prove the untidiness of the housemaids. On going to her, I soon saw that her fancied cobwebs were scraps of her own lace cap, which were falling like tinder from her head, having been singed by her stooping over the candle.

She used to spend her Fridays in going about as a sort of penance, to pay for the maintenance of the numerous illegitimate children of one of her relations.

I remained several months with Mrs U_____, looking out

in the meantime for something that might suit me better than her service did.

Through Mr Crompton, who was one of Mr G_____'s clerks, I heard that an acquaintance of his, a young gentleman who was come up to London to study the common law, wanted a housekeeper.

I went and offered myself, and was engaged. The gentleman's name was Mr H_____. He lived at his own house, in Fenchurch Street. It was too large for him, so he let the shop and part of the dwelling, and kept only four rooms. Two of his brothers were staying with him when I first entered his service, and one of them, with another brother of his, who was not then at his house, went afterwards to Jamaica. His father, with the eldest brother and sisters, had a house at Cheshunt, but were often in town, and gave me many marketings to do for them. The house was very old-fashioned, and so spacious, that every step of the staircase of the second, third, and fourth stories measured three yards in length. There was a pump of spring water on the second flight.

I went to this place in a morning, and I found it lucky, though it is not usually thought to be so. I liked the house, and I liked my master. He was a good, innocent sort of man, and very careful in his choice of companions.

His health was delicate, and when put out, he was sometimes rather pettish in his temper. When I first lived with him he had on such occasions a habit of swearing. I thought it would be well to cure him of this, so I took my opportunity.

One day, one of his brothers made an appointment with him at a ertain hour the next morning, broke it, and kept him waiting all day long.

He quite lost his temper, was out of all patience, and when

I went into the room on some business, he spoke peevishly and swore at me.

I moved towards the door.

He asked why I was going.

I said, "Sir, I see that the room is not large enough for you, and me, and your company."

He answered, "What do you mean? I have no company." "Oh, I beg your pardon, sir, but I thought, from your way of speaking, that the room was full of devils, and that I was better out of it."

He coloured up and said, "Well, Betsy, you must own that my brother is very provoking."

"That is no reason," I answered, sternly, "that you should swear at me."

He looked much ashamed, and from that hour he broke himself of the habit of swearing.

He was a very upright man, and very kind-hearted. He took pleasure in undertaking business for the poor, and would carry on their suit, and win their causes, without making any charge for his trouble, feeling well rewarded by obtaining their rights for them.

After I had been about two years with Mr H_, he had a rheumatic fever, through which I nursed him, and he got well in a few weeks.

Dr M_____, the physician, attended him. Dr. M_____'s nephew was married to one of Mr H_____'s sisters.

Mr H_____'s sisters used to come, whenever it suited them, to stay at my master's lodgings, or to take a bed there, when visiting London on business.

Mr H_____ had great confidence in me. He knew that I held to the good old adage, 'Steal a pin, steal a pound'; and that I would not touch a book of his, unless he offered it to me, although I was so fond of reading, that once, when he had lent me an interesting history, I forgot to go to bed, and sat, enjoying it, until the morning.

He used to tell me his affairs, and twice, when he fancied himself to be in love, he read to me the letters which he wrote, and the answers which he received from the young ladies.

There was a gentleman, named S_____, who had been his schoolfellow, and used sometimes to come late at night, or, I ought to say, early in the morning, and take a bed at Mr. H_____'s. My master had told him that I was perfectly honest, and Mr S_____, it seems, did not believe that any servant could be so; for he used to leave money about in the bed, under the carpet, and in all sorts of odd corners. At first, I found some silver in his room, and I placed it on the mantelshelf in my master's sitting room. This happened several times, the sums growing larger. Then I found a sovereign, which I picked up and restored, as I had done my former findings; and a five-pound note, with which I did the same. At last, I found, one morning, a fifty-pound note under his pillow. I took it at once to the two gentlemen, who were at breakfast, and said to Mr S_____, "Sir, you left fifty pounds under your pillow."

He exclaimed, "No?" feigning surprise.

I persisted, "You did, sir, and you knew it. You did it on purpose to try me, thinking I might be honest with small sums, but not with large ones. I now give you warning that if I see any more of your money left about, I shall keep it, to punish you for having distrusted me. I wonder Mr H_____ lets you come here. You are a very wicked man."

He was very good-natured, but very wild.

When Mr H____ became aware of his real character, he put a stop to his visits.

My sister Sally had married a farmer named John Jones. She would not leave my father while he lived; and, after his death, her husband continued to rent the farm, and lived in the old house at Pen Rhiw.

Their daughter Mary, at nine years old, wrote some pretty verses in her native language upon my father's death. They are printed at the end of the 'Ychydig Gofnodau am Dafydd Cadwaladr, Bala, Agraffwyd gan R. Saunderson, 1836'.[2]

In 1842, my sister Bridget paid a visit to our sister Sally, at Pen Rhiw. I went to see her off; and, on returning to my master's house, I mentioned having done so, and added, under the feeling of the moment, "I wish I was going too!"

I thought no more about it, but Mr H____ did, and he very kindly made arrangements to spare me for a week; so, in a day or two afterwards, I followed Bridget to Pen Rhiw.

My sister Gwen and her family were still living at Bangor. Our sister Mary – Mrs Nelson – had lost her husband; her only daughter was married in India, and her four sons held appointments there in the Company's service. She had a pension of one hundred and eighty pounds a year, as an officer's widow, and returned to her own country and settled at Cerrigydruidion, in Denbighshire, about thirty miles from Pen Rhiw.

---

[2] From this little work, and from the *'Methodistiaeth Cymru'*, gan y Parch John Hughes, Gwrescam, 1851, Cyfrol 1 pp. 543-49, many of the particulars of the life of Dafydd Cadwaladyr mentioned in the Introduction to the present work, have been derived.

She came over to see me while I was staying there, and then I remembered to have met her before when she was walking with Captain Nelson, and I with Major Marley, in Fort William, Calcutta.

My old master and kind friend, Mr Lloyd of Plâs yn Drêf, was still alive, and gave me a hearty welcome. Mrs Lloyd had died before I came down, not long after her return from London.

A great number of my old acquaintances had died since I last saw Bala, besides my father.

I loved my sister Sally more than ever, and I loved her husband also, for the kindnesses they had shown my father in his old age, when I was far away.

Bridget and I returned to London one after another, when our different duties called us back.

Mr H＿＿＿＿ led a very quiet life, attending daily at his office, sometimes going out to a party, or to his father's house at Cheshunt, and sometimes receiving a friend, or two or three of his nearest relatives, at his own house.

One day he set out for Cheshunt, and I did not hear a word from him or of him for a fortnight. Then old Mr H＿＿＿＿ came, and told me that my master had been badly hurt by the upsetting of a coach the day I had last seen him; that for some days he was laid up, dangerously ill, at Tottenham, before he could be taken on to Cheshunt, where he then was.

A few days afterwards, my master was brought home to London, propped up with pillows in a coach. He was impatient to come, thinking that he should get well the sooner for my nursing. His back had been injured by the fall, and his health was affected also by the shock. He was very ill; but, with great care, he revived, and quite recovered in the course of time. He had before been thin, but when he got well, after this accident, he grew very stout; but he was never strong, and he required to be carefully attended to at all times to prevent his getting ill. This delicate state of health caused him to value my services, and to depend more upon me than a person in perfect health would have done. I was, in fact, his nurse, as well as his housekeeper, for he was a poor feeble thing.

One day my master came in from the office, sat down in his chair, and complained of giddiness in his head, and of feeling very ill. He became black in the face, foamed at the mouth, and had a dreadful fit. I sent for Dr M_____, who used to attend him. He recovered, but the fit left him in a weak state, and Dr M_____ advised his going into the country, thinking that London was too close for him.

This unsettled my master. He thought at one time of taking a cottage in the neighbourhood of London, from which he could reach his office every day; but at length he determined, as the assizes were going on, and he had a cause for trial at Wrexham, and another at Dolgellau, that he would go into Wales for the present, and defer making choice of a new place of residence. Accordingly he let out the whole house in Fenchurch Street, and put his furniture into safe custody.

He had many friends in Wales, and a great deal of business to attend to in different Welsh towns, therefore he took Lloyd, his clerk, with him, and arranged that I should accompany them to Wrexham, and that I should go about on visits to my relations, keeping as near as I could to the various places where they would be to lodge, and where my master might be staying.

This was, I think, either in the year 1844 or 1845.

At Wrexham I stopped with some cousins of mine. While Mr H_____ was at Dolgellau, I stayed at Plâs yn Drêf with the Lloyd family. Old Mr Lloyd had died since my last visit.

Mr H_____ was so well pleased with Wales that he remained there, not only during the assizes, but all through the long vacation. He went about, staying with Sir R. Vaughan, at Nannau, and at other gentlemen's seats, and amusing himself with going out hunting and making excursions to see the country. When he visited Caernarvonshire, I went to my friends at Pwllheli and at LIanberis.

From Llanberis I ascended Snowdon with Mr H_____, and a large party of my Welsh friends. Among them were Mr Roberts, Mrs Jones of Bangor, Captain Evans's two daughters, and others: about twenty of us altogether. We walked up to the top in the dead of night, that we might be ready there to see the sun rise.

A glorious sight it was, and when the curtain of fog drew up, and the high ranges of mountains, and the valleys, and the rivers, and the distant country were seen outspread around us, I thought that I never in all my wanderings had looked upon anything so fine.

When my master was in lodgings at Bangor, I stayed at the house of my sister Gwen in that town. She was then a widow, and had a neat little house, and a small income which sufficed to maintain her comfortably. Her only children were two daughters, and both of them were then at home – the eldest being on a short visit to her mother from Liverpool, where she lived in service.

About this time the annual association of the Welsh Calvinistic Methodists took place at Conway, and I and all my relations and friends attended it. From thence I went by way of

Llanrwst, to Cerrigydruidion where I waited until my master and his friend, Mr David Jones, rejoined me. We travelled together to Bala, and I went to Pen Rhiw, on a visit to my sister Sarah. My old conviction of my sister Gwen's dislike to me was revived at this time by the discovery that she had been trying to persuade my master that I was not to be trusted, but might some day leave his service suddenly; her object being, I thought, to put her eldest daughter into my place as Mr H_____'s housekeeper. Gwen had seen and known very little of me since I was a child, but Mr H_____ knew that I had been with him for several years, and that he was not likely to get a servant and nurse that would suit him better.

During this visit to Wales, Mr H_____ had given me the pleasure of seeing my friends in different places, while he suited his own convenience by having me at hand, and in readiness to nurse him, whenever he might be ill.

Mr H_____'s business now required him to return to London. We travelled by railway, and took the express train for the sake of some buttermilk, which I was carrying from Pen Rhiw for my sister Bridget, who is very fond of butter-milk. She was then keeping a lodging-house at No. 4, Winkworth Buildings, City Road. Mr H_____ had neglected to provide himself with apartments, and hers chanced to be vacant at the time. He went there merely for the present; but day after day, neglecting to look out for others, he became so comfortable, and found them, as he said, 'so quiet and cosy', that he took four rooms at my sister's house, and made his home there, continuing to attend at his office in the Temple. He went out less than ever, and received fewer visitors. He had a handsome income from his business, besides two thousand pounds a year, which had been left to him by an uncle.

The year after his visit to North Wales, both his father and mother died, and he came into possession of still more property.

There was a family quarrel at the father's death, and his brothers and sisters were never afterwards good friends.

My master often said that they had used him very ill; and he told several of his friends, as well as myself, that he meant to leave the bulk of his property to me.

I used often to call on Mrs Carter, who was Mrs Foreman's sister, to inquire after Captain and Mrs Foreman. Mrs Foreman's brother was for many years foreman to Mr Apsley Pellatt, the great porcelain manufacturer. They did not make many voyages after I left them, but gave up business, sold the *Denmark Hill* to persons who wanted her for the seal trade, and settled in their own house at Sydney. Mrs Foreman died first. The old captain became quite blind, and survived her about two years and a half. He had no near relation, and her relations became possessed of a great deal of property after the captain's death.

In the year 1849, Mr H____ went to Cardiff on professional business. I was left in London, and, in a few days after his departure, I received a letter from him, ordering me to look in his desk for some papers belonging to a client of his, named John Davis, and to bring them with me on the journey which he had before arranged that I should make.

I travelled from London to Llandeilo, and spent a week there among the many Welsh friends of mine who came there, as I did, to attend the association.

From Llandeilo I went to Cardiff, and there I found Mr H____ in lodgings. He was very ill; a doctor was attending him, and he had kept his bed for three days when I arrived.

On my going into his room, he said, "Oh, Betsy, are you come?"

He was very glad to see me, and told me that his illness had been brought on by his taking a long walk, over-heating himself, and then throwing off his coat, sleeping on the sofa, and getting a chill. He spoke cheerfully, and hoped that I was come to nurse him well again. I did all I could for him, and watched him day and night. High fever came on; he became delirious and raving. He would suffer no one but me to come near him. I could not keep him in his bed. The moment that I had persuaded him to go back to it, he was out again, crying out that he wanted to go home, and that he must and would go home. I got together all the doctors of the town to attend him; but they did him no good. I feel sure that the one who was first with him did not understand his disorder, and mistreated it.

When I had nursed him for a week, he became sensible again, lay very quiet, and talked to me of his affairs. He said, "If anything happens to me, don't tell my family." The doctor told me that he thought they had now mastered the complaint, and that Mr H_____ would do well.

The next morning early he turned on his side, put one hand under his head, and fell asleep. It was a favourite posture of his when he was resting; and he had often told me, when I nursed him in formed ailments, that he thought that he should die so.

Two hours afterwards I looked at him. He was lying very still, and I saw that he was altered, his face was ghastly, and his features sharpened. As I bent over him, he breathed one short sigh and was gone.

He was forty-one years of age, and a good and handsome gentleman.

I sent for an undertaker. and ordered a shell, a lead coffin, and an outer wooden one; and I had him buried at Cardiff.

The doctors who had attended him in his last illness, Mr Griffin, the chancery clerk whom he had employed, John Davis his client, and Mr Elliott, at whose house he died, followed my master to the grave.

Chapter 5

What's hallowed ground?
'Tis what gives birth
To sacred thoughts in souls of worth.
Peace, Independence, Truth, go forth
Earth's compass round!
And your high-priesthood shall make earth
All hallowed ground.

Campbell

New Enterprises

A Fortune lost – Barbosa again – Guy's Hospital – South Wales – Illness – Occasional Employments – The Crimean War – Volunteering for Hospital Service – Supplement.

As soon as Mr H_____'s funeral was over, I returned to his lodgings at my sister's house in London.

I put his papers together, and found and read his will. By it he gave an estate near Lewes, in Sussex, to his eldest sister, Mrs M_____, and everything else that he possessed he left to me. The will was written in his own handwriting, signed by himself, and witnessed by two gentlemen who were friends of his.

Under it I was entitled to all his household furniture, which was then at his lodgings; to many thousand pounds in money, to several houses in F_____ Street, to an estate in Wiltshire, to a farm in Hertfordshire, to several farms at H_____, and other property.

237

Although Mr H_____ had enjoined me not to let his relations have anything to do with his affairs, I could not feel it right to obey him in this and the day after my return to London I went to Cheshunt. I saw Miss Mary H_____, and told her the particulars of Mr Charles H_____'s death. The next day she came with her brother, Mr John H_____, to my sister's house. They took possession of all my master's papers, with the will, his clothes, his furniture, and everything there that had belonged to him, and removed them from the house. They left me nothing but a few old things, which I afterwards sold for fifteen shillings. They and their lawyer said that the will was useless, because it had but two witnesses instead of three, and they administered to my master's property as if he had made no will.[1]

They questioned me about some of his things, and I told them what I knew about them. Miss Mary H_____ said that she had never in her life dealt with a more upright person, and that I was the most honest woman she ever knew in her life, and she should be glad to recommend me to another service.

My master had given me almost everything. They gave me nothing, and took all that he had given away from me. Instead of possessing an income of £4000 a year, I had again to rely on my own labour for support.

While I was living with Mr H_____, Captain Church one day delivered a message to me from Mr Barbosa, asking me to go back to Sydney to marry him, or to send my address that he might come to England to marry me.

After that again, about two years before Mr H_____'s death, Captain Bunster told me that Mr Barbosa had charged

---

[1] It is not intended here to impugn the strict legality of the proceedings which disappointed Cadwaladyr's expectations.

him with a message to the same purport, adding, that he would never marry anyone unless he could marry me. When I last heard of him, he was living at Sydney.

I do not know whether B_____ ever returned from the Cape, or what became of him. I never asked.

A meeting of the Calvinistic Methodist Association was being held at Liverpool about this time, I determined to attend it, and to see the old places there once more. I went, and my sister Bridget accompanied me.

Sir George B_____'s old house at the corner of D_____ Street, I found to be still standing, but used as a warehouse.

A lighthouse had been erected on the Black Rock where the *Perseverance* struck, and where Harris was lost years before.

Having been much accustomed to the sick, and to all sorts of casualties, I engaged myself, as a nurse, at Guy's Hospital, and continued there for some time – perhaps a year; I do not exactly remember how long. The doctors, finding me steady and sober, wanted me to become a night nurse, in the place of one who had behaved ill. This I refused, and thereupon left the hospital.

I next took to nursing private patients, being recommended by surgeons and physicians to whom I was well known.

I did not like nursing so well as being in service, and, hearing from one of my Welsh friends that a fellow countrywoman was wanting to take charge of a house in South Wales, I asked her to recommend me. She did so. On hearing that I was Dafydd Cadwaladyr's daughter, Lady_____ sent for me, spoke to me, and engaged me. I went down in August, 1851. In the November following I had a fever, which ended in the dropsical swelling of one leg. Lady_____ sent me to

London, in order that I might be cured at the Homoeopathic Hospital, in Golden Square; but I was very ill after the journey, and kept my bed for several weeks at my sister's house, where one of the surgeons from that hospital attended me. By slow degrees, I recovered my health.

In March, 1852, I walked, one day, to _____ Street, to ask after Lady_____ and the family. When I got there, I found that the housekeeper was just going to forward a note, which had been sent for me by her ladyship. Its purport was to ask me to come there as head housemaid, to supply the place of a person who had just been obliged to return to Wales on account of her husband's sudden death.

I set about my work there immediately.

Lord Raglan's house stood near; and often, when I was cleaning the door of a morning, I used to see Lord Raglan going out on horseback for his morning ride. He never passed me without giving me a pleasant look and a civil word, such as 'Cold morning', or 'Fine morning', and once I heard him say to his groom, "That woman's always up!" I stayed there until August, 1852, when the family left town, and my services were no longer wanted.

I returned to my sister Bridget's house as a home, and again maintained myself by going out to nurse.

I had from my early childhood a dislike to soldiers; and this dislike was aggravated by the cruel conduct of the sentries in India who prevented the young widow's escape from the suttee.

After having been abroad, I always liked to know what was going on in the world, and this curiosity made me an eager reader of the newspapers. Sitting one evening with my sister, I read in one of them an account of the battle of the Alma.

"Oh!" said I, "if I had wings, would not I go?"

"What," answered Bridget, "go to be a soldier? Well, I can
  believe anything, if you have changed your mind about
them."

I did not want to be a soldier, but to see what was going on,
and to take care of the wounded.

Then again I read of Miss Nightingale preparing to take
out nurses. I did not like the name of Nightingale. When I first
hear a name, I am very apt to know by my feeling whether I
shall like the person who bears it.[2]

I determined that I would try to go to the Crimea.[3] I dressed
myself, and set off to the solicitor named in the newspaper. I
found him by the address given. He was in George Street; and
from thence I was directed to St John's, Queen's Square,
Westminster. When I got there, I thought that I was in a
nunnery – I saw so many women, and only one man. He was
the Rev Mr Shepherd. He asked my history and occupation,
and said that if I had applied two or three days before, I could
have gone next week with Miss Nightingale and her staff; but
that now no more nurses could be sent out until after her
arrival. He took down my address, and promised to write to
me. I then returned home.

Some time afterwards, Dr Watkins – an old acquaintance
of mine from Breconshire – gave me a written
recommendation to the Ladies' Committee. I took it to Mrs
Sidney Herbert's. The servant there showed me the way to

---

[2] The peculiar tone of the heroine's mind is strongly marked by the
premonitory form of prejudice against a name which conveys to
people in general a very pleasing impression.

[3] To be near the head-quarters of the army appears to have been the
heroine's first impulse and persevering intention.

Miss Stanley's at No. 6, Grosvenor Crescent. I saw Miss
Stanley, and she asked me many questions, and wrote down a
great deal. I suppose it was my pedigree, and all about me.
Seeing that I was a Welshwoman, she told me that her
grandmother was a Welsh heiress. As to my going out, she
said she could give me but little hope.

A day or two passed by, and then I received a letter from
Mrs Sidney Herbert, telling me to call that day between ten
and twelve o'clock at her house, to settle about going to the
east. It was then two o'clock, but I went, and saw Mrs Sidney
Herbert, who told me that I was not too late. She fitted me
with a bonnet, goloshes, and cloak, and sent me to Miss
Stanley's to be fitted with a gown. Long and short was the
greatest difference between the gowns; there was not much
shape in them.

The clothes supplied to us were not sufficient for those
who had rough and dirty work to do. Two gowns were
provided, and I wore them out, and three of my own besides,
before I came back again. The aprons and other things were
also too few; and those nurses must have been badly off who
had not a stock of clothes of their own.

I went to Mr Sidney Herbert's house in Belgrave Square,
on Friday, the first of December, 1854, with the other nurses
and ladies who were to go out under Miss Stanley. We stood
while he addressed us, warning us to expect hardships and
discomforts, and to be prepared to meet many horrid scenes.
He exhorted us to obedience, and desired us to remember that
we all went out equally as hospital nurses, that nobody was to
think herself above the rest of her companions. I also
particularly recollect his using the following words, or words
which bore the same meaning:

"You are going from hence into a strange land, and according to your behaviour and obedience you will be rewarded. If you behave yourselves well, there will be a provision for you; if not, it will be the ruin of you. I want to impress this upon your minds you go out either to make yourselves, or to ruin yourselves."

As he said this, I thought to myself, "Please God, they shall never have reason to complain of me!"

There were some present whose looks I did not like, and there were many very respectable persons.

I told one of the gentlemen, that morning, that I intended to go to the Crimea. He answered, "My good woman, you must be either drunk or mad! You would be amongst our enemies. It would be quite presumptuous to think of such a thing. We have not the least idea of establishing a hospital in the Crimea."

The form of agreement was then read to us. It bound us to devote severally our whole time and attention to the duties of a nurse of the sick and wounded of the British army serving in the East; under the direction and to the satisfaction of the Superintendent of Hospitals. I do not remember that the name of Miss Nightingale was mentioned in the agreement. I believe that it was not, and I have always thought so. I have still kept my certificate, and, certainly, she is not named in that.[4]

The wages were to rise from ten shillings a week to twenty-five shillings, according to service and merit.

Miss Stanley's party consisted of fifteen nuns, called 'Sisters of Mercy'; they were chiefly Irish ladies, who had

---

[4]　See Appendix A

been in training at Chelsea for a short time; also of nine ladies, namely:

Miss E. Anderson,
Miss Shaw Stewart,
Miss Kate Anderson,
Miss Smythe,
Miss Sims,
Miss Polidori,
Miss Clough,
Miss Tebbutt, and
Miss Taylor; and of twenty-two nurses.
Mr Percy, of 77 Eaton Place, London, and Dr Meyer, who had held a medical appointment in Norfolk Island, accompanied the party.

We were only allowed one small box apiece by way of luggage, and we were not allowed to open it until we got to Constantinople. I carried a change of linen in a bag, but wearing the same outer clothes all the way; we were a very dirty-looking set.

We went by railway to Folkestone and crossed the channel to Boulogne. We then went to Paris, where we were not fit to be seen, and we stayed there over Sunday. On Monday we went to Lyons; we passed from thence down the Rhone to Valence, and went on by railway to Avignon and Marseilles.

There I went to the quay, and asked which of the ships we were to take our passage by.

The *Egyptus* was pointed out to me, having soldiers on board.

I said, "Oh, she is a perfect rolling-pin!"

I knew it by the build of her; she was too broad in the

bottom. We had a troublesome voyage in her; some thought she was out of repair, but whether that was the case or not, the fault was in her building.

Some of our company went on shore at Messina, but I did not, having been there before; but I did go on shore at the Piraeus to see it once more. At Gallipoli, two French sisters of charity joined us.

On the 17th of December, we passed Scutari and arrived at Constantinople. We left the *Egyptus* on Monday, the 18th of December, and reached Therapia early in the forenoon.

Supplement to Chapter 5

One of Cadwaladyr's fellow voyagers has kindly added the following original record, which embodies some particulars not noticed in the preceding chapter:

> After a training in one of the London hospitals, and a probation in St John's House, I was selected as a nurse to the British army, and prepared to leave England with Miss Stanley's party.
>
> We had each a certificate on parchment given to us, signed by Dr Andrew Smith, which we were told to keep about us as a kind of passport, or ticket of admission to the hospitals (they were never inquired for). I returned to St John's, and in the evening, heard an address from our chaplain, and received the sacrament of the Lord's Supper.
>
> Four of us were going from St John's – six having left with Miss Nightingale – and received before going, the benediction of the Bishop of London, whose wish it had been that the sending forth of female nurses should have

been the spontaneous movement of the Protestant Church.

Soon after four, on the morning of the 2nd, we all met at London Bridge station, and there first saw the fifteen Roman Catholic Sisters.

The leave-takings were many, but I being a stranger in London, had no kind friends to say farewell. At Boulogne we were hospitably received, by the fisherwomen taking charge of our luggage from the boat to the station. A luncheon was kindly provided at the Hotel des Bains, after which we left for Paris. We reached that city late at night, and every comfort was provided for us at the Hotel du Prince, Rue Richelieu.

Here, I must speak of the great kindness and attention shown to us by the Hon. J. Percy, and Dr Meyer, and by Miss Stanley, who had the charge of the party, numbering in all fifty-two persons.

Through Mr Percy's kindness in taking us, we went in a body to the English chapel, and many of us there partook of the Lord's Supper. In the evening we had a walk – in a procession of two abreast – people wondering what we were in our grey dresses, grey cloaks, and brown bonnets.

In the morning we started for Lyons, and on the morning of the 5th, embarked on board the steamer, but a fog coming on, we were stranded on the Rhone for two hours; then the day cleared up, and we enjoyed our voyage, with its beautiful views, and the many windings of the river.

The Duchess of Hamilton, and her children, and party were on board, on their way to Nice. Arriving at Valence, we found that we had missed the train to Marseilles, so we telegraphed to Avignon for beds to be prepared for our large party. As usual at the hotels in France, we found them prepared to receive us.

In the morning we started for Marseilles, and arrived about noon at the Hotel de l'Europe.

We went out shopping, and Mr Percy kindly acted as our interpreter.

In the afternoon of December 7th, we embarked on board the mail steamer *Egyptus,* carrying out French soldiers to the East.

We had not been out long before a storm arose, and press of weather drove the *Egyptus* into Hyeres, for some hours.

On the evening of the 8th, we went on our way. The French soldiers all slept on deck. We had high winds till December 11th, when the sea became quite calm, and at four o'clock in the morning I got up to look at Mount Stromboli. We passed close by the island, and could see a light as in a cottage window at the foot of the mountain.

In the dark night, the mountain seemed like a rock of fire in the midst of the water. Every now and then a flame burst out, and then disappeared, and a rumbling noise was heard as of falling cinders. One was beside me then, whom God has since seen fit to take to himself, and whose body is laid in the graveyard of Scutari.

Some of our party went on shore at Messina, where we anchored at daybreak. They came back full of praise of the kind reception they had met with, and the beautiful orange and lemon groves.

A second storm came on after leaving Messina, and the occupants of the fore cabins suffered much, as the skylight was washed off, the sea constantly washed over the ship, and the water had to be baled out of our cabins, whilst every moment we expected to go down. Never shall I forget that storm. The noise on deck was awful. The nurses were very quiet, but we could hear the screams of the nuns as the water rushed into their cabins.

The following morning, before it was safe to walk the deck, Miss Stanley kindly came to see us. She then exchanged berths with one of the nurses, and slept and took her food in the fore cabin for the rest of the voyage.

The garçon had been in great request, for as soon as he had baled out the water, it flowed in again. No breakfast could be got that day, and for some days afterwards the water was salt.

We put back into Navarino Bay till the storm abated. On the 15th, we anchored off the Piraeus. Some of our party went on shore, and rode nearly to Athens. It was a beautiful day – the country and the white marble ruins looked beautiful in the distance.

Here I first saw the Greek boatmen in their strange costume, and an Albanian came on board to dine with us; two officers of the Buffs, and two French Sisters of Charity also came on board, with whose cheerful manners I was much pleased; and the French soldiers in the ship seemed to look upon them as friends.

On Saturday, the 16th, we passed the Plains of Troy, entered the Dardanelles, and anchored off Gallipoli at dark. Two French Soeurs de la Charité came on board there to proceed to Constantinople.

It was only as we passed the Seraglio Point that we realized the great beauty of the view when entering the

Golden Horn, and, for the first time, looked upon the mosques and minarets of the far famed city; but our thoughts were on our fellow-countrymen, lying at Scutari, in the hospitals, and we forgot our fatigue in our desire to be with them.

The first note of welcome was from the crew of the French hospital ship, who cheered us as we passed.

At Constantinople, the two hundred and fifty French soldiers, who had come with us from Marseilles, left the ship. They were perfectly well-conducted men in all respects.

Whilst we were anxiously waiting to know what would be done with us, we amused ourselves with watching the fairy-like caïques shooting rapidly by, with Turkish women closely wrapped in feridgees and yachmacs.

Most strange to us were the many sights that passed up the Golden Horn on this our first evening in Turkey; and much disappointed we were to find that we were to sleep on board another night. In the morning, we were taken up the Bosphorus to Therapia. The scenery was ever changing, and truly beautiful; but there was a damp on our spirits at not being set to work at once, knowing, as we did, that help was so much needed – some three thousand sick being at that time in the Scutari hospitals.

On the Sunday morning before Christmas Day, we had service in the room set apart for an English chapel – part of the Hotel de l'Angleterre – but on Christmas Day we stayed at home, and had mince-pies sent for our dinner by Lady Stratford.

Roses, shrubs, and many flowers were in fine bloom, and we enjoyed much the walks in the garden of the

Embassy. Therapia is a Greek village, and one day I went to the Greek chapel. I could see little difference in their worship from the church of Rome. Each person brought a lighted candle, placed it before the picture of a saint, bowed before it, and the priest brought incense, and walked down the aisles waving it about.

One day being at the landing stage, a Greek brought a cross folded in a napkin, and the Greeks going on a journey kissed it, placed money in a silver plate, and they were sprinkled with incense. I was told the ceremony was intended to insure them a safe voyage.

On the Sundays we went to the naval hospitals, and there we first saw the poor men sent down from the front with frostbites, and every dreadful form of disease.

Some of our party went for a time to wash for them, and their clothes were then brought to our abode to be mended. Some of us were ill, and were kindly attended to by a naval surgeon.

Chapter 6

Take well whate'er shall chance, though bad it be,
Take it for good, and 'twill be good to thee.

Randolph's Precepts

Eastern Experience of Hospital Life
Therapia – Scutari – Supplement.

I was very much disappointed, like the rest of Miss Stanley's party, at being sent to Therapia, instead of having employment at once in some military hospital. I was ready to go to the Crimea, and to do my best for the poor soldiers; but I was left without knowing what I was to do, or whether I should ever be set to the work for which I had hired myself; and, like the rest, I was discontented and uncomfortable.

I knew that this state of things was harder for Miss Stanley than for any of us, for she had not only her own disappointment to bear, but ours too; besides the ill-behaviour of two or three of the party, who disgraced themselves by drunkenness, as well as the discontent and murmuring of all the ladies and nurses. Knowing that their services were really and sadly wanting at Scutari, they were being kept away from their proper work, which they had quitted home and friends to do; and were left either to pass their time in utter idleness, or to while it away in doing things of a sort which they had never engaged or intended to do.

When Miss Stanley used to go to Pera and Constantinople to see if there was any opening for us, the nurses would watch for her return, and flock around her like a swarm of bees, questioning and teasing, and speaking reproachfully among themselves, on purpose that she might overhear them. Miss Stanley bore it wonderfully. I honoured her for the patient, resolute way in which she suffered it all, and kept her own counsel without condescending to complain, or to tell us the trouble she was in. She used only to say, "I do my best to get you employed. I hope you will not have to wait long. I cannot name the day."

Often and often I have pitied her for being placed in such circumstances, and for having people almost in a state of mutiny to deal with. I never teased and pained her with such questions. I knew she could not help our situation, and no one had more cause to dislike it than herself. She had a great deal to put up with, and in my opinion, she always behaved like a lady – like a real lady, as she is.

If anybody wants Miss Stanley's character, the people from Koulali can give it; and she well deserves their praises.

While we were waiting at Therapia, Mrs Shaw Stewart brought down a large basket of the patients' linen, from the naval hospital, to be mended; but our party would not touch the things until Miss Stanley persuaded them, and set them the example.

With her permission, I took my turn among the nurses who went up to the naval hospital to wash clothes for the patients. I was glad to do anything that was of use to the poor fellows.

I am sure the committee of ladies in England did all they could to procure good nurses for the Eastern hospitals; but they were obliged to take other people's recommendations, and could not know enough of the working-classes to judge for themselves. Many women, therefore, were sent out as nurses who had never filled any place of trust before, and were really incapable of the duties which they had undertaken.

Some among them, too, were persons of unsteady habits, who, not doing well at home, hoped to fare better abroad.

Others were good women, and excellent nurses, and deserved to be trusted.

I was one of the nurses in the last set sent for by Miss Nightingale[1] from Miss Stanley's party at Therapia.

We arrived at the barrack-hospital, Scutari, on Monday afternoon. We were ready for work, but had nothing given us to do that day.

On Tuesday we had a parcel of old shirts put before us to mend, and we continued at that work until Friday afternoon.

On Thursday, I asked Mrs Barker – one of Miss Nightingale's own nurses – when they were going to the wards. She said, "We are not going until one of the Sisters of Mercy comes and calls for us. This they usually do from half-past ten to half-past eleven, and they stay about half-an-hour in the wards."

She also told me that they must not speak to the patients excepting through the Sisters of Mercy, or else they would be sent home by Miss Nightingale.

I never was allowed to visit any of the wards, but I saw the

---

[1] "Miss Nightingale" – according to a statement made or authorized by herself – "had been placed by the Government in two positions of trust – each quite independent of the other. She had been appointed superintendent of the nursing establishment, and she further had received authority as almoner of the free gifts; to apply them, or any other funds derived from private sources, in the war hospitals." – See 'Statements Exhibiting the Voluntary Contributions,' &c., pp.19, 20. Printed by Harrison, St Martin's Lane, W.C., 1857.

patients in the long corridor, through which I passed in and out. On Friday morning Mrs Bracebridge came to me, and said she wanted me to go into the stores from two o'clock until five, to sort the linen with other nurses. I think there were five of them. When I got into the stores, really I was shocked to see the condition they were in. If there was a pound of rotten linen, there were thirty tons. I do not speak at random, for I am used to the weight of goods.

I remarked to one of the nurses, "What a sin and shame it was to see so much linen spoiled."

She answered, "Don't talk about that. Go to the mainguard stores, you will see everything, from a baby's shirt to a man's great coat – a hundred tons, if not more – not worth a pin."

"Whose stores are they?" I asked.

"They call them Miss Nightingale's stores," she answered. I never was in them, but I believe what she told me. All those I saw had water under them, and water over them, for it thawed that day, and the melted ice and snow came down through the roof. The linen, good and bad, as it had been mixed together, was all rotten. Mr Bracebridge's little pony was there. It was his stable.

On Saturday morning I saw Mrs Bracebridge, and said I wanted to speak to her. I told her I wished to go home if I could not go to the Crimea, for I saw I was of no use where I was. I said I had no work to do.

"Not yet," she answered, "There is no room."

I said, I understood there were from eleven to thirteen hundred men in the hospital, and that I should think there must be plenty of work to be done.

She said, "We must see what you are able to do."

"You'll never see that," I replied, "in my mending old

shirts, and you may get me a ship as soon as you like. It's an imposition on the country,[2] and I'll go home and tell the country the reason why I return."

She then promised to speak to Miss Nightingale. I had as yet never seen Miss Nightingale.

On Monday, at noon, Miss Nightingale sent for me – after speaking very politely, and telling me to sit down, she said, "I understand that you have been upsetting my nurses."

I said, "No, I have nothing to do with anybody but myself, but I want to go home if I can't go to the Crimea."

She inquired, "Why?"

I said, "Because I don't like this place, nor anybody in it, nor do I like the system."

"You don't like me, then?" she said.

"No, I don't,'" said, "but I never saw you before."

"Before I go any further," said Miss Nightingale, "I want to impress one thing particularly on your mind. If you do go to the Crimea, you go against my will." [3]

---

[2] This expression has been used by other labourers in Scutari Hospital, who knew that they were restrained from doing work which urgently required to be done there. The helpless lay unfed and famishing by day, the dying called in vain through their last weary nights for attentions, which ready hearts and skilful hands were longing to render. Surgeons asked for nurses and were refused, while nurses sat unemployed.

[3] This repugnance to sanction nurses in volunteering for the Crimea, is attested by many individuals besides Mrs Davis. A dread of their escape from systematic control appears to have been its incentive; for objections founded upon the dread of dangerous insecurity in a hostile country, and excessive privation, must have vanished at Lord Raglan's application for eight women to assist the army surgeons at Balaclava.

This she repeated over and over again, adding, "Another thing which I wish to impress upon your mind is, that, if you misbehave yourself, there will be no home for you here, and you will be sent straight to England from the Crimea."

This put up my Welsh blood, and I told her that neither man nor woman dared to accuse me of misbehaving myself. I had too much regard for my employers to do that, even if I had none for myself.

She informed me that she had made me over to a new superintendent, and I said (my Welsh blood being up again), "Do you think I am a dog, or an animal, to make me over? I have a will of my own."

I persevered in my intention of going to Balaclava, and she observed, "Well, Mrs Davis, I can't let you go without some one to overlook you. If you do go," she added, joining her open hands sideways together, and then forcibly dividing them, and spreading out her arms by her sides, "I have done with you and your new superintendent *entirely.*"

In spite of all this, she said she would get a ship as soon as she could, and thought it might possibly be ready to sail the next day.

After that, I assisted in making clothes for Mrs Gibson, while I remained in constant expectation of setting off.

I was altogether ten days at Scutari. On Monday night, at ten o'clock, I saw Miss Nightingale, a second time. She was passing to the wards, carrying a little tin and a lantern, followed by her maid, whose name was Roberts;[4] I was then

---

[4] Mrs Roberts acted as personal attendant to Miss Nightingale, but was a government servant. Mrs Roberts was a professed and experienced nurse.

walking about a little for exercise before going to bed. Twice afterwards, about the same time of the night, or very near it, I saw Miss Nightingale again going her formal rounds.

Every day, during my stay at Scutari, I, and the other nurses, dined on the filaments of the meat, which had been stewed down all night long to make soup for the patients.[5]

Miss Nightingale had a French cook, and three courses of the best of every kind of food were served up everyday at her table for Mr and Mrs Bracebridge, and her friends.

The 'free-gift' stores were said to be freely used there, but my informants believe that she knew very little about where things came from – even what were on her own table – or how other delicacies were disposed of.

Supplement to Chapter 6

The following remarks on the state of the Scutari Barrack Hospital, written early in December, 1855, by a diligent labourer in its wards, tend to corroborate Mrs Davis's narration:

---

[5] The author of '*Eastern Hospitals*' says, (third edition, pp.53-54) "We suffered greatly from want of proper food. Our diet consisted of the coarse, sour bread of the country, tea without milk, butter so rancid we could not touch it, and very bad meat and porter; and, at night, a glass of wine or brandy. It was an effort, even to those in health, to sit down to our meals; we forced the food down, as a duty; but some of the ladies became so weak and ill, they really could not touch it. For one, in particular, we tried to get a little milk, or an egg, but both these articles were scarce. A small quantity of both was regularly taken into Miss Nightingale's and Mr and Mrs Bracebridge's rooms; but they were not furnished to the rest of the party. Occasionally, Miss Nightingale kindly sent some light dish from her own table to the sick ladies."

About the middle of January, 1855, I went to Scutari, and was employed under Miss Nightingale. My duty was to attend on the sick in the division of the hospital to which I was attached. A short time after I joined, the 'free gifts', sent out by the British public, began to pour in. At that time the Government Purveyors'Department was not in the efficient state it is now in. For a long time, everything that was required was furnished from the *Times'* Fund.

When the fund was nearly exhausted, the system of making requisitions on the 'free gifts' came into force. An order was promulgated that nothing could be issued from the 'free-gift' stores without a requisition signed by two medical men. The medical men did not like to make requisitions on Miss Nightingale.

There were several objections to the system. First, it made it appear that the government purveyor was not in a position to supply what was wanting; and next, it gave unnecessary trouble. For instance, if the surgeon in my division of the hospital wished a patient to be served with jelly, he gave me a requisition, and on presenting it to Miss Nightingale, she gave an order for its being supplied. The surgeon intended, most likely, that the patient should continue to receive his jelly until further orders; but a second supply could not be got from Miss Nightingale's department, unless the requisition was repeated. The Staff Surgeon, or Deputy Inspector General of Hospitals, had important duties to perform, and could not always be found to countersign a requisition. When most things could be obtained from the government purveyors, it was unlikely the surgeons would make requisitions on Miss Nightingale, unless it were for some luxury not procurable from the government store.

The surgeons did not object to anything that contributed to the comfort of the sick being given from Miss Nightingale's stores of 'free gifts', but they did object to making requisitions.

The articles most needed by the men, at the time I refer to, were handkerchiefs. I have often torn up pieces of linen and calico, into convenient sizes, and given them to the men. The quantity of 'free gifts' was enormous; they arrived in ship loads. A good deal was worthless – old rags – quite rotten – Miss Nightingale and Mrs Bracebridge were sometimes bewildered at the quantity, and were put out when captains of transports came to deliver lists of packages they had brought. Some of the 'free gifts'used to be stowed away in No. 3 store, which was considered to be Miss Nightingale's private store. It contained books, fine shirts, and wearing apparel of superior quality; hot water comforters for the sick, tea, jams and jellies, spirits and cordials, preserved meats, soups, biscuits, &c. Miss Nightingale used to sit in the store and transact business, and write letters, when she wished to be alone.

There was another store in C. corridor, which we called the 'Rev. Mother's Store', because it was in charge of the Superior of the nuns. It contained a great quantity of articles arranged in compartments, and ticketed. At first the reverend mother freely gave what was wanting out of her store, but subsequently she was more particular, having been commanded not to give anything without a requisition. She had in her store, preserved meats, soups, jams, arrowroot, vermicelli, feather pillows, mittens, corn. forters, flannel, woollens, &c.

There was also a Queen's store, a general storeroom, opposite the mainguard.

Also a store on the ground floor of Lady Alicia
Blackwood's hospital, and another on the ground floor of
the wash-house. In the last named places, the packages were
merely placed under cover; but they were not protected in
any way: there was no sentry placed over them. Soldiers
and soldiers' wives, and children, passed freely in and out.

My duties did not admit of my working at the stores.
There were nurses who worked there regularly, opening
the packages, and sorting and arranging the contents.

The nurses used to have some of the eatables served out
to them from the 'free gifts', such as jams, herrings,
sausages; but these things had often been kept until they
were bad, before the nurses got them.

The plum-puddings which the good people of England
sent out for Christmas Day, were never distributed to the
sick soldiers; but long after, when they were quite mouldy
and spoiled, and had spoiled everything they were packed
up with, they were placed on the nurses' table.

I observed that in the hospitals they were using new linen
for poultices; so I made it my business to let Mr and Mrs
Bracebridge know that it was desirable they should use old
linen in preference to new. I then went to the reverend
mother's store, and found Vickery, the orderly, at work,
stowing away preserved meats. I asked, were any of the
nuns there, for I wanted some old linen. Vickery said, 'Here
is a sheet I am going to throw away.' Preserved meats had
been wrapped up in it, and it was dirty. I took it to my own
room, and used portions of it as I wanted them in the wards.
This will show the freedom of action that existed. Miss
Nightingale, of course, knew nothing of all this: indeed, I
don't see how she could know, with all she undertook to do.

Chapter 7

Wafting glad tidings to the sick man's couch.

Graham's *Sabbath*.

**Crimean Experience of Hospital Life: Part I
The Hospital Wards at Balaclava – The Extra Diet Kitchen
at Balaclava under Miss Langston and Miss Shaw
Stewart– Lord Raglan.**

On Friday morning Miss Langston, (also called the Mother
Eldress) who was our new superintendent, Mrs Gibson, Mrs
Whitehead and myself left Scutari on board the *Melbourne.*

The other ladies and nurses for Balaclava, came from
Therapia, and joined us at Constantinople, accompanied by
Dr Hanbury, a surgeon. There were Mrs Shaw Stewart, Miss
Clough, Mrs Noble and Mrs Disney.

We arrived on Sunday, but did not disembark until
Thursday after dinner, between two and three o'clock.[1]

We went to one of the Russian houses which was empty in the
hospital, adjoining the surgery. Next day the superintendent and
I went to visit the wards and the sights I saw, I shall never forget
as long as I live. I was there from half-past eight in the morning

---

[1] The reader is referred to Appendix B for an account of the conditions
of Balaclava Hospital at this period. It was been carefully compiled
from official documents. The general hospital at Balaclava was
established in September 1854, on the British occupation of the town.
It was attended by female nurses from January 1855 to June 1856,
when the British forces were withdrawn from the Crimea.

until twelve at night. On setting out, the superintendent told me
that I was not to speak to the patients. When I got to No. 5 ward,
poor fellows! "God bless your face!" they cried out. The first
man I met with, I asked how he was. She scolded me for doing
so, and repeated her order, that I should not speak to them.

I began to open some of their wounds. The first that I
touched was a case of frostbite. The toes of both the man's
feet fell off with the bandages.

The hand of another man fell off at the wrist. It was a
fortnight, or from that to six weeks, since the wounds of many
of those men had been looked at and dressed.

They had only two surgeons in attendance, Dr White of the
8th Hussars; and Dr Cross, of the 11th Hussars; Dr Wilson of
the 72nd, used to attend there occasionally.[2] There were, I
suppose, from three to four hundred patients under their care,
besides their respective regiments.

Dr Hanbury came with us to assist them.

One soldier there had been wounded at Alma by a shot
which passed through his left breast, above the heart, and came
out below the shoulder-blade. His wound had not been dressed
for five weeks, and I took at least a quart of maggots from it.

From many of the other patients I removed them in
handfuls. When the wounds were regularly attended to, these
men soon got well. I do not believe that maggots ever occur
in cases where the wounds are properly cleansed and dressed.
I always consider their presence as a proof of neglect. In my
experience, I have always found it so.

Not a man there had a bed. They lay upon bunks (tressels
and boards), having one blanket under, and a blanket and rug

[2] See Appendix B.

over each patient. Their great-coats were their only pillows, and they had no sheets. The sick and the wounded were alike neglected, unclean, and covered with vermin.

That first day I only washed wounds, applied fresh poultices, and tried to relieve the poor creatures a little. That evening I inquired for the ward-surgeon. They told me he was at No. 9, behind the Pack Stores. I found him there, and asked him if beds and bedding could be had.

He said that he did not know, and I must go to the purveyor.

I asked where he was.

The surgeon said that he was at the other side of the yard.

I left him, and inquired of some of the men, who pointed out the office.

I went there, and found the deputy-purveyor, Mr Fitzgerald. I asked him about bedsteads and bedding for the hospital patients.

He told me that he had plenty.

I inquired whether I could have three hundred or four hundred sets by eight o'clock the next morning, and he said, "Yes."

By that hour the next morning he had them all put ready for me. I immediately set the orderlies about washing, combing, and changing the clothes of the poor men – getting one set of orderlies to help another all through the wards,[3] and thus having four at a time in each ward. Two men from the Government stores removed the bunks, set up the iron bedsteads, and spread the mattresses. I made the beds, with

[3] The 47th Regulation for the Management of Army Hospitals declares that, 'The duties of an orderly-man are to attend on the sick, administer their medicines, and comforts, keep their wards clean and make himself generally useful.' In the General Hospital at Balaclava only two orderlies were then allowed to each ward.

blankets, sheets, and pillows, all clean; and then the orderlies got the men into them.

I had all this done myself: the superintendent did not interfere. She just came and looked at what was going on. That was my Saturday's work, until twelve at night.

On Sunday, Mrs Shaw Stewart, Mrs Noble and I went to look after the wounded before we went to church. The superintendent saw us home, and then she returned to church.

In the afternoon, Lord Raglan and his staff came down from the camp. When he came in, the first words he said, before he spoke to anyone else, were addressed to me, "I know you. Did not you live in Stanhope Street?"

"Yes, my lord."

"Then you know me?"

"Yes, my lord."

"The best woman I ever saw for getting up in the morning."

After having spoken with Mrs Shaw Stewart, and Miss Clough, he remarked to me that he already saw the fruits of our arrival in the hospital. He talked a good deal.

I thought that as Miss Nightingale disclaimed us, it might be well to have such a powerful friend as Lord Raglan to apply to, in case of any danger or other emergency, so before he went away, I said to him, "If you please, my lord, I wish to speak to you before you go away."

He said, "Well, what is it?"

"I want to put myself under your protection, and Dr Hall's." He asked why I wished to do that.

I said, "Because, my lord, we came here against Miss Nightingale's will."

He asked whether any of the others also wished it.

All the other nurses then present arose, and said the same. The superintendent was still at church, while this was going on. The Deputy Purveyor told me afterwards that Lord Raglan often said, "What a blessing it is that those women came!"

The superintendent, who was usually called Mother Eldress, apportioned the attendance among the nurses. While I was still in charge of the wards, by her desire and that of the doctors, I went to nurse Captain Johnson, who was ill of a fever at his own house. I watched him two days and two nights, and then Mrs G_____ was sent to succeed me. In a few hours she was found insensible from intoxication on the floor on his room. Mrs D_____ succeeded her: she also drank to excess.

I had the charge of Wards Nos. 1,2,3,4,5,6, and 7, for three weeks, under the superintendence of Mother Eldress.

After that time Mrs Whitehead took charge of Nos. 1,2,3 and 4, and I kept Nos. 5, 6 and 7. In No. 5 there were then 39 patients; in No. 6, 43; in No. 7, 45.

In Nos. 1 and 2 were 32 beds – 16 in each; in No 3, 17; in No. 4, 28. In the two huts there were 36 beds; in one marquee were 13, and in the other 10; and at this time also 49 of the orderlies lay sick in the three Russian houses.

The patients in the wards were placed so close together, that I could not put my foot straight down between their beds, and was obliged to pass sideways.[4]

About the middle of February, fever prevailed among the

---

[4] The 57th Regulation for the Management of Army Hospitals enjoins that 'In order to prevent the Hospital from being crowded, every man is to have a separate bed with a space of five feet at least allotted to it and of two feet between each bed; and if the apartment be less than ten feet high a greater space is to be allowed.'

orderlies, and the Deputy Purveyor applied to Lord Raglan for new ones. We were four days without them, getting such help as we could from the Ambulance Corps, who were tipsy fellows, and ate and drank the supplies which they ought to have carried to the patients.

When I had been about six weeks in the wards, the cooking for the patients was so much neglected, that they were left two days running, without their dinners; then Mother Eldress asked me to come from the wards, and undertake the charge of the extra-diet kitchen.

Lord Raglan used often to stand and talk with me there. It distressed him to see the wounded men carried the long distance between the camp and Balaclava; and he always looked forward to having a hospital there in the front.

Upon the first Tuesday in March, Mother Eldress established me in the kitchen, and gave me the entire charge of it. She said she saw I should do well, and could trust me; therefore, as she had much writing and many other things to do, she should not often come there. That very day she was taken ill, so she never afterwards visited the kitchen. I used to report to her by word of mouth, every evening during the three weeks which she remained. Miss Erskine then came to fetch her back to Scutari, and Mrs Bull, the nurse, went with her, when Miss Langston left for England.

Mrs Shaw Stewart acted as superintendent when Mother Eldress left, and under her direction things began to work well in this place. She was just and firm, though arbitrary and odd now and then. She never spared herself, but would work all day, and watch the sick at night. I think she was the only lady who went to the East in all respects really capable of a nurse's duties.

I do not undervalue the services of any of the ladies, but real, high-born gentlewomen are not accustomed to hard manual labour, and are not strong enough for it. In performing servile offices they put constraint upon themselves, and hurt the feelings of the men, who were acutely sensible of the unfitness of such work for persons of high station. Ladies may be fit to govern, but, for general service, persons of a different class, who could put their hands to anything, were more useful.

If ever anyone deserved well of her country, Mrs Shaw Stewart did.

Often have I followed her out night after night in the dark, through the bad weather and along the worst roads possible, to visit the sick and wounded, and to carry lemonade and other drinks from our kitchen to the huts. We used to set out at ten o'clock, and one night we got into a hole up to our waists in snow, and were not at home again until four o'clock in the morning. We both had Balaclava boots on. General Estcourt gave twelve pairs to the hospital, and they were used by such of the nurses as had most need of them.

About eight o'clock in the evening of the first Saturday in April, a Captain Clarke called, who commanded a ship. He stated that he had ninety bales and boxes, besides other packages on board, and that there was twenty pounds due for their freightage. They were Free Gifts from England, especially directed to Miss Nightingale, for the use of the army in the East. Miss Nightingale had refused to pay for them, and so he brought them from Scutari to Balaclava.

Mrs Shaw Stewart received them, and paid the twenty pounds out of her own pocket. They were landed on Monday. We did not know where to put them, so that they stood out that night, and the next day we bundled them into our house, and into the extra-diet kitchen.

Mr Fitzgerald soon knocked up a little store for her to put some things in, and he gave Mrs Shaw Stewart the key. He never grudged anything that would do good.

On Wednesday, Mrs Shaw Stewart began to open the goods. She sent all the wine into the kitchen to me. She made the orderlies give in lists of the patients' wants through the nurses, and also went herself through the wards to ascertain them; and she not only gave out the things required through the nurses, but generally carried them in loads to the patients. Every man who needed, received two flannel shirts, two cotton shirts, two pairs of stockings, two pocket handkerchiefs, two pairs of drawers, a waistband or two, and a throat comforter.

I used to see the fatigue parties waiting before Mr Fitzgerald's door to be set to their work. Some of these men were without stockings; others had worn their flannel shirts for six weeks. I often asked them if they wanted anything and told them to come to me when their day's labour was over at five o'clock. I then made out lists of their wants to Mrs Shaw Stewart, and she gave the things for each man.

She was so kind in doing this, that, like a true Welshwoman, I determined to make the most of the opportunity, and told the men of the fatigue parties to inquire who wanted anything in the camp. They soon brought down lists, signed by their officers, and Mrs Shaw Stewart gave me the clothes and other comforts to send back to their comrades. In this way two hundred shirts were sent to the 39th Regiment, alone. She used to be amused at my being so busy about distributing the things, and often laughed, knowing what I came for, when I knocked at her door.

The kits were always examined on the admittance of the patients, properly supplied with clothings, and given back to each man, when he recovered and was dismissed.

Mrs Shaw Stewart and Mrs Noble went out with the intention of going backwards and forwards in the ships between Balaclava and the other hospitals; having heard of the dreadful sufferings of the sick and wounded men, from neglect on the passage from the Crimea to Scutari. They altered their purpose merely because they found that they could be more useful in the hospitals. Mrs Shaw Stewart never wished to be a superintendent.

Lord Raglan urgently wanted her assistance at the new hospital, which he had instituted at the Castle, for the reception of the wounded alone, and she, with Mrs Noble, a nurse, went thither early in May.

By the day of her departure, all her clothing goods had been distributed, except a few, which taken together would scarcely have made up a bale; and every single book had been given away. She left behind at Balaclava a large quantity of preserved fruit, and other useful stores, for which she had paid fifty pounds to Captain Wilson of the *Paramatta* on the last Saturday in April. She paid that sum out of her own pocket, and bought the things only for the benefit of the patients in the Balaclava Hospital.

Lord Raglan, General Estcourt, and Sir Richard Airey had all of them a high esteem for Mrs Shaw Stewart. Miss Nightingale sent three nurses to the Castle to Mrs Shaw Stewart; and two to Balaclava – Mrs Sandhouse and Mrs Lawfield. They were dissatisfied at being held back from their proper business at Scutari, and in one way or other got sent on to the Crimea.

Lord Raglan used to come down three times a week to visit the Hospital, besides doing so on other occasions. He never failed to visit the kitchen, to see how we got on. He looked at the arrowroot and the other food prepared for the men, and often told me in jest to send nothing out without plenty of brandy and wine in it, for he was sure the country grudged nothing to the soldiers.

All the surgeons who came from the camp, visited the kitchen, approved of what I did, and wished they could have had me and the kitchen up there.

After Lord Raglan's death, I never saw a commander-inchief at the hospital, nor any members of the staff sent from him.

The patients used frequently to ask me to pray with them, and I always gave them a few words of Scripture to think of.

It made me weep when I could not speak, to be understood, one religious word to the poor Maltese and Sardinians when they were dying.

The chaplain was the only clergyman of the Church of England, in the hospital. He was diligent, but there was more work than he could do.

Mr Crozier succeeded Mr Heywood at Balaclava. Mr Parker was chaplain at the Castle Hospital. There were many Roman Catholic priests.

Before I left London, Mr Phillips, of the Bible Society, gave me a dozen or two of Testaments – some of them Welsh and English, and others English. He told me, at the same time, that he was going to send out two bales of Bibles and Testaments to Balaclava, for the use of the soldiers.

I gave away the Welsh Testaments to Welshmen in the hospital, and the English ones to Englishmen. All were very glad to have them, and when they recovered and returned to the camp, many of their comrades there came or sent down to ask me for more. I had no more, and I often inquired for the two bales which had been promised, but never could hear of their arrival.

The chaplain of the hospital did not like the British and Foreign Bible Society, and would not distribute their books; but I do not know that he ever received those bales.[5]

It is a melancholy fact that the Superintendent of the Female Nursing Staff did not recognize *any religious intercourse* between the nurses and patients. Whatever did take place was without her authority, and in most instances without her knowledge.

The principle of having nothing to do with their souls was avowed. That care was wholly left to the few chaplains and priests.

The instructions from the War Office accorded with this practical exposition of the system of non-interference.

---

[5] The author of the tract on Kaiserswerth remarks. pp. 18. 19: 'One great reason which deters women of education from this work of love is that having seen the unutterable dullness of a common hospital they say to themselves, 'If I am to have no moral or spiritual work to do, if I am only to sweep, and comb out dirty heads, and dress loathsome wounds, as I have no idea of buying heaven by such works, I may as well leave them to those who must earn their livelihood and not take away their trade.' Let such as feel this go to Kaiserswerth and see the delicacy, the cheerfulness, the grace of Christian kindness, the moral atmosphere, in short, which may be diffused through a hospital by making it one of God's schools, where both patients and nurses come to learn of Him.

No one can seriously believe that Christian influence is not desirable in times of sickness, as well as at other times. It is the abuse of this influence, it is un-Christian influence which causes the fear and the jealousy we so often see. No one can seriously believe that the word let fall by the nurse, during a restless night, has not a better effect upon the suffering patient than the set visit of the chaplain. Educate, qualify the nurses to exercise this influence, to drop the word in season, and this jealousy will fall away of itself.' Ibid, – pp. 15, 16.

The 'jealousy' appears to refer to the fear entertained by 'many surgeons' lest their patients should be 'excited by pious nurses'.

At p.17, some particulars are given of the system pursued by the pastor in instructing the nurses 'how they are to approach the hearts of the patients, without assuming the tone of a father confessor, how they are to act in cases of emergency; and at all times they have access to him to ask his advice.'

The author then illustrates by instances, 'how ready these women become to seize the moment for making an impression on the hearts of their patients.'

Chapter 8

Ponder not
The form of suffering; think of what succeeds.

Cary's Dante.

Crimean Experience of Hospital Life: Part II
Sleeping Accommodation – Daily Duties – An Inquisitive
Visitor – Miss Nightingale's First Visit to Balaclava –
Rejection of the New System – The Sardinian General.

Miss Wear succeeded Mrs Shaw Stewart as superintendent at
Balaclava. She, too, was a good creature, and would have
things to give to a poor fellow. After her arrival, she allotted
the ward No. 6 to the use of officers only. Before this they
generally stayed at the regimental hospitals, and only a few
were to be found among the privates in the hospital wards;
afterwards, they were glad to come in.

I worked well with Miss Wear. She was active at all hours,
and would sometimes herself watch the sick six nights out of
the seven, making no difference, but giving her care and
attention to whoever was in the greatest need, whether officers
or men. French, Sardinians, and Russians were nursed there as
carefully as our own soldiers and civilians. Miss Wear went
every morning through the wards, to see that the orderlies had
put everything that was requisite within reach of the respective
patients, and to add anything that she thought might be
conducive to their comfort.

During the early part of my residence at Balaclava, I, and the five other nurses, slept in one room of the house adjoining the surgery. We had neither a table nor a chair between us – and we all of us ate and drank together on the floor, in that one room. The adjoining one was occupied by the Mother Eldress, and Mrs Shaw Stewart.

The rats were very troublesome. I have often been awakened by their climbing about the bed, and several times have found them coiled up fast asleep upon my shoulder.

Miss Wear was so much annoyed by the rats that she could not bear to remain in this house. Mr Fitzgerald, therefore, had two huts built on the top of the hill, about forty yards from the General Hospital – one for Miss Wear, and the other for the nurses.

From the time of my removal from the wards, I used to sleep in the extra-diet kitchen, where the rats were as bad as in the former sleeping place; I think they came there to do their exercises.

This extra-diet kitchen was a hut, but not a *wretched* one. After the partition had been taken away, and the part formerly used as a Protestant church was let into the kitchen, I found it sufficiently spacious and comfortable.

The huts built on the hill were pitched and white-washed, and covered with tarpaulin. Unfortunately, the roof of the extra-diet kitchen was not thus protected, and I had often, by day, to select a spot where I might find shelter from the rain, while giving out the rations. At night, I have frequently had to lay soaking, with the rain pouring down upon me; and the following morning have been obliged to dry my bed and bedclothes out of doors in the sunshine on the rocks.

There was no oven in my kitchen.

Peter Frank, a Scotch man, who was an old pensioner, had charge of the General Hospital Kitchen. He had three orderlies and a cutter-up to assist him; they cooked for the patients who were on full diet, and for the hospital orderlies.

There was an in oven in Peter Frank's kitchen, to which I could send things to be baked. When I had too many for this purpose, I used to send puddings, &c., to the large public oven, kept by Mr Primrose, the government contractor.

I had five braziers at work in my own kitchen every day while the cold weather lasted; and when hot weather came, I had them placed out of doors, and employed them there.

Lady Stratford De Redcliffe sent a stove with two ovens for my kitchen, but some of the flues and fittings were lost on the way, and the stove could not be put up for want of them. It lay about for a long time, and at last, Stevens, the ward-serjeant, took it up to the Monastery, to try what he could do with it in that building.

Lady Stratford De Redcliffe was always ready to befriend the soldiers, and to help the ladies and nurses in their efforts to serve them. I have a very great respect for her, and so have all who know what she did for the cause.

Among the patients was one named Hargrave, belonging to the Grenadier Guards. He had lived in Lord M_____'s service, as confectioner; and Lady M_____ repeatedly sent him presents of mercery, needles and pins, and other useful things. He was grateful for the attention which I paid him while he was suffering from fever, and being an oven builder as well as a baker, he planned a stone oven for me, with the intention of building it in the very place where the Sisters of Mercy afterwards had one.

Hargrave exerted himself too soon in assisting Mr

Primrose, brought on a relapse of fever, and was sent to Scutari; so I never had the oven.

I did not like the painted tin drinking-cups which I found in use, for the sick men; and complained of them to Mr Fitzgerald. He told me to send them and other old things to him by the orderlies. Fresh supplies were then given out of bright tin vessels, and new knives and forks. Each patient had a cup, a plate, a knife and fork, a large spoon and a tea spoon. Six bright tin panikins with handles, were also allowed to each ward, for the patients to receive drink from in the night.

Every morning at eight o'clock I served the soldiers' breakfasts to the orderlies of the wards, and the officers' breakfast at nine.

At ten I gave out luncheon for the extra-diet patients, and at noon I served the dinners – dividing each man's portion separately, and delivering them all to the orderlies of the wards.

As soon as this was done, I prepared dinner for the officers, and then I followed the orderlies who carried it in, that I might feed the patients who could not lift their hands to their mouths.

At five, I got tea ready for them; and at seven or eight o'clock, according to their need, I sent the suppers in.

At ten at night, I gave out drinks and arrow-root for the bad cases. The doctors used to come backwards and forwards with orderlies, from nine to eleven o'clock, ordering wine and other things to be given – perhaps every ten minutes, to some patients.

I never got to bed before twelve, and was generally out of it four or five times in the course of the night, to attend to the orderlies, before five o'clock in the morning. At that hour I always rose to go about my daily business.

Sometimes I took my turn in watching the sick all night,[1] I and always did my daily duties, just the same as usual.

It was no time to save oneself when so many were suffering.

The patients, officers, gentlemen of the civil service, and all, used to call me "Mother", always behaved to me with respect, and said they were grateful to me. Many have told me since, that they owed their lives to the care I took of them.

I had an orderly to assist me in the kitchen until June – a quiet, useful man; he became very ill from the thick smoke and charcoal dust accumulating in his chest, and was obliged to go into the hospital, where he lay sick for a long time. I had afterwards two, one succeeding another, but they were idle, tipsy fellows, so I preferred going without such assistants, and did all the work myself. I generally called in two orderlies, or Araba men, from the yard, to lift the great pot for me.

Between dinner and tea, Miss Wear used to come to the kitchen and employ herself with whatever work was most needed. At that time we made the jellies for the patients, and prepared other things.

Fruits often arrived in ship-loads from Malta, and elsewhere; and Miss Wear and I had to sort it, to pick it, and to wash it all, before it was fit to be distributed in the wards.

After the first start, I never found any difficulty in getting proper shirts, both cotton and flannel, for the patients. Socks

---

[1] At Scutari Hospital night nursing was formally prohibited. At Balaclava it was most beneficially practised by and under the superintendence of Miss Wear, although at an expense of strength which might have proved fatal to the devoted women, who voluntarily compensated by excessive personal exertions for the want of a sufficient number of labourers.

and stockings were supplied abundantly, according to the wearer's choice. Every patient had two pocket-handerkerchiefs, and hundreds remained in the Free Gift Store.

Three washing-stands belonged to each ward, excepting No. 7, which had only two. Every man who kept his bed had a separate washing-basin for himself.

Two round roller towels, and six separate hand towels, were delivered clean to each ward every week. No. 9, was, in my time, a pack store ward. From ninety to one hundred dozen towels were washed for the hospital every week; and a pillowcase and pair of sheets were allowed for every patient.

When I received orders from the doctors, they never gave the name of the patient, but merely the number of his ward, and of his bed in that ward. I was not ordered to get double-signed requisitions. Mrs Shaw Stewart, or Miss Wear, wrote an order for such things as I required, and I took it to the serjeant in command of the stores, who sent them immediately; or, if they were delayed, I used to go and give his men a good scolding.

The medical officers gave the orderlies requisitions upon the kitchen for necessaries, which were in my keeping, and I supplied them at the proper times and seasons.

It was on one of the last days in March, that I first saw Mr. S_____, who called himself Miss Nightingale's uncle. He was said to be connected with the London newspapers, and certainly appeared to come on purpose to spy about and pick up information.

I met him at the purveyor's office.

He asked me if I was one of the nurses.

I replied, "A Jack-of-all-trades, doing any work that was to be done."

He enquired whence I came.

"From the Principality," I answered.

"Where is that?"

"Oh, not here!"

I disliked the old gentleman directly I met him – I thought he looked like an old fox.

He asked my name. I said, "I'll tell you some of my letters – E – C – Y – R –; there, spell that; what do you make of it?" The purveyor's clerk did not like him better than I did; for he was always prying into everybody's business.

On the following Tuesday, he came into my kitchen, exclaiming, "Oh, you are here!"

"Oh, yes, I am here, there, and everywhere!" I replied.

The great pot was then on the fire, which required two men to lift it on and off. Mr S_____ walked towards it, and put out his hand to raise the lid of the pot. I asked if he wanted to put anything in.

"No," said he.

I told him to have the goodness, then, to leave it alone; but that if he wanted to have anything cooked, I would do it for him.

He professed a wish to know how we got on, that he might let the public know; then asked many frivolous questions of me about washing his linen.

I have read paragraphs in a London newspaper about Balaclava, which must, I think, have been written by him. He used to borrow horses and mules to carry him backwards and forwards to the camp; I believe he never hired any, although he was reputed to be rich. He had two sons, who were also prying about. He was a little man, in a wig. He got Miss Wear to let him make a bed of the soldiers' coat chest to rest upon, after wearying himself with his rambles.

He went very often to and from Scutari. I think he was the means of first bringing Miss Nightingale to Balaclava.

There was a Mrs Smith, who was housekeeper at Miss Nightingale's private residence at Scutari, and three other ladies, said to be cousins of Miss Nightingale, were also there. I do not know their relationship to Mr S_____, our 'Paul Pry'.

Nobody there liked this old man. He accused us of extravagance because we supplied the real wants of the patients, and all his reports of us were unfavourable.

I know that the lives of many poor fellows were saved by careful attention in feeding and nursing them night and day. Many must have died without proper attendance at night.

We thought, at Balaclava, that Mr S_____ was the means of inducing Miss Nightingale to come thither to establish her system, and to set up her authority beyond its former boundaries, which did not reach farther than Turkey.[2]

---

[2] On this subject we can quote Miss Nightingale's own statement. 'Miss Nightingale's superintendence, which commenced Novr., 4, 1854, the day of her arrival with her party of sisters and nurses, extended over the Female Nursing Establishments of the barrack and general hospitals, at Scutari, of those at Koulali, and of five general hospitals in the Crimea. She resigned the management of Koulali in April, 1855, and the nursing establishment of the general hospital at Balaclava was not under her superintendence during the period between October 1855, and March 1856. See *Statements*, printed by Harrison, 1857.

The extent of her superintendence does not appear to have been defined by government, until a short time before the hospitals closed.'

C. A. WINDHAM, Chief of the Staff.
Head-quarters, March 16.

'No.1. It is notified, by the Secretary of State for War, that Miss Nightingale is recognized by Her Majesty's Government as the General Superintendent of the Female Nursing Establishment of the

Although Miss Wear was the superintendent, it was not with her, but with Mrs Shaw Stewart that Miss Nightingale communicated on the subject of her purposed visit to Balaclava.

In May Miss Nightingale first came to Balaclava. She continued on board the ship four or five days after her arrival, before she disembarked. On landing she went up at once to the camp, but returned to sleep on board at night.

That day Lord Raglan and his staff came to the kitchen, and talked with me as usual.

I said, "I understand, my Lord, that Miss Nightingale is gone up to the camp?"

"Thank God! I am very glad of it," he replied.

Colonel Somerset remarked, "You do not like her?"

I answered, "No; and I don't know what she wants here." What pleased Lord Raglan was the arrival of more nurses, for they were badly wanted.

I did not see Miss Nightingale until the Friday after her landing. She went through the hospital on that day with Miss Wear, and came to the kitchen where I was very busy, saying, "How do you do, Mrs Davis?"

Military Hospitals of the Army. No Lady, or Sister, or Nurse is to be transferred from one hospital to another, or introduced into any hospital, without previous consultation with her. Her instructions, however, require her to have the approval of the principal medical officer in the exercise of the responsibility thus vested in her. The principal medical officer will communicate with Miss Nightingale upon all subjects connected with the Female Nursing Establishment, and will give his directions through that lady.' – *The Times,* Tuesday, April, 1856.

I answered, "Very well, thank you," without raising my head from my work. In a minute or two I looked up and exclaimed, "Oh! Miss Nightingale!"

"What! did you not know me?"

"Yes, ma'am; but I should as soon have expected to see the Queen here, as you."

She afterwards went out of the kitchen. The next day I was told she had a violent quarrel with Mrs D_____, a tipsy nurse. On the same day, Miss Nightingale was taken ill, on board ship, and carried up, as a patient, to the Castle hospital.

Miss Nightingale objected to my cooking for the officers, and using government stores for them, saying that they ought to find their own. However, I went on doing what I thought best, for they were then as much in need as the privates, although some of them were gentlemen of large fortune.[3]

Lady Stratford De Redcliffe arrived, and was on board the *Caradoc,* with Lord Stratford De Redcliffe, and the Bishop of Gibraltar. They used to come to the kitchen to see what went on, and I sent soup for them up to the hut, which was called the church, where they took their luncheon. I told Lady Stratford De Redcliffe about Miss Nightingale disclaiming me and others for insisting on coming to the Crimea, and then following us, and looking upon us as subject to her. She said that she herself

---

[3] 'In consequence of the absence of any provision for sick and wounded officers in hospital. by the War Office Regulations, the cooking for their service in the Castle, and General Hospitals in the Crimea, was entirely done by the female staff; part also of the materials for their use being supplied from private sources. And by the express desire of the medical officer in charge, the superintendent drew for them, wine, bread, and meat under the head of Nurses.' – Miss Nightingale's *Statements,* p. 28.

wished to retain me where I was, and that she considered Miss Nightingale to have no authority whatever at Balaclava.

Miss Nightingale called together a board of medical officers at the Castle Hospital, and herself took the chair when they assembled, although Dr Hall was there. Her object was to propose her new system for the management of the hospitals in the Crimea; but Dr Hall and Dr Anderson refused to entertain it.

On the Saturday before Miss Nightingale left Balaclava, after this first visit, Mr Bracebridge came to me in the kitchen, and said that he had settled with the other nurses, and was come to settle with me, and to pay me my wages, at ten shillings a week, from Miss Nightingale. I declined to have anything to do with him, and told him that I was not under Miss Nightingale,[4] that I did not wish to receive my wages until I returned to England, and that rather than accept so low a rate as ten shillings a week, which the most useless of the nurses could claim, I would go without them altogether.

He opened all the bales, of which Mrs Shaw Stewart had paid the freight, before he could find linen fine enough for Miss Nightingale's use on her voyage to Scutari. He took out table cloths – one being an Indian damask, four yards long – sheets, pillow. cases, linen chemises, long nightgowns, fine towels, and stockings, of which some were of lambs' wool, and others of cotton.

Mrs Bracebridge came from Scutari to fetch Miss Nightingale, who was still an invalid, and they returned together on board Lord Ward's yacht to Scutari.

On her return to Scutari, she sent Dr Hadley and Dr O'Connor

---

[4]   Mrs Davis always thought that Miss Nightingale's authority was limited to Turkey, and supported that opinion by referring to the certificate. Appendix A.

to superintend all the hospitals in the Crimea. They tried her system, and it came into operation there on the 15th of July, 1855.

The pitiful quantity of three quarters of a pound of arrowroot, was sent to me as the allowance for the supper of eighty-three men: before it came, however, I had fortunately made preparations for that meal in my usual way.[5] The next day I received a hundred and thirty-five screws – little paper parcels such as grocers put up – they contained rice, arrowroot, sago, sugar, and such things, and were sent to me from the stores under the new system adopted by the medical staff.

I arranged all the little packets on the table, and was going out to call Mr Fitzgerald to come and look at them, when I saw Dr Hall and two other gentlemen riding up the hill.

I asked him to come in. He did so, and his companions, Dr Taylor and Dr Hadley, who were then strangers to me, came in also. He inquired, "Mrs Davis, who has put your Welsh blood up today?"

I answered, "It would have been enough to put your Scotch blood up too, if you had been here."

I showed him the 'screws', and declared, as to this new plan, that I would not put up with it, and that I refused to obey such orders.

Dr Taylor said it would never do, and Dr Hall promised that things should be altered.

I was very angry, and said, "I wish I could but see that Hadley, I would give it him! A fellow come here to fatten himself upon what the poor men ought to have!"

---

[5]   Compare this and the following passages with *Eastern Hospitals*, 3rd edition, p. 313. 'During the whole day *little bits of rice, and grains of sugar* were continually arriving to be made into rice puddings; or scraps of arrowroot to be cooked, &c:'

Upon this, the three doctors burst out laughing – Dr Hadley, a little spare man, being one of them, although at that time I did not know him by sight.

On the following Saturday, Sergeant Gamble, of the 23rd, ran and called to me, "Nurse, nurse, here is Dr Hadley going up the yard."

"I asked, 'Which?'"

"That one on the grey horse."

The doctor turned to the surgery, and I said to him, "If you please, sir, is your name Hadley?"

"My name is Dr Hadley."

"Beg your pardon, sir, for not entitling you."

I then asked about the allowance of wine. One extra bottle was ordered to be kept in hand for urgent cases; the rest of the wine, spirits, arrowroot, and other medical comforts, were to be kept with the stores; leaving me with nothing else to supply any call that might be made for it at night. I used formerly to have abundant supplies of all these things ready in the kitchen.

I said, "I understand I am to be placed under the superintendent of the medical staff?"

"Certainly'," he replied.

"There are three of them," I remarked, "one between fifteen and sixteen years of age, one seventeen, and the other nineteen."

I knew their ages, for I had before asked the boys, and they had themselves told me.[6] I, therefore, refused to act under such

---

[6] Possibly the young surgeons might have understated their age on purpose to teaze Mrs Davis. The ignorance of many inexperienced medical officers as to the properties of different kinds of nutriment. and of the quantities proper for particular cases is mentioned by a friend of hers, one of the most efficient of the Female Nursing Staff – as causing much injury to the patients, and most lamentable waste in the consumption of provisions.

inexperienced persons, and said I would rather go home than do so. I added, "You will see whether I put up with such arrangements. I shall go to Miss Wear, and you shall know whether or not I procure the things which are required."

Miss Wear gave me a requisition – that is to say, a simple order on the store-keeper, signed by herself – and I had six dozen of port wine, six dozen of sherry, six dozen of brandy, a cask of rice, one of arrowroot, and one of sago, and a box of sugar.

When I had seen these things put ready for me, noticing the doctor in the purveyors office, I said to him, "Now, doctor, this is your new shop. Stop here five minutes, and you will see it all going into the kitchen."

As I went out, I overheard Mr Fitzgerald say to him, "That woman would be cheap to the government at a thousand a year."

Mr E_____, a clerk there, told me afterwards, that Dr Hadley had answered, "We must not let her go home just now. We must indulge her a little. "

One day after that, I went into the purveyor's office, and saw Dr Hall, and other medical officers, and joked with them about Dr Hadley, 'indulging' me.

From that time I went on in my old course, and got what I liked from the purveyor, for the bad cases. Dr Hadley and I were afterwards very good friends.

I had all that were left of Mrs Shaw Stewart's stores in charge, to give out at my own discretion. All the free gifts were disposed of in the same way, by the superintendent's orders, to the nurses, or else sent by the fatigue parties to the camp.

There was no deficiency in supplies from Mr Fitzgerald. He

was always ready to furnish what was asked for him from his stores; and when things were wanting there, he was diligent in buying them from the ships, or elsewhere. He was a good and kind-hearted man, and a clever, hardworking man, who did his duty well. He spoke several languages, and was thus enabled to talk to the different people, and to be very useful. When he showed the kitchen to visitors – which he often did – he used to remark, "There is cleanliness, and no waste."

In one thing only I adopted the new system. I allowed the orderlies to procure the fowls which the doctors ordered, and to feather and truss them ready for cooking. Their doing so saved me trouble, and I was glad to be relieved from it, for there was much to be done in that kitchen at Balaclava.

The fowls were killed in the fowl-house yard, and brought ready feathered to the kitchen. I never but once saw a fowl that had been skinned. It was done by a new orderly, who was ignorant of his work.

As long as I remained at Balaclava, I cooked the fowls myself.

If provisions were brought in too late, whether fowls or anything else, I refused to cook them that day. This taught the orderlies to be punctual.

I always liked Dr Hall. He would listen to reason.

Dr_____ was the greatest simpleton I ever saw in a hospital, or anywhere else. He did not know what a diet roll was, and I have been three days together without receiving one from him.

I could speak only my native Welsh, and English, although I understood a few phrases in foreign languages.

Miss Wear spoke not only English, but also French and Italian.

She was therefore highly valued in the hospital as an intepreter.

General Ansaldi arrived at the camp with the first division of the Sardinian army. He was a noble-looking old officer, more than seventy years of age.

As he was riding out on horseback one day, he was shot by a chance ball above the knee. The ball was extracted, and he was kept roughly nursed at the camp for ten days. He suffered dreadful pain, and consented at last to be brought down to the General Hospital.

Miss Wear had contrived to hang up white calico in the ward, so as to give to each bed the appearance of a little separate chamber.

The general was very ill, and Miss Wear and the doctors were very attentive to him. He had exerted himself too much, and striven against suffering until his strength quite failed. I used to visit him, and to feed him, for which he always tried to show that he felt obliged to me. He was a good man, and very gentle and polite in his manners.

In dressing and poulticing his wound, I noticed that the bone was touched, and, considering his age, and exhaustion, I feared that he could not get over it.

His aides-de-camp and friends sat up with him the first two nights, and Miss Wear herself sat up with him through the third night.

The following morning she came to me, and said that since daybreak the general had slept for an hour, that he had less pain, and that she thought him a good deal better.

She asked me to come and see him, and I went. Three doctors were with him. The wound was uncovered, and they were looking at it.

I said to Dr M_____, "How is the general, now'?"

As soon as the general heard my voice, he put his hand out, to shake hands with me.

Dr M_____, answering my question, said cheerfully,

"He is a great deal better."

I remarked softly, "I don't like the look of his face, it is too blue." He seemed to be free from pain, and I saw by a glance at the wound that mortification had taken place.

It was then about eight o'clock, and I told the doctors that I thought he would not live four hours.

He died at half-past eleven the same morning.

He was very much beloved by his own countrymen. The officers of his staff used constantly to come down from the camp to make inquiries after him. When they arrived that day and heard that he was gone, they cried as if they had lost their father. Many of them alighted, went in, looked at him, and kissed him.

Afterwards, they returned in form, with General La Marmora, and a guard of honour, to fetch away the corpse for burial. Miss Wear spoke with them in Italian, delivered up the dead general, and received the thanks of the Sardinians for the kindness and care which had been shown to him in the hospital.

Supplement to Chapter 8

The writer having applied to Miss Wear, the late superintendent of nurses at Balaclava, for some particulars connected with Mrs Davis's account of the Sardinian general, has been favoured, in return, with a letter which contains, among other things, the following interesting statement:

'In May, cholera cases rapidly increased in our hospital. On the morning of the 24th, Captain Tossetti was brought to me. As it was too early for the authorities to be on duty, I had to take upon myself to receive him in the best manner I could. No officer having, as yet, been in hospital since I had been at Balaclava, there was no place but the general wards. I hastily chose a corner in No. 6, had it cleared out, and prepared, with my own hands, a comfortable bed; added a little table, chair, clean towels, &c., &c., and thus my poor patient was quickly and comfortably lodged. The authorities quite approved of all I had done, and allowed me to put up table-cloths, &c., thus screening off the rest of the ward, and leaving a square corner, which took in a large window. This was the first beginning of the Officers' Ward in Balaclava Hospital.

'Captain Tossetti only lived thirty hours. I sat up through the night, as did also, by turns, two medical men. He was prepared for burial like the men, being sewn up in a blanket, and left in the dead-tent. The next morning, six or seven brother officers came to accompany the cart that took his remains to interment. I went with them to the tent, and lest there might be any mistake (for there were many there), I had the blanket opened, and the Sardinians gazed on the face of their dead comrade in sadness. They thanked me very much, and I hurried away, sick at heart, not to give way to my own feelings, but to go to my trying daily work.

'The little corner in No. 6, was quietly occupied again, others came, and other little divisions were made. Ultimately the whole ward was given up to officers, being divided into six compartments. The next most painful death was that of Colonel de Rossi. He was brought to me on the evening of the 17th of June. Never can I forget the sad hours I passed by the bedside of this much loved and regretted officer. It was a moment of general excitement – everyone who could be spared, or who could get an animal, was mounting to go and see the preparations for the next day's engagement. Colonel de Rossi's case was one of the most violent cholera I ever witnessed. He was lead colour, and the cramps so violent that it was all his aides-de-camp, and another soldier could do to rub him. There was from the first no chance of saving him. The doctor of the ward remained all night – only reposing for an hour or two on a mattress in the church – and I never went to my hut until the following evening. In the night, I sent for the clergyman. My poor patient remained sensible to the last, spoke to me of his wife and mother, and appeared to die resigned. In the morning some Sardinians came into the ward, but did not approach the bed. I was considered rash in continuing to attend him, but, thank God, no fancy of danger ever came into my mind. He died between one and two p.m. I performed the last offices for him, and then returned to my work. The hospital, which had been almost deserted during the night, was now becoming a scene of great bustle. Many will remember the fatal 18th of June, 1855. I was worn out in body and mind, but there was no rest for me. Poor Mr Stowe came down from the camp that day, alas! to die.

* * *

'I hope Davis is well. She is ever to be depended on, good, honest and devoted.

May 14th 1857.'

Chapter 9

Here let us
Review the series of our lives, and taste
The melancholy joy of evils passed;
For he who much has suffered much will know,
And pleased remembrance builds delight on woe.

Pope's *Odyssey*, Book XV, p. 423

Crimean Experience of Hospital Life: Part III
Miss Nightingale's Second Visit to Balaclava – Failure of
the Heroine's Health – Visit to Sebastopol – Departure
from Balaclava – Supplement.

Early in October, Miss Nightingale came again to Balaclava.
She and her maid,[1] who was always following like her
shadow, slept at our hospital on the first night after their
arrival. The very day she landed, she came to me in the
kitchen, about eight o'clock. I always know the hour by
remembering what I was doing at the time. She had just
ordered me to shut both the doors, as she was going to place
great confidence in me, when her maid came after her, and
said, "My dear lady, you must have something to eat. You
have not eaten anything for the last three days."

---

[1] For an account of Mrs Roberts, and just encomium on her previous
services, the reader is referred to a pamphlet, entitled 'Facts
concerning Hospital Nurses', written by Mr South, Senior Surgeon of
St. Thomas's Hospital.

Miss Nightingale said, "No; go and get your own supper. I will take a little arrowroot with Mrs Davis."

The maid chose bread and cheese, with which I supplied her, offering her at the same time brandy and water, or wine and water. Beer was out of my department – of this I only received sufficient for the nurses. She raised her hands in silent amazement at my having such things to offer, took what she required, and then went to their rooms.

Miss Nightingale had some arrowroot, which I made for her with port wine in it. She said that it was beautiful, and asked if I made it thus for the men. I told her that I did. She asked, "Is it not too thick for them?" I answered, "Not a bit."

When she had eaten it, she resumed the subject of her confidence which she was about to place in me, and requested me to fasten both the doors.

I said I could not do that from within; but that, if I shut them, it would do as well – no one being allowed to come in without knocking.

She said that I must not prejudice her nurses, and added, "I want to know your opinion of them – I have sent the best here."

I answered, "You know more about them than I do."

She enquired, "Do you think the reports about them are true?"

"I have heard no reports; but all I can say is they are very fond of drinking; and if these are your best, your nurses are not good for much."

"Whose fault is it?" Miss Nightingale asked.

I replied that I supposed drinking too much must be their own fault; and said, "You know nothing about me. I don't want you to place confidence in me."

She said, "I have heard a great deal about you. About Mrs D, did you see anything wrong? She is one of my best nurses."

"I only wish you had never sent her here; and if you wish to know more, you must apply to Miss Wear."

She inquired about Mrs L. I said I did not think she was a clever nurse. The she asked, "What was the crime of Mrs S?"

I told her that I did not know of any crime she had committed, and again referred to Miss Wear, the superintendent, as I did not desire to prejudice her.

She next inquired how Mrs W had broken her leg.

I said, "Mrs W need not have done it: she was not sober."

Miss Nightingale checked me, saying, "Mind what you say!"

I replied, "I know what I say, and I will stand to it. You had better not ask me questions, unless you wish to hear the truth."

On the following Saturday Miss Nightingale again came to the kitchen to have a confidential conference with me. She asked if I had heard anything about the nurses at the Castle.[2]

I said I did not doubt that if the walls could speak, they could tell tales. I knew things only from hearsay; by the men talking together about the surgeons and nurses.

Miss Nightingale afterwards sent Miss Wear to fetch me to confront Dr J, and to speak before him of what was going on at the Castle ruins. I denied having mentioned his name, or any one else's, and declared that I knew only of what people did generally, and by report.

---

[2] In the winter after the establishment of the Castle Hospital, two hospitals were set up at Karani, for the use of the Land Transport Corps. Female nurses were employed in them from March 1856, until the end of June.

Dr Hall having given orders to build the wooden hospital in front of the camp, Miss Nightingale came over this second time to establish her authority there.

She had a hut at the Castle,[3] and used to walk down to the General Hospital, to visit Miss Wear. She scarcely ever entered the wards – never, except on special occasions. One day she went there to see a French officer, who was a patient in No. 6.

She did not in any way interfere with me.

I learned from the orderlies that she did not visit the wards at the Castle Hospital, nor interfere with its arrangements. It was said that she spent her time chiefly in writing.

Miss Nightingale used sometimes to come to the extra-diet kitchen. Once she said that she wished to see the extras given out, and inquired the hour at which it was done.

I said, "At ten o'clock."

She stated her orders were that none should be given out at that hour.

I told her that I did not attend to anybody's orders when I did what I knew was for the best, being acquainted with the wants of the poor men.

---

[3] This was the second in date of the Crimean hospitals. It was opened in April 1855, and constantly attended by female nurses until June 1856. In Guthrie's *Tour through the Taurida*, p. 111, this place is described as follows:

'On the mountain to the right, as you enter this port from the sea, you discover the ruins of a Genoese fort, the works of which, running all round the brow of the hill, seem to have been of such extent as to contain a small town within it. This outwork, or fortified wall, was once defended by twelve or thirteen turrets, three of which are much larger than the rest, more particularly one, which seems to have been a second fort of itself.'

One day about twelve o'clock, which was the dinner time, Miss Nightingale and her maid came in from the Castle. I was busy sending out the extras for the patients on half diet.

I was irritated at being interrupted, and said, "You must please to walk out. I don't want petticoats here."

There were perhaps as many as thirty orderlies in the kitchen, and I was cutting up fowls and putting things ready for them to carry away.

Seeing the necessity of the case, she went away; and when the hurry was over, she came back again, and said, "You were in a bad humour, Mrs Davis."

I denied it, for I did not consider just displeasure as bad humour. She said, "I thought you were. You spoke very sharply."

I told her that I was very busy, and thought that she would not like to be there among the common men. So she went away again. Miss Wear used to go up to the Monastery[4] once a week to overlook what was going on there. A horse was provided for her, and she rode there and back. She was an excellent horsewoman.

Hearing that the great attack was to be made upon the Redan, and knowing that the camp itself would be the most

[4] In Guthrie's *Tour*, Balaclava is mentioned (p. 109) as 'the most unhealthy spot of all the Taurida'. The third volume of the *Cambro Briton*, pp. 332-5, contains a letter signed 'Geirion', which treats of the Taurica Chersonesus as the Gwlâd yr Hâf, or Summer Land, from which the Cymry came to Britain, and assigns a Celtic origin to the word Balaclava. i.e. 'Bala', signifying an efflux or outlet; 'claf', sick or ill, and 'a', a termination, denoting collection or production. 'Geirion', having met with Mrs Guthrie's description, found there what appeared to him a confirmation of his previous conjecture.

suitable place for assisting the wounded men, Miss Wear and I offered our services to go up – but they were not accepted.

Dr Fraser wished me to come, but Dr Hall decided that I had better not quit the General Hospital at Balaclava until the new arrangements were completed.

Miss Wear waited for the arrival of the Sisters of Mercy from Koulali to succeed her at Balaclava, before she removed to the Monastery to undertake the office of superintendent there.

I can testify that during her stay at the General Hospital, soldiers and civilians, of all ranks and of all nations, were equally cared for, and nursed with unremitting attention, and impartial kindess.

Strong as I was, I overtasked my strength at last, for I got too little rest at night.

My health became very bad. The atmosphere of the hospital was unhealthy and everybody saw that I had been working too hard. I suffered from diarrhoea and dysentery.

Dr Hall was very anxious that I should have change of air, and he advised that I should be sent to Smyrna, Malta, or the South of France; fearing that if I went to England I should not return from thence, and wanting me at the new hospital at the front.

He told Miss Nightingale that my health was failing; she came down, and proposed to send me to whichever of those places I might choose, and at her own expense.

Seeing that I was bent on returning to my own country, she gave me a week to consider the subject, hoping that I should change my mind. When this time had elapsed, she came again to learn my decision.

She inquired whether I had made up my mind to go to Smyrna, Malta, or the South of France.

I told her that I had made up my mind to go home, and

nowhere else, for I thought I should not live long, and I did not like the idea of dying in a foreign land.

She desired me to promise to return to her when I got better. I said that I would promise Dr Hall and Miss Wear, if I got better, to go to them.

She said, "You won't come to me then?"

I told her that if I lived to come back, I could not go to both, and I would go to Dr Hall.

She then said that she would settle with me, and pay me my wages, adding, "Your wages are ten shillings a-week."

This was the lowest rate at which any nurse could be paid, under the agreement made with Mr Sidney Herbert.

I said, "If I cannot have what I am entitled to, which is more than that, I will have none at all. I do not want money here, and I would rather wait and be paid in England."

Miss Nightingale told me that no one could pay me but herself, and that I must go without the money if I did not take it then. At last she yielded, and said that she would make it up at the rate of eighteen shillings for two months, and the rest at ten shillings, and that she would atone for that by giving me five pounds as a present.

I said I could earn more in England, and that the doctors could recommend me to the Government.

She said, that one word from her would have more effect with the Government than all that the doctors could say. She then promised to look out for a ship, in which I might have a passage to England.

I did not wish her to do so, and observed that Mr Fitzgerald could find me a ship.

She then went away. She afterwards wrote to Miss Wear, and named a ship for me.

Miss Wear went to see it, and would not allow me to embark in it, for there were none on board but men.

I did not give up the charge of the extra-diet kitchen, until the day before I came away from Balaclava.[4] On the arrival of the Sisters of Mercy, I cooked for them. They afterwards had the possession of my kitchen; and, acting under the new system, to which I never would submit, they found the inconvenience and discomfort attending it.

Miss Nightingale had brought to Balaclava ten cart-loads of packages, which were taken to the storehouses, where the goods from the *Paramatta* had been stowed. All I ever saw were four bales. They were brought into my kitchen, for want of any other place of stowage, and Miss Wear requested me to let them come. The lower parts of the wrappers were rotten. I did not know what they contained, until afterwards, when Mrs Bridgman, the Superior of the Sisters of Mercy, came one day to examine them. The bottoms of the bales were placed uppermost, and were open from rottenness. She took out two new shirts, one of blue striped cotton, and one of brown calico, and unfolding them said, "Look here, nurse!"

They dropped in four pieces each, in the creases. Mrs Bridgman, Sister Mary Chaucer, and myself turned up the bales and read the inscription on each. It was "Free Gifts. New Shirts".

The first bale was small, it contained eighty-seven; another contained ninety-nine; another ninety-seven, and the largest a hundred and two. They were all in the same state, and so far as we could see, were rotten throughout.

They were not injured at Balaclava, but appeared to have been brought in that state from Scutari. All the shirts were new, and some of them fine.

Mrs Bridgman said while looking over them, "What a shame, and what a pity!"

One day before this, Miss Nightingale had come to the kitchen, and touching the bales with her parasol, asked me what they were.

I said, "You should know, I don't. They are not good for anything." I spoke myself to Captain Heath, the harbour master, about my passage home. He told me that I should go in a first-class ship, for I deserved it.

My passage was taken on board the *Calcutta*. The Friday before she sailed, ill as I was, I went in an Irish car with some of my acquaintances, to see Sebastopol. On a steep and narrow part of the cliff, as we went up, we met a Sardinian waggon, heavily loaded, coming down. The road was not wide enough for the car and the waggon to pass each other properly, and the wheel caught and tore one of my feet; both were hanging over, and must have been torn off, had not the waggoner suddenly whipped his horses, which started aside, and fell with the waggon and its load headlong over the cliff.

I walked about to see the ruins, notwithstanding my wounded foot, but it afterwards inflamed, and got very bad.

My friends wanted to detain me on account of it, and the doctors came about me like bees, trying to persuade me not to embark until the wound got better; but I was determined to go.

Miss Wear came with me on board, and charged the surgeons and nurses to take good care of me.

It was on the Saturday morning when I left Balaclava, that Mrs Grundy came hastily down from Miss Nightingale, who was still at the Castle Hospital. Mrs Grundy came with me on board, and stayed until after Miss Wear had gone on shore.

She then said, "Oh! Mrs Davis, I have a parcel for you from Miss Nightingale. I think it is money." She took a packet out of her pocket and gave it to me.

I opened it, and found, I think, £3 16s. in it, besides an order on Mr. Glyn's bank for £36 12s., leaving one week short unpaid for. There was also a memorandum, recommending me to the War Office for a gratuity of one year's pay, at eighteen shillings a week.

The *Calcutta* sailed from Balaclava, and brought me back an invalid to England.

When I was a little girl, attending the day and Sunday schools at Bala, Mr Charles gave me a small Welsh Bible, as a reward for my attention to learning. That Bible has been my constant companion ever since, and has guided and kept me right through all my wanderings.

Supplement to Chapter 9

I meant to have ended my history with my return to England from the Crimea, but I have since made some discoveries connected with the British Army Hospitals, with which, I think, the public ought to be acquainted. I have mentioned in the eighteenth chapter, that I spent some days in the Barrack Hospital at Scutari, that I saw there nurses waiting in vain, like myself, for employment, while the wards and corridors were filled with grievously sick and wounded men; and that I also found there articles of clothing and use, and delicacies of diet, kept from the patients, who were the true owners, to their hurt, and rotting to waste, while the poor soldiers suffered from the want of them.

I heard at that time much more than my short stay allowed

me to see of the miserable mismanagement going on in the hospital. Since I came back to England, I have often conversed with ladies, nurses, and patients from Scutari, and I have found the opinion I at first formed of the 'system' which was pursued there, confirmed and strengthened.

While I was in the Crimea, working under Mrs Shaw Stewart, and Miss Wear, in succession, the Free Gifts which reached Balaclava Hospital were distributed fairly and freely among the sick and needy. But, compared with the quantities sent out and received at Scutari, very few were delivered to us, and some of these were good for nothing from want of proper care and stowage.

It often troubles me to think how many poor soldiers might have been comforted by the clothes and food which were thrown away unfit for use.

I lately paid a visit to a friend of mine at Woolwich. I found that Government Stores and Free Gifts were selling there by whole sale. Crowds of Jews and dealers came from far and near to purchase them. Articles of clothing had been returned from the Crimea to Woolwich; and articles of food, such as flour, biscuits, cocoa, &c., to Deptford.

I went to a shop at Woolwich, and asked if they had goods on sale from the Crimea? The man answered, "Plenty."

He showed me various things, and I bought of him as curiosities several articles of wearing apparel, both linen and calico – the cast off clothing of rich people – from among the Free Gifts. I have also bought new clothes and handkerchiefs, which I knew to be Free Gifts.

I think the poor soldiers, or the widows and children of those who died in the war hospitals, ought to have the worth of all the valuable things which were sent out for their benefit, as they did not have the things themselves. I hope they will have it.

I know that large sales by auction of Free Gifts, consisting of cutlery, hosiery, mercery, eatables, wearing apparel, and blankets, are taking place in London. I have an auctioneer's placard, advertising goods as 'Direct from the Crimea'; and there are several shops, in obscure parts of the city, where such things are kept for sale, some by wholesale, and others by retail.

Notice

In the decline of life and with broken health, the Heroine of this narrative is left unprovided for.

She is anxious to obtain employment in some public institution, and is still fully capable of executing any office of trust and vigilant inspection.

Benevolent readers who may wish to constribute to the comfort of her latter years, can pay in subscriptions for her, either to Mr Murgatroyd, 18, Stafford Row, Pimlico; or to Mr John Brown, 9, Hans Place, Sloane Street.

Appendix A

Testimonials

Miss Wear to Mrs Davis (Elizabeth Cadwaladyr)

General Hospital, Balaclava,
October 3rd, 1855.

My Dear Mrs Davis,

Trusting it may be for the benefit of your valuable health, I consent to part with you, but your going away is a serious loss to me. I cannot hope to find anyone who will do all you have done so long, so untiring, and often where all others equally ill would have remained in bed; for never, for one single day, during six months in this climate, and in the pestilential air of this hospital did you desert your post: up early and late, and ever preparing comforts for between two and three hundred sick!

Should it please God to restore you to sufficient health and strength, I should indeed be happy to have you again with me, and your position at the Monastery would not be so fatiguing as here. Do not fail to let me hear of you; and trusting you may have a safe journey, and be as well as I wish you,

Believe me ever,
Your sincere friend,
Margaret Wear

* * *

Miss Wear to the Hon Mrs Sidney Herbert

General Hospital, Balaclava,
October 3rd, 1855.

Madam,

May I hope you will forgive my recalling myself to your remembrance? In doing which allow me to express my gratitude for having been recommended by you to this mission. However anxious I was to come out, I am now still more anxious to remain – so completely am I devoted to the undertaking, and grateful to you for having been the means of placing me here.

I now take the liberty of strongly recommending to you the bearer, Mrs Davis, who has acted as diet cook during my residence in this hospital. Nothing that can be said would be more than is justly due to this 'faithfulest of Her Majesty's Nurses', this respectable and truly good woman, who has sacrificed her health, almost life, for the good of her suffering countrymen.

I trust to your kindness to afford her the protection and patronage she so justly merits; and begging to apologize for these few lines,

I remain, Madam,
Your most obedient servant,
M. Wear [1]

* * *

[1] On Mrs Davis's personal delivery of this letter, Mrs Sidney Herbert returned it to her, saying, "Should I hear of anything likely to suit you, I will let you know." Nothing has since been done for her, and she has not heard further.

I have much pleasure in recording my opinion of the extreme merits of Mrs Davis. Since her arrival here in January, she has been in charge of the Extra Kitchen of the hospital. In winter, I have seen her up at six and seven o'clock in the morning; and at my departure from the hospital at night, at and after eleven o'clock, I have left her up and doing. Throughout the night her services were available – willing and cheerful on all occasions. In the heats of summer her services were equally extensive and unremitting, amidst fires and numerous calls. She was extensively trusted; and my most minute observation could only trace in her the utmost honesty and steadiness. Many a patient appreciated and thanked her kindess of disposition and heart, and in every particular she has proved herself to be of most excellent character. I cannot too highly speak of her, or recommend her to the favourable consideration of the authorities, now that she leaves for England, unable longer to continue her valuable services from ill-health, occasioned by her zealous and continuous application to business.

> *David Fitzgerald,*
> *Purveyor to the Forces,*
> *General Hospital,*
> *Balaklava.*
> *November 3rd, 1855.*

* * *

Mrs Davis has been nurse, and in charge of the Extra Diet Kitchen, during the six months I have been in superintendence of the hospitals at Balaclava, and I cannot speak in too high terms of Mrs Davis's universal good conduct, and her unremitting attention to the sick during this period. Mrs Davis's health having suffered of late – she goes home at her own request.

> *Henry Hadley*
> *Staff Surgeon,*
> *Principal Medical Officer of Balaclava.*
> *Balaclava, November 3rd, 1855.*

* * *

> *War Department, Pall Mall,*
> *December 26th, 1856.*

Mrs Davis,

His Imperial Majesty, the Sultan, having been pleased to place at the disposal of her Majesty's government a sum of money for the benefit of the ladies and nurses, who served in the British hospitals on the Bosphorus, and in the Crimea, I am directed to inform you that the share of each paid nurse, entitled to participate in this gift, is £ 7 4s. 3d., and the general agent, Sir John Kirkland, has been directed to issue that sum to you accordingly.

I am to add that the Secretary of State for War has much pleasure in conveying to you the approbation of her Majesty's government, of the services you rendered to the soldiers of the British army, in our hospitals in the East.

I am

Your obedient servant,

> *B. Hawes.*

* * *

Memorandum of agreement, made this 1st day of December, 1854, between Miss Nightingale on the one part, and Mrs _____, of _____, on the other part:

Whereas the said Miss Nightingale, superintendent, has undertaken to provide female nurses for the sick and wounded of the British army serving in Turkey; and in carrying out this object, she has engaged to employ the said Mrs _, in the capacity of nurse, at a weekly salary, varying from ten to eighteen shillings, according to merit; and also to provide board and lodging; also to pay all expenses attendant upon the journeying to or from the present or any future hospital that may be appointed for the accommodation of the sick and wounded of the said army; and to pay all expenses of return to this country, should sickness render it necessary for the said Mrs_____ to return, save and except such return shall be rendered necessary by the discharge of the said Mrs _____ for neglect of duty, immoral conduct, or intoxication, in which case the said Mrs_____ shall forfeit all claim upon Miss Nightingale from the period of such discharge. And the said Mrs_____ hereby agrees to devote her whole time and attention to the purposes aforesaid, under the directions, and to the satisfaction of the said superintendent, the whole of whose orders she undertakes to obey until discharged by the said superintendent.

Signed

Witness, Elizabeth Herbert.[2]

---

[2]   The whole of the above document was in lithograph, excepting the date, signatures, and figures, which were written with pen and ink.

In the form of this agreement signed by Roman Catholics, a clause was inserted binding them not to speak on religious subjects, excepting with patients of their own persuasion. It was understood that professors of all creeds might be accepted for the work, but no other restriction was laid on Protestants, previous to quitting England, than 'a general caution not to interfere with the faith of others'.

* * *

Copy of the Nurses' Certificate
I hereby certify that Mrs Davis has been appointed to act as nurse under the orders of the superintendent of female nurses for the British army hospitals in Turkey, under the control of the chief medical officer of the hospital at Scutari, or elsewhere in the East.
   Andrew Smith, M.D., Director-General,
        Army and Ordnance, Medical Department.

* * *

OFFICIAL CIRCULAR
To the Nurses about to join the Army Hospitals in the East

It having been stated that the Nurses who have gone to the East, complained of being subject to hardships and rules of which they were not previously informed, and of having to do work different to what they expected, it has been thought desirable to state several points relating to their duties and position as Nurses, under the new and hitherto untried circumstances of female attendants in Military Hospitals, of which they must necessarily be ignorant.

In the selection of Nurses for this purpose the utmost pains were taken to secure such as would be competent for the service required, and who possessed testimonials of high principles and good character. It is a subject of painful regret that in many instances these testimonials have not been borne out by the results.

1st – It seems hardly necessary to state, that at the very outset, in the journey itself, there will be many trials, notwithstanding all the care taken for the comfort of the party. Those accustomed to travel can hardly realize the inevitable difficulties and annoyances of travelling with a large party – the crowded accommodation, the hurry and fatigue which must be borne, the different tempers and habits of a large band of strangers brought together suddenly, which will cause a constant and hourly demand for the exercise of mutual forbearance and self-denial, and cheerful and ready submission to orders, without which all will be confusion.

Undertaken and borne in the right spirit, on the other hand, the journey may become a bond of union amongst those who were previously unknown to one another, and who then meet for the first time on a common mission.

2nd – It must be remembered that although the object for which the Nurses are engaged is to nurse the soldiers in hospital, it is impossible to foresee from day to day what may be required from those who are to fulfil that duty in a Military Hospital in a foreign country.

It is therefore very important that none should undertake this duty who are not prepared and willing to perform every branch of work which lies within a woman's province, such as washing, sewing, cooking, housekeeping, house cleaning – all these have been in turn required from those who have already gone out, and may be again.

3rd – In case of illness amongst the Nurses, it is hoped that the patient herself will endeavour to bear the inevitable privations and inconveniences to which she will be exposed, with patience and cheerfulness, and that her fellow-workers will consider it a part of their duty as well as a pleasure, to give her every attention and assistance possible.

4th – The rules of each Hospital will vary according to circumstances, of which none but the Authorities on the spot are fully informed; the Nurses must therefore bear in mind that such rules must be implicitly obeyed, whatever their own habits and judgment may be.

What may appear strict and unnecessary to them, is probably imposed in consequence of finding that a less rigid rule would not suffice for the maintenance of order and discipline. For instance, the Nurses are not allowed to leave their quarters for exercise, or even for their appointed work, unless two go together.

5th – It has been the intention of Government throughout to include persons of all creeds in this labour of Mercy, and it is earnestly requested that all will endeavour to work together in Love, bearing one another's burdens, and so fulfilling the law of Christ.

In order that no difficulties should arise respecting religious intercourse with the patients, the War Office has recently issued the following Instructions to Lord W. Paulett and other Commandants of the Hospitals in the East; to the effect:

'That no Protestant or Roman Catholic Chaplain should, in any way, directly or indirectly, interfere with the religious opinions of any person whatever belonging or professing to belong to a Church or Creed different from that of which the Chaplain, Protestant or Catholic, is an appointed minister.

'And that with regard to Protestant Ladies or Nurses attached to the Hospitals, it is to be a clear and well understood Rule, that they are in no case to be used as religious instructors or teachers by direction of any Protestant Chaplain, and that they are not to enter upon the discussion of religious subjects with any patients other than those of their own faith.

'With regard to the Roman Catholic Nuns, or Sisters of Mercy, they are strictly to confine themselves also within the rule, which is laid down for their guidance by the proper authorities of their own Church, and to which they distinctly assented when nominated to the office, the duties of which they undertook.[3]

'Your lordship will accordingly make these rules generally known, with the clear understanding that anyone holding an office in the Hospital who shall infringe them, must at once be suspended, and finally removed from their respective situations.

'Lord Panmure, however, trusts that no such painful duty will be imposed upon him, and that all parties will consider it a paramount duty to abstain from interfering with the religious faith or opinions of those of a different Church or Creed from

[3] 'The greatest caution being necessary on all hands in the matter of religion, the Sisters of Mercy will hold themselves free to introduce such subjects only with patients of their own faith.' – *Extract from the War Office Document. Signed by Dr Grant, R.C. Bishop of Southwark, October 24th, 1854.*

their own. Unless, indeed, such a course is strictly observed, it is clear the Hospitals may become the scene of religious dissensions and animosities, not more injurious to the peace and welfare of the sick, than calculated to mar the efficacy of those works of mercy and charity so pre-eminently inculcated upon us by the common religion we profess.'

In conclusion, all are intreated to remember the responsible position in which an Englishwoman going out to nurse her countrymen in a foreign country is placed.

On the one hand, by any misconduct, she brings discredit on her sex and countrywomen – on the other, by doing the work as unto God, with all her heart and mind and strength, she will be doing honour to her Queen and her country.

July, 1855.

* * *

In a letter addressed to _____ and dated from the War Office, October 21ˢᵗ, 1854, Mr Sidney Herbert said, alluding to the numerous ladies who had offered themselves to serve as nurses in the military hospitals:

'Nor even if capable in other respects would they always be ready to yield that implicit obedience to orders so necessary to the subordination of a military hospital.

'The government have come to the conclusion that the best mode of obviating these dangers and inconveniences would be to appoint some one person, on whose energy, experience and discretion they can rely, who should be the one authority to select, to superintend, and direct in the British General Hospitals in Turkey, a staff of female nurses, herself acting under the immediate orders of the medical authorities. Miss

Nightingale, who has, I believe, greater practical experience of hospital administration than any other lady in this country, has, with a self-devotion for which I have no words to express my gratitude, undertaken this noble but arduous work. She will act in the strictest subordination to the chief medical officer of the hospital; and the nurses who accompany, or who follow her, will, in the same manner, be placed completely under her authority, nor will anyone be admitted as a hospital nurse except she have a certificate signed by the Director General of the Army Medical Department upon Miss Nightingale's recommendation, or that of some person deputed by her. I trust that all confusion will be avoided by this arrangement.'

Guardian, October 25th, 1854.

Appendix B

Immediately a place
Before his eyes appeared, sad, noisome, dark –
A lazar-house it seemed, wherein were laid
Numbers of all diseased; all maladies
Of ghostly spasm, or racking torture – qualms
Of heart-sick agony, all feverous kinds
Convulsions, epilepsies, fierce catarrhs,
Intestine stone and ulcer – cholic pangs,
Demoniac phrenzy, moping melancholy,
And moon-struck madness – pining atrophy,
Marasmus and wide-wasting pestilence
Dropsies and asthmas, and joint-racking rheums.
Dire was the tossing, deep the groans; Despair
Tended the sick, busiest, from couch to couch;
And over them, triumphant Death his dart
Shook, but delayed to strike, though oft invoked
With vows as their chief good and final hope.

Paradise Lost, Book xi., 477-93.

Balaclava Hospital
Observations on the State of Public Feeling during the Crimean War – Appointment of a Commission of Inquiry into the State of the Military Hospitals in the East – Depositions relative to the Sick and Wounded and the Buildings – Accommodation and Supplies at the General Hospital, Balaclava.

In order to enable the reader to realize the scenes and circumstances described in the latter part of Elizabeth Davis's narration as well as to estimate the difficulties of her position, and the importance of her services, it is necessary that some additional facts should be distinctly brought forward.

The regular and speedy communications established between Britain and many distant regions, the rapid transmission of intelligence from Turkey and the Crimea, and the activity of the public press in the home diffusion of foreign news, during the late Eastern war, tended constantly to keep alive the attention of the British public, and thus to secure more general and kindly sympathy for our soldiers, than was ever before manifested for any troops on foreign service.

The long preceding peace of Europe, the unbroken practice of industrious arts and quiet labours, the existence of a majority among the population to whom war was known only as an old tradition, or a distant rumour, caused surprise to mingle with compassion at the first information which reached Britain of the occurrence of the sufferings inalienably incident to warlike operations. The aggravation of those sufferings, by the addition of needless privation, disease, anguish and death, soon wrought those kindly feelings into a furious storm of popular indignation against the most conspicuous persons whose incompetence had produced these diastrous results: but every attempt subsequently made to alleviate the miseries of our Crimean army was viewed with favour, and applauded with enthusiasm.

The appointment of Miss Nightingale to the superintendence of the volunteer gentlewomen and nurses going forth to be employed in the British hospitals in Turkey, was generally received as a pledge, that henceforth the comforts and consolations of home, would encompass there each sick and wounded soldier.

Meanwhile, a committee was appointed to investigate the affairs which had been obviously misconducted in Turkey and in the Crimea, and to suggest fit remedies for existing evils. The Commissioners first named, were Dr Alexander Cumming, M.D., Dr Thomas Spencer, M.D., and Mr P. Benson Maxwell.

On the death of Dr Spencer, Mr P. Sinclair Laing took his place, and assisted in the final preparation of the Report.

In the Report made by the Commissioners to the Duke of Newcastle, upon the condition and wants of the sick and wounded of the British army in the East, and their hospital accommodation and provision, from the invasion of the Crimea, Sept. 14th, 1854, to the date of the report. Feb. 23rd, 1855, the Commissioners divide the subject into four collateral parts.

The first relating to the means of transport, provision and treatment, on the earliest occurrence of sickness or wounds.

The second, relating to the hospital accommodation, provision, and treatment in the field, and at Balaclava.

The third, relating to the same on board the transport ships, which conveyed the sick and wounded from the Crimea to Turkey; and the fourth, relating to the accommodation, provision and treatment in the established hospitals in Turkey.

We proceed to extract from this blue-book a short series of passages, which we have so arranged as to present a clear view of the condition of the patients of Balaclava Hospital, previous to, and immediately upon the arrival in the Crimea of female nurses from England.

It would have been easy to relate the painful narrative

succinctly, but in a case of this kind the evidence in detail of eyewitnesses and agents is invaluable.

At page 118 of the appendix to this report, Dr Marlow, surgeon to the 28th Regiment, after some preliminary observations, states:

'I am inclined to enumerate, amongst the chief causes of disease:

1. Inadequate shelter when off duty.
2. Irregularity in the rationing.
3. Want of sufficient clothing.
4. Almost incessant duty, and consequent exposure.

The last of the causes assigned is, as a matter of course, unavoidable, and may be at once dismissed. But with regard to the first, a few words may be said.

The tents at present in possession of the regiment have nearly all been in use since April, and many of them are quite worn out, decayed, full of holes, and as pervious to water as a sieve. The men return from a fatiguing day's duty in the trenches, cold and wet through, and find the floor of the tent in which they have to sleep a mere puddle; until very lately, their single wet blanket answering for bed and bedding; they have now two.

Second, irregularity in the rationing. There have been days, both in this month and the preceding, and not a few on which a short allowance of biscuit and meat has been issued; occasionally there has been no sugar, and latterly no rice at all. With respect to the coffee, it is given out in its green state. The fuel is next to be looked for by the men themselves, however tired they may be; means for roasting the coffee have then to be found, and the result is generally a compound, resembling so much charcoal and hot water, and about as nutritious. A few instances of undoubted scurvy have occurred; but the scorbutic diathesis is apparent in many of the men; and it is much to be wished that lime juice could be issued as a preservative measure, as on long sea voyages, before the disease has time to develop itself; not to mention the prejudicial influence such a state of the constitution would be likely to have in all cases of wounds and accidents.

Third, want of clothing. Until very lately the men were literally in rags, swarming with vermin, the boots, in many instances, useless, and the so-called 'great coat', threadbare. After the chief burst of the sickness had occurred, a supply of warm clothing was distributed. But the field hospital soon became so crowded (our means of transport being a mere cipher), that the assistance of the French ambulance was solicited, by the aid of which this great accumulation of disease, filth, and misery was handed over to the medical department at Balaclava in hundreds. It would thus seem, that while the causes of disease would appear to have received scarcely sufficient attention, the efforts of the medical officers to remedy the evil have neither been supported, nor at all times justly appreciated.'

The preceding deposition describes the manner in which sickness was produced, and suffering increased, and the state and circumstances under which sick and wounded soldiers were consigned to the hospital at Balaclava.

The following paragraphs describe the buildings and accessories of that institution in the words of the Commissioners.

'The General Hospital at Balaclava was formerly the village school, and consists of two parallel ranges of buildings about forty feet apart, situated on the side of a hill, the building which was the school dormitory being on the higher level.

There are two smaller buildings, one roofless, and both in bad repair, at right angles to these, but not connected with either, one of which is allotted to the medical officers for their quarters, and for the purveyor's stores, while the other is occupied as a pack store. The schoolrooms, three in number, are in good repair, with the exception that a few panes of glass were broken when we visited it. The rooms are heated by stoves of Russian construction.

Two of these rooms are 29 feet 9 inches long, by 27 feet 5 inches, and 14 feet 5 inches high; the third is 28 feet 8 inches long, by 21 feet 9 inches broad, and 14 feet 5 inches high. The school dormitory consists of four rooms, measuring each 33 feet 3 inches, by 19 feet, and 10 feet in height.

The kitchen has three coppers, two of which are used for soup, and one for the preparation of extras and tea. The flues are carried round the coppers, by which means a saving of fuel is effected. Over the coppers is a cupola, which collects the steam, and transmits it through three openings into the chimney.

The smell from the drains is offensive, and has been, according to Dr Anderson, the cause of fever and bowel complaints among several surgeons who lived in the immediate vicinity. The pack store was roofless, unprotected against depredation, and in great confusion.

Two marquees stood in front of the hospital, and four wooden huts, each measuring 28 feet 2 inches, by 16 feet 2 inches, were in course of erection near them, while we were at Balaclava, the first three weeks in January.

The whole number of patients, therefore, which, in our opinion, the hospital at Balaclava could properly accommodate, is 110. This hospital has been used not merely

for the treatment of the sick, but also for the reception –
frequently for a single night – of sick and wounded men, on
their arrival from the camp at too late an hour for
embarkation.' – Report of the Duke of Newcastle's
Commissioners, February 23rd, 1855, page 14.

'When the sick and wounded are carried from the camp to
Balaclava, they are either admitted into the hospital in that
place, or they are embarked on board vessels for Scutari.' –
Report of February 23rd,1855, page 14.

Under examination by the Commissioners, January 14th,
1854, Mr Jenner, purveyor of Balaclava, deposed:

'I have reported the want of glazing of the windows and
the drainage to the engineer in charge here. I told him I had
glass, but required labour. He wanted putty, which I could not
procure, and the windows have not been mended. I reported
to the Commanding Officer, Royal Engineers of the British
Army in the Crimea, through Dr Hall, that the whole of the
roof was out of repair, and the drainage. Nothing has been
done.' – Appendix, p.338.

Under examination by the Commissioners, January 10th,
1855, Dr Anderson, the principal Medical Officer at
Balaclava, said:

'The hospital at Balaciava is not large enough for the
number of patients I have. The building is in very indifferent
repair; one wing is roofless. The roof of the rest is very
defective. The windows are, in many cases, totally deficient of
glass. I have reported it to Dr Hall. It is unsuited for the
treatment of sick. The smell of the drains is very offensive.' –
Appendix, p. 336.

On January 14th, 1854, Mr Jenner the purveyor at
Balaclava, stated:

'When I first got here, I kept my stores on board the *John Masterman*. The ships which brought me goods usually delivered them on board of her. They were slow about it. On one occasion, the *Medway* sailed away after having disembarked a part only of my stores. She came back afterwards and delivered the rest. I have always received by post an invoice of goods sent from Scutari, but never of goods which have come from England. I do not know whether the things which I have then got without invoice were intended for me or not; perhaps they were destined for the authorities at Scutari, and were brought on; but by Dr Hall's directions I have taken possession of all hospital stores I could find. I got goods in this way from the *Medway* only, and the boards and tressels on board the *Manilla*.

I boarded the *Pedestrian* when she arrived about a fortnight ago, and asked the captain if he had any stores for me. He said he did not know, as he had not any invoice of the goods on board, and that he intended disembarking everything on the shore, and let the owners claim them. I make it a practice to go on board any vessels of whose arrival I hear, as often as I can, but I have no boat and find the greatest difficulty in doing this.' – Appendix, p. 338.

'Till October 11th,'says Mr Jenner, in his deposition, 'no diet rolls were kept. I fed all the patients in the hospital down to that time on the verbal order of Dr Hall, without any vouchers. Since then, diet rolls have been kept, but so incorrect, that I doubt if correct stoppage accounts can be made out. In some cases, the same man is entered on different days as belonging to different regiments. No morning *states* were furnished to me until January 1st, and these are so incorrect, that I can do nothing with them.' – Appendix, p. 339.

'According to the ordinary practice, when a regimental surgeon is in want of medicines and medical comforts, he applies to the principal medical officer of his division for a supply. This officer, if he approves of the requisition, countersigns it, and the required articles are issued by the apothecary, or the purveyor's clerk in charge of the stores attached to the division. When the stock of medicines and medical comforts in these stores began to fail, the regimental surgeons endeavoured to get their wants supplied by the apothecary and purveyor at Balaclava, where the principal stores in the Crimea are kept. The practice entailed upon these latter gentlemen a great addition to their ordinary labours, and upon the surgeons in the inconvenience of sending several miles for their supplies. This inconvenience became gradually aggravated in proportion as it became frequent, and its frequency became more and more necessary as the quantities that were dealt out at a time to them, in answer to their requisitions, became smaller. The practice, under such circumstances, of requiring the counter-signature of the medical officer in charge of divisions, operated very vexatiously.' – Report of Feb. 23rd, 1855, pp. 11-12.

'From the evidence of Dr Hall, Dr Anderson, Messrs Jenner, Kersey and Fernandes, it would seem that the want of medicines, medical comforts, and of several articles of hospital furniture, was attributable partly to tardy and imperfect compliance with orders and requisitions on Scutari, and partly to the difficulty of ascertaining on board what vessels stores were laden, and of landing those stores when such information was attained.

The imperfect state in which we found Smith's and Clarke's stretchers, in the camp, was stated by Dr Hall to have been owing to the fact that different portions of them were shipped on board different vessels. The frames, it would seem, arrived at Balaclava by the *Jura* last November, while the legs were sent by the *Robert Lowe,* which did not reach that harbour until the end of December.' – Ibid, p. 12.

'By an oversight, no candles were included among the stores brought to the Crimea. Lamps and wicks were brought, but not oil. These omissions were not supplied until after possession had been taken of Balaclava, and the purveyor had an opportunity of pur chasing candles and oil from the shipping, and the dealers in the town.' – Report of February 23rd, 1855, p. 9.

The Commissioners state:

'We found a great want of bedsteads, stretchers, and every other means of raising the men above the ground. Even of the small supply of Smith's and Clarke's stretchers at the disposal of the surgeons, only a portion was used, owing partly to the insufficient number of marquees and tents available for hospital purposes, and partly to the incompleteness of the stretchers, many of which were without legs and without the transverse bars which keep them stretched.' – Ibid, p. 10.

With respect to the medical attendance given to this hospital from the time of its being opened, September 27th, 1854, to the time of the Commissioners' visit, the Report states merely their failure in ascertaining the number, and disingenuously avoids the declaration of the fact that it was utterly inadequate to the patients' requirements.

The following depositions complete the miserable picture of Balaclava Hospital.

Under examination by the Commissioners, at Scutari,

February 20th, 1855, Mr Tucker, purveyor of the Barrack Hospital there, stated:

'I think Miss Nightingale came into the office not a week ago. She stated there was a great want of shirts at Balaclava – that she had heard not a patient in hospital had a shirt, and asked if we were sending any of these stores to the front. I said that rested with Mr Wreford, that I had no information that any were required. She asked whether shirts could be sent. I asked what number. She said that 4,000 would be required altogether. I said that I understood Mr Wreford was making arrangements to send things to Balaclava. She went on to say that she would send some shirts herself, and a small quantity of barley.'

– Appendix, page 343. At the same time and place Mr Wreford testifies: 'I met Miss Nightingale the day before yesterday. She asked me if I had flannel shirts; I said I had. I had 1,000 five or six days ago. She made no demand for any; she observed that if I had them, she would not issue any.' – Appendix, page 344.

On February 20th, 1855, Miss Nightingale deposed before the commissioners at Scutari:

'The men who come from the Crimea are in such a state of filth, that the shirts have to be cut off from them; and when they leave the hospital they are allowed to take away their shirts on their backs. I could not refuse it.' – Appendix, page 342. The Commissioners say: 'The loss of their kits, which had been made so frequently the subject of complaint to us at Scutari, appears one of the chief causes of the vermin, which was, if not general, at all events not uncommon among them. This loss arose principally from their having, in obedience to orders to that effect, left their packs on board the vessels which transported them to the Crimea, and from their having being unable to recover them afterwards.' – Report of February 23, 1855, page 12.

A growing confidence of victory was shown about the time when Mrs Davis reached Therapia, in the wish expressed by Lord Raglan to retain the sick and wounded in the Crimea, and to have female nurses sent to assist in taking care of them. All circumstances, excepting the adverse chances of war, favoured the establishment of hospitals near the scene of action; and as the fear of failure wore away, sufferers were saved in greater numbers from the agony and risk of removal, until at last, the hospitals of Turkey received but a few casual patients, and the hospitals of the Crimea became the principal receptacles of the sick and wounded.

Appendix C

Withhold not good from them to whom it is due, when it is in the power of thine hand to do it.

Prov. iii. 27.

Remarks on the System of Administration in the War Hospitals of the Crimean Army

The recital of Mrs Davis's experience in the four last chapters of her Autobiography tends to show the ill effects of the system of countersigned requisitions when brought to bear upon the British War Hospitals of the Crimean Army. It touches also upon some other particulars concerning the discipline and employment of the female nursing corps, which may assist considerate minds in forming distinct opinions of past occurrences, and in eliciting principles for the future guidance of benevolent enterprises.

A pamphlet, which has lately been issued to the donors of free gifts, written either by Miss Nightingale herself, or by her authority, supplies the means of offering here the fairest and clearest view of her system of administration.

In writing a commentary upon it, the adoption of a reviewer's style will best suit the subject and prevent the appearance of invidious personal criticism.

The writer is unacquainted with Miss Nightingale, but shares the feeling of the country in honouring superior natural endowments, and mental acquirements, wherever they may be found, and more especially when dedicated to the public service.

'Statements exhibiting the voluntary contributions, received by Miss Nightingale, for the use of the British War Hospitals in the East. With their mode of distribution in 1854, 1855, 1856. London, printed by Harrison and Sons, St Martin's Lane, W. C., 1857.'

Miss Nightingale and her coadjutors have won for themselves the gratitude of their country, and honourable renown in the history of their time.

Far be it from us to detract from the merit of their noble self devotion, or to take a narrow view of the results of their labours.

But we must recollect the importance of collecting the ripe fruits of experience for the use of future war hospitals.

Acknowledging, freely and fully, the good that has been done under the superintendent of the female nursing establishment, we must not refuse to examine the question, 'Whether the adopted method of administration really produced the largest amount of benefit which could possibly be conferred by the means at its command?'

We have carefully pursued this inquiry through the Blue Book, containing the Commissioners Report and Appendix of February 23rd, 1855; the Parliamentary Returns on Scutari and other Hospitals, of August 1st, 1855; the public newspapers, various pamphlets, several volumes of published records, and various unpublished documents and letters concerning the British War Hospitals of the Bosphorus and Crimea. We have conversed often and freely with many persons who shared the arduous toils and painful sufferings of the period. We have conscientiously endeavoured to attain to a just and impartial view of well attested facts; and have made ourselves acquainted with the ordinary arrangements of British hospitals, both civil and military.

Bringing this previous preparation to bear upon the pamphlet now before us, we proceed to examine its contents.

Five pages of introduction define the object of the remaining sixty-eight to be – 'Simply to render to those who committed to the charge of Miss Nightingale their contributions, in kind or in money, for the use of the sick and wounded in the war hospitals of the East, a concise account of the mode in which such contributions have been applied.'

The introduction also contains her acknowledgement of the effective assistance rendered by her fellow-labourers, of the cooperation of the medical officers, and of the sanction and support which she uniformly received from the war department, and from the military authorities, in carrying out her plans.

The 'Report,' included in the 'Statements', says, at page 19, that: 'Miss Nightingale had been placed by the government in two positions of trust, each quite independent of the other. She had been appointed Superintendent of the nursing establishment, and she further had received authority as Almoner of the 'free gifts,' to apply them, or any other funds derived from private sources, in the war hospitals.'

An extract from a War Office document, at page 10, shows that Miss Nightingale, as almoner of the 'free gifts,' was only 'subject to the opinion of the Inspector-general and the Commandant.' It does not appear that these personages ever interfered, *unless in compliance with her own request.*

The combinations of these two important trusts of Superintendent and Almoner brought upon their possessor such numerous, various, and complex duties, that nothing but a most comprehensive capacity of business, a most exact division of subjects, a choice of subordinate agents capable of carrying on affairs 'currently and constantly,' a confiding delegation of executive power, and ever vigilant supervision, could possibly ensure their successful administration.

In the first page of this 'Report,' the following paragraph occurs:

'Although the army had been encamped at Scutari in the month of May, 1854, no office for the reception and delivery of packages for its use, was established at Constantinople or Scutari until the end of March, 1855.'

After detailing the 'delay, difficulty, and confusion' consequent upon this omission, and upon the manner in which some of the packages were addressed, Miss Nightingale's 'Report'says (page10): 'These circumstances will sufficiently account for the non-arrival at her hands, and consequent non-appearance in the annexed schedules, of a large amount of the donations, which were possibly destined for her distribution by the senders.'

'In the spring of 1855,' says the same Report (p. 10), 'the late Major Campbell (then Deputy-assistant Quarter-master general at Scutari) assigned a distinct building close to the Main Guard or Barrack Hospital Gate, for the reception of the contributions *in kind,* which were called the free gifts. Two small stores in the interior of the hospital were also attached to the Sisters' Quarters for the same purpose.'

The first great benefactor of the suffering army, was Mr Macdonald, the administrator of 'the *Times* Fund'. In the destitution of all things, and the despair incident to the loss of the *Prince,* and the stores with which that ship was laden, Mr Macdonald supplied Miss Nightingale with the necessary articles of nutriment, clothing, and hospital accommodation from the middle of Nov., 1854, until January 1st, 1855. The

1100 wounded men from Inkerman were thereby saved from perishing for want. This was the period at Scutari when need was most general, most appalling, and most urgent; and the fact of its relief by the intermediation of Miss Nightingale has set the halo round her head.

We are informed by the Blue Book of the Duke of Newcastle's Commissioners, that Mr Macdonald, the almoner of the *Times,* 'had not, like Miss Nightingale, inquired of the purveyors before sending his donations to their destination, whether the goods were in store or expected.' – page 35 of their Report, Feb. 23rd, 1855.

At pages 18 and 19, Miss Nightingale explains the plan on which she issued a 'small proportion' of the free gift stores on her own responsibility, including allowances to invalids and convalescents on leaving the hospital, additions to the extra diets of the patients, restoratives to the sick and wounded on their arrival, and supplies entrusted 'according to their own requisition, to the female superintendents, who were (always at the desire of the principal medical officers) stationed at the various hospitals.' These ladies were desired to issue the stores upon requisition, and under similar restrictions to those which Miss Nightingale imposed upon herself.

At page 26 in the two last paragraphs of a note, we are told that, 'she (Miss Nightingale) exacted, and she rendered adherence to rules to a large extent, and she strictly reverted to them when any emergency, during which at the instance of authorities she had departed from them, had ceased. A position, such as hers, necessarily exposes the holder to attacks from different quarters, upon opposite grounds. While previously existing authorities are disposed to complain of all novel expenditure as lavish, and tending to the relaxation of discipline by over indulgence; others, who feel themselves checked or restrained by regulations in the distribution of comforts according to their ideas of benevolence, will naturally object to the obstruction, in their view unnecessarily interposed, to the current of public liberality. While the experience of all who have conducted the operations of any extensive charity proves that the application of the ordinary axioms of business is the only road to success, it also sufficiently shows that such application is surely attended by no small measure of unpopularity.'

Schedule A presents a list of articles of hospital furniture, supplied to the Scutari hospitals from Nov. 10th, 1854, to July 1st, 1856, by Miss Nightingale, on requisition.

Pages 54–59 are occupied with lists of supplies furnished on requisition by Miss Nightingale to the 'War Hospitals of the East, the Depot at Scutari, and various corps in the Crimea.'

If the numbers of patients officially registered as admitted and dismissed during that period are considered, and if the testimony of eyewitnesses to the actual condition of those patients is believed, the supplies entered in these tables will appear to fall far short of what their need required.

Lists of pecuniary subscribers, collections, and contributors, and an account of the assistance given to the wives, widows, and children of soldiers, occupy the last pages of the pamphlet; but the proportion borne by the donations either to the almoner's receipts, or to the hospital distribution, must remain for ever indeterminate.

A section of this report opens at page 61 under the head of 'Distribution of Free Gifts', with the following paragraph:

'The instructions issued by the government to Miss

Nightingale contained a provision that neither she nor her nurses should interfere in any way with the medical treatment of the patients, or with the general discipline of the hospitals.

On her arrival at Scutari, the following alternatives were open to her:

1. The requisition system. The rule of a military hospital is that nothing shall be supplied but in compliance with a written requisition signed by one, and in most cases by two medical officers, and made upon the medical store-keeper, or the purveyor, to be forwarded, in the latter case, in certain instances to the commissariat, the engineer, or the barrack master respectively.
2. To act partly on the requisition system, and partly on personal discretion; or
3. To be guided solely by personal discretion in the distribution of the free gifts.

That there are partial advantages in the two last alternatives is evident, but they are open to these objections:

a. The abrogation of the ordinary rule of military hospitals.
b. The impossibility of preventing irregular issues, or at least of disproving the charge, unless by the system of official requisition.
c. The unfitness of a large proportion of the women, who efficiently discharge the duty of nurses; to be the judges of the wants of soldiers, and distributors of the supplies to them; and farther the abuse which some would undoubtedly make of the power. To those to whom the charge of dishonesty would not apply, religious partiality either would, or what in matters of this kind, is only less mischievous, would be believed to apply. These objections

are, if possible, still stronger to giving patients other food than that ordered by the medical officers. It is needless to state to any sensible person, even without hospital experience, the manifold dangers of issuing to nurses, whether ladies, sisters or nurses, stores, or facilities for procuring stores, to be distributed at their own discretion through the wards.

Therefore, from the first, Miss Nightingale issued the free gifts, or the various stores entrusted to her distribution, solely upon the requisition of the medical officers, excepting a small proportion, the responsibility of which rested with herself.'

With reference to what is here termed Miss Nightingale's first alternative, it is necessary to remark that the rule laid down for the general guidance of military hospitals, is really less stringent than this statement represents it to be.

The 'Regulations for the Management of Army Hospitals at home and abroad', are ushered in by a paragraph which closes with the following emphatic words:

'Though framed principally with a view to home service, (they) should be also observed on foreign service *whenever it may be practicable.'*

This virtually implies the admission that occasions might occur in which their observance would be impracticable.

In a case of this kind, the terms injurious, inexpedient, and impracticable ought to be equivalent.

In fact, the Regulations, like the medical formulary annexed to them, while discouraging needless deviations, are not intended to preclude the adoption of such measures as may be called for by emergencies.

Let it be remembered, that in the hospitals of the Bosphorus and of the Crimea, the Regulations were openly and constantly violated with regard to the proportionate number of orderlies in attendance upon the patients, the space allotted to each bed in the wards, and in other important particulars.

If the plea of necessity is admitted as a sufficient apology for those violations of military rule which lessen the comforts of the patients, its application cannot consistently be denied to such variations as were pronounced by competent judges, and proved by experience, to be replete with benefits.

The Report of the Duke of Newcastle's Commissioners, Feby. 23, 1855, distinctly recommends the abolition of requisitions, and the substitution of receipts as vouchers.

Nevertheless, although the 'rule' was avowedly flexible – although the Commissioners officially announced their opinion, 'that the practice of issuing on requisition is vicious' – the Superintendent of nurses, Almoner of the free gifts, rejecting the option of acting solely upon personal discretion, and the middle course of a qualified system of requisitions, deliberately determined, in defiance of an order of the medical board, to persevere in adherence to the strict military rule of doubly-signed requisitions.

The grounds which she assigns for this choice, simply show the self-protective principle of rigid observance, in securing regular issues of supplies, and their due acknowledgement.

It is always right to preserve the means of proving our own integrity, but we think that the Almoner of the free gifts erred in making this the first object of her administration. It ought, undoubtedly, to have been secondary and subservient to the steadfast purpose of doing the greatest possible good with the means entrusted to her distribution.

This avowed warp in the intention, accounts for many

lamentable facts. But we have yet to consider more particularly a part of those grounds which formed the basis of her official conduct. The alleged unfitness, dishonesty, and religious partiality of the subordinate members of the nursing staff (§3), and their inability 'to be judges of the wants of the soldiers, and distributors of the supplies to them,' involves matter for careful consideration.

To all sane persons, however silly they may be, the perception of want suggests the need of supply. It is obvious that any 'women who efficiently discharge the duties of nurses', must be capable of judging that, if a wretched sufferer has no shirt, he needs one; and that if he is obliged to lie naked in his bed while that one shirt is washed, he needs another; that the beverage suddenly asked for at midnight by a dying person, must be given at once, or never.

Information derived from eyewitnesses, numerous, and unconnected with each other, convinces us that the enforcement of the rule of requisitions produced in the ladies and nurses a conflict between their feelings of natural duty and of formal restriction, and ended in general and conscientious disobedience.

Ladies and nurses of thorough and long-proved integrity, declare that, in the sight of urgent want on the one side, and of open bales of undistributed free gifts upon the other, they did infringe upon the Almoner's exclusive privilege; that they did supply the naked with clothing, and the dying with the refreshment they desired. The strictness of the 'rule' ensured its practical abrogation.

A detailed account of the miseries incident to its exact observance, may be found in *Eastern Hospitals*, 3rd edition, pages 44–45, and pages 52–53.

Those instances show that even the most kind and strenuous efforts of the medical officers, could not prevent the dreadful evils attendance upon the rule of the countersigned requisitions in the General Hospital at Scutari.

The author of the account of the Institution of Kaiserswerth (Hookham, New Bond Street) satirizes, at page 14 of that pamphlet, 'regulations made without experience'. How much more worthy of censure are regulations maintained in defiance of experience!

In the words which Lord Stanley of Alderley used at Manchester, in January, 1856, we can say of such a 'system':

'It is not rules, not forms, not paper checks, or guarantees, that make an enterprise prosper; it is the living, unfettered human energy.' – See the *Times* of January 18th, 1856,

Nevertheless, we believe that the modified adoption of the regulations in use at Guy's Hospital, or those of any similar establishment, might have been better than the 'system'; for in them the principle of trust, in well-chosen agents of graduated ranks, forms the basis of every course of action,

The author of the 'Statements' says:

1. It is to be remembered that the employment of women in army hospitals is recent; that many experienced and able surgeons are opposed to it;

2. that among these some are honestly, and some unscrupulously prone to find objections to it, and to exaggerate mischiefs arising from it; that the surgeon can, to a considerable extent, allow the nurse to be useful, or force her to be comparatively useless in his wards;

3. that the war hospitals are a bad field for investing the nurse with power and offices which she never exercises in civil hospitals, of the system of which she is an established part,

recognized as indispensable. On these grounds, as strict an adherence to existing rules as was possible appeared to be the only course.'

With reference to the first part of this paragraph, we must remark that the occasional employment of women in army hospitals long preceded the establishment of the female nursing staff at Scutari. Mr Sidney Herbert, then Secretary at War, in his letter to Miss Nightingale, dated October 15th, 1854, seems, nevertheless, to be ignorant of the clause which authorizes their admission under special circumstances.

The 43rd Regulation for the Management of Army Hospitals at home and abroad, is as follows:

'Besides the hospital sergeant borne upon the establishment of each regiment of cavalry and battalion of infantry, orderly-men are to be employed, according to the number and wants of the sick. For a number not exceeding 10, one orderly-man, and for any greater number an additional orderly for every 10 patients. A nurse shall not be employed in lieu of an orderly, except under special circumstances, nor unless with the previous sanction of the Secretary at War; but if a nurse be allowed, a soldier's wife, of sober, careful, cleanly, and active habits should be selected; and when not otherwise occupied, she is to wash and mend the hospital bedding and towels, if this be not done by the barrack department.'

The allusion to the medical officers in the same paragraph, ought to be explained by some of those who held authority at Scutari.

Judging merely from the evidence afforded by the books, ladies, and nurses which we have met with, this charge would appear to be unfounded.

We certainly know that surgeons frequently applied for the assistance of nurses, and that their applications were refused.

We also know that the Superintendent of nurses set not always an example of submission to medical authority.

For instance, Miss Nightingale states, February 20th, 1855, at Scutari:

'With regard to the wine, I used to issue arrowroot without wine, even after the medical officers made requisitions on me, and I insisted on the men putting into it the port which they got from the purveyor. I did not issue the wine until the medical officers said the port was so bad.' – Appendix (p. 343) to the Report of the Duke of Newcastle's Commissioners.

With regard to the powers and offices to be exercised by nurses in Army Hospitals, we consider that the distrust which prevented a judicious delegation of the powers, and proper appointments to the offices, produced myriads of evils and prevented much good.

The inorganic form, or disorganized condition of Scutari Hospital may be inferred from the fact that in the list of hospital servants appended to the printed forms of the 'Monthly Returns of the Sick', the order of gradation is

"Sergeant"

"Nurse"

"Orderlies"

while neither the nominal system nor practical deviations from it, placed the nurses in command of the orderlies.

We are told that, 'The whole number of nurses who left England for the service of the military hospital in the Crimea, and the Bosphorus, under Miss Nightingale, was 125; viz:

1st party 38
2nd " 47

3rd "	8
4th "	7
5th "	4
At different times	7
	111
From the establishment at Smyrna	3
From that of officers' nurses	2
From that of Koulali	9
	125

Happily for the patients, there were among the volunteers some women of strict principle, possessing sufficient judgement and energy to shape their several courses, and to work out their own notions of duty. Force of character won for them the confidence of the medical officers, and thus their opportunities of usefulness were increased. To such women, and among them to Elizabeth Cadwaladyr (Davis), the gratitude of their country is due for ever. She did, as the direction paper of one of our metropolitan hospitals expresses it, 'assist in promoting, by every means in her power, the wellbeing of the patients'.

Others who remained comparatively useless, or were sent home as inefficient or disgraced, might, under a different system, have achieved praiseworthy deeds. Many a structure which alone would totter and fall, stands safe and useful as one among others.

The nuns have been praised as the most useful labourers in the war hospitals. Their superiority appears to have consisted simply in their combination and subjection to established control among themselves. As individual labourers, some Protestant nurses could not be surpassed.

A project originating in the purest and most zealous benevolence was marred from the first by injudicious accessories. Equality was proclaimed among labourers, whose only possibility of combined usefulness lay in the most exact subordination.

In the midst of attempted conformity to military rule, its essential elements, graduated rank, and deputed authority, were cast aside. The female army was allowed to have only a field-marshal, colonels and privates.

An expression in Mr Sidney Herbert's letter of October 15th, 1854, suggests the idea that the superintent of female nurses was, from her very first appointment, shackled by her own resolutions and by his friendly injunctions, and thus involved in a predetermined and prescribed course, within which she subsequently framed her own little codes and corollaries, and from which she punctiliously dreaded to deviate. Circumstances compelled deviations, and 'the system' was practically reduced to a series of inconsistencies, even by its framer and expositor, while skilful and diligent labourers dreaded only its prohibitory force.

We know that it is easy to find fault, and easy to judge, when a whole case lies before us, of details which came out day by day with most puzzling complexity; but the faculty of skilful adaptation to circumstances belongs to capacity for governing. We can easily imagine that in the midst of her overwhelming occupations and responsibilities, the Superintendent of the Female Nursing Establishment might have felt that to give up her system would be like leaving hold of a rope in a shipwreck. We sympathize with the weakness of the woman, but we deplore the incapacity of the public functionary.

We are conscious of no bias, no partiality, no prejudice. Our investigations have fairly led to the conviction that the method of administration did not produce the largest amount of benefit which ought to have been communication by the means at its command; and that the Barrack Hospital at Scutari continued to present the greatest amount of least alleviated misery of any war hospital belonging to the British Army of the East.

Postscript

> Yet History has her doubts, and every age
> With sceptic queries marks the passing page;
> Records of old, nor later dates are clear,
> Too distant those, and these are placed too near!
>
> Crabbe's Library.

In footnotes throughout the work, much illustrative matter has been brought to bear upon various points of Cadwaladyr's history.

While the *Autobiography* has been passing through the press, some additional information has been gleaned from the wide fields of the Heroine's adventures, and this is garnered in the present chapter.

In the seventh chapter of the first volume of this *Autobiography*, she narrates several particulars of her mistress's proceedings which may appear to many persons highly improbable.

Parallels may, however, be readily found. Mrs S_____'s fast day habitude was not singular, nor local, nor has it become obsolete.

Individuals are now living who avowedly deem it 'foolish to fast and inconvenience oneself, when merely saying a benediction over the meat and fancying it to be fish does just as well!'.

The Trinidad transaction, and more especially the pecuniary part of it, receives elucidation from *La Semaine Religieuse*, T. 7, No. 172, which contains the address and instructions of MM. les Vicaires Généraux Capitulaires, administrant le diocèse de Paris, le siege vacant, au clergé et aux fidèles du diocèse, for the proper observation of Lent.

The following quotations from this high authority will suffice:

'Après en avoir conféré avec nos vénérables confrères les chanoines et chapitre de l'église de Paris, nous avons ordonné et ordonnons ce qui suit:

'Art.I. Nous permettons l'usage des oeufs pendant tout le Carême, a l'exception des trois derniers jours de la Semaine Sainte. Nous permettons l'usage de la viande les Dimanche, Lundi, Mardi, et Jeudi de chaque semaine, depuis le Jeudi après le Cendres, jusqu'au Mardi de la Semaine-Sainte inclusivement. Cette dispense ne s'applique pour ceux qui sont tenus au jeune, qu'au principal repas, le Dimanche excepté. A la collation, nous continuons à autoriser l'usage du lait et du beurre, a l'exception du Mercredi des Cendres et du Vendredi-Saint; cette permission s'étend a tous les jours de jeûne de l'année.

'Les personnes infirmes qui auraient besoin de dispenses plus étendues pourront, comme les années précédentes, s'adresser à leurs curés respectifs ou à leur confesseurs, que nous autorisons à cet effet. Celles qui vi vent dans les communautés, collèges, ou hospices, s'adresseront aux supérieurs, aux premiers aumôniers ou chapelains investis du même pouvoir.

'Art. 2. Toutes les personnes qui profitent de la dispense de l'abstinence, doivent, selon leurs facultés, faire en faveur des pauvres une aumône, qu'elles remettront à MM. les curés. Moitié de cette aumône sera versée au secrétariat de l'archevêché, pour être appliquée aux écoles chrétiennes libres, fondées dans l'intérêt des pauvres des paroisses. La dispense n'est accordée qu'à cette condition. Une autre aumône est due également par tous ceux qui profitent de l'autorisation de faire usage du lait et du beurre à la collation. Cette aumône sera distincte de la première. Elle sera consacrée aux besoins généraux du diocèse.

'MM. les curés devront séparer l'aumône destinée aux pauvres de celle qui sera appliquée aux besoins généraux du diocèse, et qui sera remise au secrétariat de l'archevêché.

'Art. 3. Nous accordons pour la prèsente année, comme pour les annees précédentes, en égard à la difficulté des temps, la dispense de l'abstinence pour le jour de Saint Marc et les trois jours des Rogations. Les fidèles seront exhortés à compenser cet adoucissement de la discipline par quelques bonnes oeuvres et quelques aumônes.

'Art. 4. Pour l'exercice de dévotion en l'honneur de la Passion de Nôtre-Seigneur Jésus-Christ et de la Compassion de la sainte Vierge, on se conformera à ce qui a été prescrit les autres années. (1.) Nous invitons tous les fidèles à assister à ce pieux exercice, soit à Nôtre-Dame, soit dans les églises de leurs paroisses respectives, soit dans les chapelles des différentes maisons où il est autorisé.

'Nous leur rappelons que, par divers rescrits des souverains-pontifes, Léon XII et Grégoire XVI, des indulgences sont accordées a tous ceux qui, remplissant les conditions prescrites, pratiqueront dans les susdites églises et chapelles, la dévotion que nous venons d'indiquer.

'Art. 5. Tous les Dimanches du Carême et le Dimanche de Quasimodo, il sera fait dans l'église métropolitaine, à une heure après midi, une conférence sur les véritiés fondamentales de la religion. Elle sera précédée d'une messe basse.

'Art.6. Le temps fixé pour la communion pascale commencera le Dimanche de la passion et finira le second Dimanche de la Quiquagésime; publié et affiché partout où besoin sera.

'Donné à Paris, sous notre seing, le sceau du Chapitre, et le contre-seing du Sécretaire-général de l'Archevêché, le 19 Février, 1857.

'L. Buquet, Vicaire-général capitulaire, Archidiacre de Nôtre-Dame.

'A. Surat, Vicaire-général capitulaire, Archidiacre de Sainte-Geneviève; G. Darboy, Vicaire-général capitulaire, Archidiacre de Saint-Denis.

'Par mandement de MM. les Vicaires-capitulaires, E. J. Lagarde, Chan. Hon. Secret. Gén. de l'Archevêché.'

A note appended to Art. 3 makes the matter still plainer. It says:

'Ces conditions sont, pour gagner l'indulgence plénière, l'assistance à l'exercice, la confession et la communion faites avec les dispositions convenables. Pour gagner une indulgence de 300 jours, il suffira qu'étant contrits de coeur, les fideles suivent l'exercice, et récitent cinq Pater et cinq Ave, avec cinq Gloria Patri, en mémoire de la Passion de Notre-Seigneur. Cette même indulgence sera gagnée, aux mêmes conditions, par ceux qui ne pourraient se render à l'église, ou chapelle, s'ils en ont été empêchés pour cause d'infirmitié, ou quelque autre raison légitime. L'indulgence plénière et l'indulgence de 300 jours sont applicables, par manière de suffrage, aux âmes du purgatoire.

'L'une et l'autre peuvent être gagnées à l'église métropolitaine par tous les fidèles indistinctement, mais elles ne peuvent être gagnées dans chacune des paroisses que par les fidèles de ces mêmes paroisses, et dans chacune des communautés ecclesiastiques et religieuses, et dans les maisons d'éducation, que par les personnes qui en font partie.'

A tangible, and, in one sense of the word, a *venerable* monument of similar practices may be seen in the south-west tower of Rouen cathedral, built A.D. 1485-1507, with money paid for indulgences to eat butter in Lent, and still known as the Tour de Beurre.

[This is a directive to the clergy and lay members of the Paris diocese for the proper observation of Lent. It gives permission for various dietary rules to be broken, setting out the conditions under which absolution can be granted and the charitable donations which are required in return.]

In the eighth chapter of the first volume, and in the first chapter of the second volume, of the present work, Elizabeth Davis mentions her visit to 'Mr Cartwright, the magistrate' at Liverpool in Australia.

The *Sydney Morning Herald* of Tuesday, December 23, 1856, contains an obituary notice, derived from the Goulburn papers of the preceding Saturday, relating to this gentleman – the Rev. R. Cartwright, senior chaplain of the diocese. It will be seen that place and time both agree with her narration.

'This aged minister of Christ expired at his residence in Goulburn, on Sunday last. We cannot permit him to depart from among us without a reference to his long ministerial services in this colony, in which he had faithfully pursued his vocation for upwards of forty-six years. He was born in Shropshire, in the year 1771, of a highly respectable family, his mother being of the Powys Castle family, and connected with the leading families of that aristocratic county, viz., those of Lord Hill, the Earl of Denbigh, &c. After dedicating some time to mercantile pursuits, and visiting Constantinople, in company with his brother (who was British consul at Algiers), he returned to England through Wallachia, the very scene where the late war broke out. After this he seems to have turned his attention to the ministry, having become deeply impressed with the necessity of a change of life, and a thorough dedication of his heart to God. For this purpose he became a student of St Edmund's Hall, Oxford, but did not continue long enough to graduate. After leaving the University he was ordained curate of Bradford, in Yorkshire, where he was eminently popular and beloved, as can be testified by one person residing at this moment near Goulburn, who heard him preach his last sermon in that town – an event much to be remembered when we look back nearly fifty years, and contemplate the missionary taking leave of a beloved congregation, to undergo the perils of an Australia voyage. A hymn was expressly composed for the occasion, a copy of which now lies before us.

'Hymn sung at Bradford Church, April 16th, 1809, the last time the Rev. Robert Cartwright preached, before he went as Chaplain to the Colony at New South Wales.

> *With all Thy power, O Lord, defend*
> *Him whom we now to thee commend;*
> *Our faithful minister secure,*
> *And make him to the end endure.*

Gird him with all-sufficient grace;
Give to his footsteps paths of peace;
Thy truth and faithfulness fulfil;
Preserve him, Lord, from every ill.

Before his face protection send;
O love him, save him to the end;
Nor let him as Thy pilgrim rove,
Without the convoy of Thy love.

Enlarge, inflame, and fill his heart;
In him Thy mighty power exert;
That thousands yet unborn may praise
The wonders of redeeming grace.

Praise God from whom all blessings flow, &c. [1]

'Induced, then, by zeal for the spread of the Gospel, at the instigation of the late Rev. S. Marsden, he left the town of Bradford in the year 1809. At that period it required no ordinary amount of moral courage and ministerial fidelity to leave a land where his prospects were cheering, and his services fully appreciated, for a country only lately reclaimed from the possession of the savage, and where he must of necessity follow the work of the ministry among the offscourings of the human race. These discouraging reflections did not prevent him following the bent of his mind, being, under Providence, cheered on his way by the prayers of

---

[1]   Though void of poetic merit, these verses are remarkable for the prayer which they contain, and the fulfilment which it found.

such men as Wilberforce, Thornton, and other great and good men, who ever took a lively interest in the moral and religious welfare of this land.

'On his arrival, or soon after, he was appointed to minister on the Hawkesbury – at that period the boundary of the colony; he afterwards reluctantly consented, at the solicitation of Governor Macquarie, to be appointed a magistrate of the territory for the same locality, the duties of which important office he discharged with diligence and fidelity. After leaving the Hawkesbury he was appointed to the district of Liverpool, where he had the superintendence of the Orphan School, and also an establishment for the instruction of the children of the aborigines, which we believe was not attended with more success than has unfortunately attended many similar undertakings.

'Upon the death of the Rev. R. Hill, he was removed to St James's, Sydney, where he remained nearly two years. In the year 1837 he resigned his incumbency, with the intention of proceeding to England upon family affairs; but in making his arrangements for that purpose, having had occasion to visit the counties of Murray, King, and Georgiana, he was so impressed with the lamentable want of religious observances in those extensive districts, that he determined to become an itinerant minister. This course he pursued with admirable perseverance for some years, having travelled upwards of twenty-five thousand miles, or over a greater space than would reach round the globe; then, when old age and infirmities began to creep upon him, he contracted his labours, which were, for the latter years of his life, confined more particularly to the districts of Gunning and Collector.

For some years he had desired to transfer his laborious

duties to some faithful assistant, but for a long period he was unable to find one, from the difficulty – even now much felt – in procuring clerical aid. During the whole course of a life, frequently chequered by painful trials, and extended far beyond the ordinary duration of human existence, he faithfully preached the truth as it is in Jesus; and the earnestness of his manner, his venerable appearance, and the beautiful intonation of his voice, gave a charm to his public and private ministrations rarely to be found. He was not only tolerant but liberal, both in his opinions and his purse, towards different bodies of Christians; highly esteeming those of whatever sect they might be, who agreed with him in the great fundamentals of our holy faith. That he had failings and imperfections is only what may be predicated of the best of mere mortals, but amidst the infirmities of old age his reliance upon the Rock of Ages was firm and immovable.

'The close of his life gave an encouraging lesson to the waiting Christian: 'Tell them,' said he just before his dissolution, 'that take an interest in my death, that my only reliance is upon, and my only desire is to be with, my Saviour.' These words, if not literally the same, convey his meaning as nearly as his imperfect utterance would allow his hearer to catch them. He was conscious to the last. His mortal remains left this town attended by his two sons, Mr Waddell, and Mr Craig, on Tuesday afternoon, for Liverpool, where it is expected they will be interred in the family vault, this day (Saturday).'

In Volume II, chapter seven, Mrs Davis relates the first part of her Crimean experience of hospital life.

The testimony of Sir John Hall, her Majesty's Inspector-general of Hospitals, to the valuable services rendered by Miss Langston and her coadjutors, including Mrs Davis, must not be omitted here.

Dr Hall's medical report, dated March 2nd, 1855, addressed to Lord Raglan, and mentioning the General Hospital at Balaclava, says:

'The huts in the vineyard in front of the hospital have relieved the hospital, and prevented the necessity of crowding it so much as we were formerly compelled to do.

'The ventilation, too, of the main building has been improved, by boring two rows of large auger holes through the wooden ceiling of the wards.

'Mr Hanbury, and the medical officers doing duty under him, are very attentive to their patients.

'The sick have also the benefit of the care of Miss Langston and the nurses under her, who are a great comfort to them.' (Captain Sayer's *Despatches and Papers*, p. 109).

A narration slightly touching the mere surface of a life, which was exclusively a life of action, may, nevertheless, afford much scope for deep and fruitful thought.

The writer desires that it may prove both entertaining and useful. The higher of these aims will not be entirely frustrated, should the work merely serve to check the misdirected current of public feeling which now strongly bears against the whole class of hospital nurses, and more especially against the paid nurses of the late military hospitals.

A ban of reprobation, wanting only force to be exterminating, has already been fulminated against hired nurses; while schemes, not aerial but mistily terrene, are projected for the entire reconstruction of the class out of new and softer materials; plastic to the touch of Scutarian education.

It has been said that one great object of the Government in sending out Miss Nightingale and the Female Nursing Staff, was to pacify the excitement of the public, and to turn away attention from the sufferings of the army, as well as from the errors which had increased and multiplied them.

This may possibly be true, for human motives are often complicated, and philanthropy and policy were not, in this instance, inconsistent.

The measure certainly succeeded in accomplishing this secondary purpose, but at a deplorable cost of subsequent sorrow and obloquy to the nurses who had assisted in carrying it through.

Elizabeth Davis and some few other courageous and strong-minded women have indeed escaped with their good names untarnished, but they suffer and feel aggrieved by the brand which has scarred their class.

All who were dismissed – the sick and the untrained, the weak, the wicked, and the good – have alike been regarded as castaways.

Yet a gentlewoman, who long lived and laboured in the Hospital at Scutari, can testify of the hired nurses in general that, 'They were uniformly kind and good to the sick and wounded men, and needed only a better system to make them better women.'

With regard to the religious training of nurses – a subject of immense importance to the sick – all that can be done is to provide the means of grace, and to apply those means with kindly sympathy and unostentatious example.

While many of the children and servants brought up in pious households remain unimpressed, it is not surprising that less thorough and less constant teaching should fail of due effect upon hospital nurses.

In a gentle, candid, and most benevolent spirit, the author of *Hospitals and Sisterhoods* has brought together a vast quantity of evidence bearing upon the spiritual wants of English hospitals, and the general attempts made to remedy the evil, and also upon Protestant sisterhoods, and the religious orders of the Roman Catholic Church, with respect to their charitable ministrations.

The professional training of nurses for public establishments appears, as far as we can judge, to be carried on with great success in the principal hospitals of London, where candidates for head-nurses' places officiate as probationary volunteers, and share in those practical lessons which contribute to form our most skilful medical and surgical practitioners.

Upon this subject the pamphlet written by Mr South, senior surgeon of St Thomas's Hospital (published by Richardson, Cornhill, 1857), may be advantageously consulted.

As professional schools for nurses, Mrs Fry's Institution of Nursing Sisters, founded in 1840, and the Training Institution of St John's House, founded in 1848, appear to be working prosperously.

Mrs Davis's own case might appear at first sight to be isolated and exceptional.

Like Moses Primrose in the *Vicar of Wakefield*, she received 'a sort of miscellaneous education', with the important difference that his took place at home, and hers in ranging abroad.

The education wrought by various and extraordinary

circumstances through a long series of years, and a course of practical experience in Guy's Hospital to conclude, fitted her in an especial manner for energetic and useful action in perilous times and scenes of dire calamity.

But let it always be remembered that, besides Elizabeth Davis, many other faithful nurses laboured to alleviate human misery in the War Hospitals of the East; working with the love of God in their hearts, and with His blessing upon their heads; although necessity obliged them, like her, to receive wages for their services.

Among them were some who wept at night for having accomplished less good during the day than they could and would willingly have done. Among them were several who strenuously devoted their whole time and strength to the work, and cheerfully sacrificed to it all ordinary enjoyments, rest, and health.

The graveyards of the English in Turkey and in the Crimea contain the remains of several nurses, who lost their lives in the fulfilment of their arduous duties.

One of these, Mrs Drake, a person of delicate and fragile appearance, and quiet, unobtrusive demeanour, had been trained in St John's House, and accompanied the superintendent of the nurses to Scutari, early in November, 1854.

Grieved and disappointed by the restraint there placed upon her, she at last expressed to a sympathizing inquirer her mental misery, adding, "If I cannot go to the Crimea, which I am trying to obtain leave to do, I will return to England. Perhaps at Balaclava I may be allowed to work. Here we are only eating the bread of idleness, while the wards are full of sick and wounded men requiring aid, which we ought to give but dare not."

A few days afterwards Mrs Drake received permission to embark for Balaclava. On arriving there she entered diligently upon active duty as a nurse, and won the esteem of Miss Wear and her fellow-labourers, and the gratitude of the patients.

She had been about a fortnight there, when, at her earnest request, Miss Wear one day permitted Mrs Drake to accompany her on one of her visits of superintendence to the Monastery.

The heat was excessive, and notwithstanding the precautionary care of Miss Wear and two orderlies, Mrs Drake suffered much from it. A disease, termed by Mrs Davis the 'sun fever' came on, and notwithstanding the skill of the surgeons, and the kind attentions of Miss Wear and the nurses, at the end of ten days she died.

She was an efficient nurse, gentle, kind, and trustworthy. A tombstone, inscribed with her name, and the date of her death, August 9th, 1855, was forwarded from Scutari to Balaclava – a tardy but durable acknowledgement of her worth.

In order to assist the readers' memory in recalling the chronology of the principal events of the late war, we subjoin the following dates, on the authority of Captain Sayer's *Despatches and Papers* published by Harrison, 59 Pall Mall, 1857.

1854

Landing of the Allied Armies in the Crimea	Sep. 14
Battle of the Alma	Sep. 20
First Bombardment of Sebastopol	Oct. 17

Battle of Balaclava	Oct. 25
Battle of Inkerman	Nov. 5
	1855
First Assault of Sebastopol	June 18
Death of Lord Raglan	June 28
Battle of the Tchernaya	Aug. 16
Capture of Sebastopol	Sep. 8
Battle of Kars	Sep. 29
	1856
Evacuation of the Crimea	July 12

Additional Notes

p.22   *Hon. Daines Barrington* – (1727/8 – 1800), English lawyer, antiquary and naturalist, Judge of Great Sessions for North Wales, member of the Royal Society of Antiquaries.

p.23   *Whitfield and Wesley* – George Whit(e)field (1714-70), English Anglican preacher, one of the founders of Methodism. John Wesley (1703-11), Anglican cleric and theologian; with his brother Charles, a founder of Methodism.

p.26   *Bardd Cwsg* – *Gweledigaethau y Bardd Cwsg* (Visions of the Sleeping Poet), a satire by Ellis Wynne (1671-1734), published in 1703.

p.26   *Taith y Pererin* – Welsh translation of John Bunyan's *Pilgrim's Progress*

p.29   *Dr Doddridge's Rise and Progress* – *The Rise and Progress of Religion in the Soul* (published 1745), a very influential book by Philip Doddridge (1702-51), an English non-conformist clergyman and hymn-writer.

p.36   *Archimago* – a sorcerer who uses his magic to deceive in Edmund Spenser's *The Faerie Queene* (published 1590-96).

p.37   *St Patrick's Purgatory* – an ancient pilgrimage site on Station Island, Lough Derg, County Donegal, Ireland. In legend, Christ showed St Patrick a cave on the island that was an entrance to hell.

p.47   Her brother was *taken prisoner with the rest at Flushing* – he was a member of the British force in the disastrous Walcheren Campaign of 1809.

p.58   *Bishop Luxmore* – John Luxmore (1766-1830), English bishop of St Asaph.

p.60   *Lady Huntingdon's Connection* – Selina Hastings, Countess of Huntingdon (1707-91) was prominent in the eighteenth-century religious revival and strongly associated with the Calvinistic Methodist movement.

p.60   *We own cousins to the ninth degree in Wales* – medieval Welsh law (the Law of Hywel Dda) laid responsibilities on family members 'to the ninth degree' – i. e. up to and including fifth cousins

p.63   *I...adopted my father's Christian name instead* – the traditional way of forming Welsh surnames by deriving them from the father's first name, e.g. Dafydd ap Gwilym.

p.67   *Mr Canning* and the *1812 election* – George Canning (1770-1827), Foreign Secretary and Prime Minister.

p.68   *John Elias* – (1774-1841), a famous and very popular Calvinistic Methodist preacher from Anglesey.

p.72   *Mrs Siddons* – Sarah Siddons (1755-1831), famous Welsh-born actress and tragedienne.

p.77   *Restoration of Louis XVIII* – he was restored to the French throne in 1814, removed after Napoleon escaped from exile on Elba and returned to France, and after the battle of Waterloo was restored to the throne for the second time.

p.78   *Young Napoleon* (in 1815) – the son (1811-32) of Napoleon Bonaparte; was named Emperor at the age of four after his father abdicated but was later forced to abdicate himself.

p.79   *Talleyrand* – (1754-1838), diplomat and Prime Minister of French Republic; supported in turn Louis XVI, Napoleon and Louis XVIII.

p.81   *Lloyd of Beaumaris* – Richard Lloyd (1771-1839), Calvinistic Methodist minister and preacher.

p.94   *Miss O'Neill* – (1791-1872), Irish actress, tragedienne.

p.94   *Mr C. Kemble* – Charles Kemble (1775-1854), Welsh-born manager of Drury Lane Theatre, brother of Sarah Siddons.

p.100   *Sir Sydney Smith* – (1764-1840), English admiral, fought in wars of American Independence and against Revolutionary France.

p.109   *Demerara and the commotion about Smith the missionary* – John Smith (1790-1824) was an Anglican missionary who went to work in Demerara (now part of Guyana) under the auspices of the London Missionary Society in 1817. After the 'Demerara rebellion' of 1823, in which over 10,000 slaves rose against their masters, he was arrested and found guilty of inciting the rising and failing to inform the authorities that it was imminent. He was condemned to death, and died in prison before his reprieve arrived. His death provoked outrage and was a milestone in the campaign for the abolition of slavery.

p.112   *Dr Buchan's book* – William Buchan (1729-1805) was a Scottish doctor whose *Domestic Medicine* (1769) was very widely read; it went through 22 editions, sold 80,000 copies and was translated into many European languages.

p.114   *Van Diemen's Land* – now Tasmania.

p.118   *Mrs Fitzherbert* – (1756-1837) secretly married the future George IV, but the marriage was illegal because it had not received royal permission; she later married a rich Catholic sixteen years younger than her who died in a riding accident three months after the wedding. As a result she was generally regarded as a scandalous figure.

p.121   *St Jago* – now Santiago, in the Cape Verde Islands.

p.128   *Free or bond?* (asked by two constables who "seized hold of" Cadwaladyr in Hobart, Tasmania) – their question asked whether she was free, or a transported convict who had been released from prison etc. because of good behaviour but couldn't leave a specified district without permission from a magistrate.

p.134   *Whampoa* – the old English transliteration of the modern name Huangpu in Guanzhou district, China.

p.142   *Sir Robert Peel* – (1788-1850), leader of Tory party, twice British Prime Minister, founder of modern British police force.

p.145   *Rowland Hill* – (1744-1833), English evangelical preacher, supporter of the British and Foreign Bible Society and the London Missionary Society.

p.145   *Griffith of Nefern* – David Griffiths (1756-1834), Welsh Methodist minister and preacher, connected with the Countess of Huntingdon's Connection.

p.147   *Translation by G. G.* – Gwenynen Gwent, the bardic name of Augusta Hall, Lady Llanover (1802-96), ex-employer of Betsy Cadwaladyr and friend and patroness of Jane Williams.

p.148   *King John the Eighth of Portugal* – King John the Eighth of

Portugal did not exist. The last King John (João) of Portugal was the Sixth, who reigned from 1816-26 and is probably the king referred to here. Jane Williams had read extensively about the history of the Portuguese and Brazilian royal families, as her note to Chapter 2, Part 2, shows; the fact that the error remains suggests that Betsy Cadwaladyr was certain in her own mind that Barbosa had claimed to be the nephew of João the Eighth and refused to accept documentary evidence that he could not have been.

p.150 *Paul and Virginia* – lovers in the novel *Paul et Virginie* by Jacques-Henri Bernardin de St Pierre, which was first published in 1788 and set in Mauritius.

p.175 *The war between the Patriots and Spaniards* (in Peru) – the Peruvian War of Independence began in 1821 and ended in 1824 when the forces of Spain were defeated at the Battle of Ayacuche; this marked the end of colonial Spanish rule in South America.

p.180 *A thing like the head of an eight-day clock* (used during a Catholic Mass) – a monstrance, in a sunburst shape, used to display the Host (the consecrated bread).

p.206 *Lady Macbeth in the sleeping scene* – presumably this should be "the sleep-walking scene" (*Macbeth*, V, i).

p.220 *Lord Brougham* (1778-1868), lawyer, M. P., Lord Chancellor.

p.239 *Night nurse* – an untrained woman who watched over patients from 11 pm to 7 am and called a doctor or experienced nurse if a patient's condition deteriorated, etc.

p.239 *Lady _____* – this is almost certainly Augusta Hall, Lady Llanover (1802-96); she was the only titled Welsh woman with houses in London and south Wales who was living in the same street as Lord Raglan at this period (see Chapter 5, Part 2).

p.240 *Battle of the Alma* – September, 1854; the British forces suffered major losses, and the wounded had no adequate medical care.

p.241 *Mr and Mrs Sidney Herbert* – Sidney and Elizabeth Herbert were old friends of Florence Nightingale and her family. Sidney Herbert, a Tory MP, became Secretary at War, responsible for Army organisation and administration, and in that capacity recruited Florence Nightingale to organise army nurses at Scutari.

p.242 *Miss Stanley* – Mary Stanley (1813-79), at first a friend of Florence Nightingale who later quarrelled with her over nursing services in the Crimea.

p.243 *Sisters of Mercy* – a religious order of women founded in Dublin in 1831 to help people in poverty and sickness

p.244 *Norfolk Island* – in the Pacific Ocean, between Australia and New Caledonia; colonised by Great Britain in 1788 and a penal settlement until 1855 except for the period 1814-25, when it was abandoned.

p.245 *St John's House* – at Chiswick, London; the home of an Anglican Nursing Sisterhood founded in 1848.

p.248 *The Buffs* – The Royal East Kent Regiment

p.254 *Mr and Mrs Bracebridge* – Charles and Selina Bracebridge, friends of Florence Nightingale who accompanied her to Scutari and the Crimea to help with secretarial work, etc.

p.264 *Dr Hall* – John Hall (1795 – 1865) British Army Inspector-General of Hospitals during the Crimean War

p.266 *The extra-diet kitchen* – the kitchen which produced food for soldiers too weak or ill to stomach British Army rations

p.313 *Lord Panmure* – (1801-74); Secretary of State for War from early 1855 to February 1858.

p.331 *The loss of the 'Prince'* – the *Prince* was a Royal Navy store-ship, sunk in a storm off Balaclava in November 1854; the loss of its cargo meant that British troops had to endure a harsh winter without suitable clothing.

p.332 *Inkerman* – battle on November 5th, 1854, in which the Allies (Britain, France and the Ottoman Empire) defeated the Imperial Russian Army. It was followed by the Siege of Sebastopol.

p.338 *Kaiserswerth* – the Institute of Kaiserswerth (in Dusseldorf) had been founded by a Lutheran minister in 1836; it was a hospital which housed and trained deaconesses, and influenced Florence Nightingale's views on the training of nurses.

Glossary

Araba a wheeled carriage

Biscuit a crisp, dry bread, usually hard

Block large stone etc. used by riders for mounting and dismounting from horses, etc.

Blue books – official reports of the British Parliament or the Privy Council which were published in dark blue covers in the 19th and early 20th centuries.

Briton (here, used by English people of Betsy Cadwaladyr) a Welsh woman

Buttermilk the liquid that remains when the butter has been churned

Calabash the hollow shell of a gourd or pumpkin used for holding liquids

Clock (of stocking) an ornamental pattern in silk thread worked on the side of a stocking

Co-adjutors co-worker or assistant.

Commit ("You *commit y*ourself") You've just given yourself away and ensured you'll be sent to prison.

Convict hulk an old, worn-out ship used as a prison; usually moored within sight of the shore.

Creole in the West Indies and Mauritius, someone born in that country but of Spanish, French or African origin

Cuddy small cabin, often for passengers on a merchant ship

Diolch yn fawr i chwi (Welsh) thank you very much

Dropsy an illness caused by retention of fluid

Entitle to address someone using their correct title

Factory (the English *factory* at Canton) the trading house of a merchant company

Fatigue parties groups of soldiers given extra duties (often as punishment)

Feridgee a long loose robe worn especially by Turkish women

Froward difficult to deal with or please, ungovernable

Garret a room under the roof, an attic

Galoshes rubber overshoes

Grog a mixture of rum and water, sometimes with added lime and sugar, which was issued on Royal Navy ships from the mid-18th century to the later 20th.

Hessian boot boots made of strong coarse cloth (usually jute)

Hy-day-gies a dance popular in the 16th and early 17th centuries

Inmate (fellow) lodger

Interlude (Welsh *anterliwt*) : a play acted at a fair or in a tavern, often satirical and including parodies, etc.; popular in the 18th century.

Issue a discharge of blood or pus; the dressing put on it

Journeyman a qualified craftsman (i.e. no longer an apprentice) who worked as an employee for someone else

Juggernaut the image of the god Krishna, drawn in procession

Late something which was in the past but is not now; ex-.

Marasmus the wasting away of the body, especially because of lack of nourishment

Mercery fabrics

Misdoubt to have doubts about someone's character

Mor ddrwg (Welsh) so naughty

Nankin/nankeen cotton cloth, originally made in China.

Negus a sweetened mixture of wine and water

Note-of-hand a written promise to pay a certain amount of money on a certain date

Old faggot! A term of abuse or contempt applied to a woman

Palanquin a framework containing a bed or seat and surrounded by curtains, which was mounted on poles and carried by four or six men.

Passage-boat a small boat which ferried passengers between two places, at sea or on a river or canal

Pelisse a long cloak.

Supercargo an officer on a merchant ship who supervised the cargo and the commercial transactions during the voyage

Tippet a short coat or cloak, often with hanging ends.

Tirewoman a dressmaker

Viaticum Eucharist administered to someone who is dying or in danger of death.

ABOUT HONNO

Honno Welsh Women's Press was set up in 1986 by a group of women who felt strongly that women in Wales needed wider opportunities to see their writing in print and to become involved in the publishing process. Our aim is to develop the writing talents of women in Wales, give them new and exciting opportunities to see their work published and often to give them their first 'break' as a writer. Honno is registered as a community co-operative. Any profit that Honno makes is invested in the publishing programme. Women from Wales and around the world have expressed their support for Honno. Each supporter has a vote at the Annual General Meeting. For more information and to buy our publications, please write to Honno at the address below, or visit our website: www.honno.co.uk

Honno, 14 Creative Units, Aberystwyth Arts Centre
Aberystwyth, Ceredigion SY23 3GL

Honno Friends

We are very grateful for the support of the Honno Friends:
Jane Aaron, Annette Ecuyere, Audrey Jones, Gwyneth
Tyson Roberts, Beryl Roberts, Jenny Sabine.

For more information on how you can become a Honno
Friend, see: http://www.honno.co.uk/friends.php

Titles published in this series:

Jane Aaron, ed.	*A View across the Valley: Short Stories by Women from Wales 1850-1950*
Jane Aaron and Ursula Masson, eds,	*The Very Salt of Life: Welsh Women's Political Writings from Chartism to Suffrage*
Elizabeth Andrews,	*A Woman's Work is Never Done* (1957), with an introduction by Ursula Masson
Amy Dillwyn,	*The Rebecca Rioter* (1880), with an introduction by Katie Gramich
	A Burglary (1883), with an introduction by Alison Favre
	Jill (1884), with an introduction by Kirsti Bohata
Dorothy Edwards,	*Winter Sonata* (1928), with an introduction by Claire Flay
Margiad Evans,	*The Wooden Doctor* (1933), with an introduction by Sue Asbee
Menna Gallie,	*Strike for a Kingdom* (1959), with an introduction by Angela John
	The Small Mine (1962), with an introduction by Jane Aaron
	Travels with a Duchess (1968), with an introduction by Angela John
	You're Welcome to Ulster (1970), with an introduction by Angela John and Claire Connolly
Katie Gramich and Catherine Brennan, eds,	*Welsh Women's Poetry 1460-2001*
Eiluned Lewis,	*Dew on the Grass* (1934), with an introduction by Katie Gramich
	The Captain's Wife (1943), with an introduction by Katie Gramich
Allen Raine,	*A Welsh Witch* (1902), with an introduction by Jane Aaron
	Queen of the Rushes (1906), with an introduction by Katie Gramich
Bertha Thomas,	*Stranger within the Gates* (1912), with an introduction by Kirsti Bohata
Lily Tobias,	*Eunice Fleet* (1933), with an introduction by Jasmine Donahaye
Hilda Vaughan,	*Here Are Lovers* (1926), with an introduction by Diana Wallace
	Iron and Gold (1948), with an introduction by Jane Aaron
	The Soldier and the Gentlewoman (1932), with an introduction by Lucy Thomas
Jane Williams,	*Betsy Cadwaladyr: A Balaclava Nurse* (1857), with an introduction by Deirdre Beddoe

Clasuron Honno

Honno also publish an equivalent series, *Clasuron Honno*, in Welsh, also recently re-launched with a new look:

Published with the support of the Welsh Books Council

Welsh Women's Classics

Series Editor: *Jane Aaron*

Formerly known as the *Honno Classics* Series, now renamed and relaunched for Honno's 25th Anniversary in 2012.

This series, published by Honno Press, brings back into print neglected and virtually forgotten literary texts by Welsh women from the past.

Each of the titles published includes an introduction setting the text in its historical context and suggesting ways of approaching and understanding the work from the viewpoint of women's experience today. The editor's aim is to select works which are not only of literary merit but which remain readable and appealing to a contemporary audience. An additional aim for the series is to provide materials for students of Welsh writing in English, who have until recently remained largely ignorant of the contribution of women writers to the Welsh literary tradition simply because their works have been unavailable.

The many and various portrayals of Welsh female identity found in these authors' books bear witness to the complex processes that have gone into the shaping of the Welsh women of today. Perusing these portrayals from the past will help us to understand our own situations better, as well as providing, in a variety of different genres – novels, short stories, poetry, autobiography and prose pieces – a fresh and fascinating store of good reading matter.

> *"[It is] difficult to imagine a Welsh literary landscape*
> *without the Honno Classics series [...]*
> *it remains an energising and vibrant feminist imprint."*
> (Kirsti Bohata, *New Welsh Review*)

> *"[The Honno Classics series is] possibly the Press'*
> *most important achievement, helping to combat*
> *the absence of women's literature in the Welsh canon."*
> (*Mslexia*)